Front Cover:
*Church of San Pedro,
detail of the apse turrets,
Teruel.*

Museum With No Frontiers (MWNF) Exhibition Trails

ISLAMIC ART IN THE MEDITERRANEAN | **SPAIN**

Mudéjar Art
Islamic Aesthetics in Christian Art

The MWNF Exhibition Trail *MUDÉJAR ART: Islamic Aesthetics in Christian Art* and this related guide are part of the cycle *Islamic Art in the Mediterranean*. The realisation of the Itineraries in the Autonomous regions of Andalucía and Extremadura, undertaken within the framework of the "Gateway to the Mediterranean" project, was co-financed by the European Union through the European Regional Development Fund (ERDF), Article 10, pilot action Spain-Portugal-Morocco.

Funding was also received from the General Directorates of Fine Arts and Cultural Heritage and of Co-operation and Cultural Communication of the Ministry of Education, Culture and Sports. Furthermore, the project could count on the support of the National Archaeological Museum.

The following entities have collaborated in this project:

Cortes of Aragon	Municipality of Guadalupe
Provincial government of Aragon	Municipality of Guadix
Junta of Andalucía	Municipality of Jerez del Marquesado
Junta of Castilla-La Mancha	Municipality of La Calahorra
Junta of Castilla-León	Municipality of Lanteira
Junta of Extremadura	Municipality of Llerena
Provincial government of Granada	Municipality of Madrigal de las Altas Torres
Provincial government of Seville	Municipality of Maluenda
Provincial government of Saragossa	Municipality of Mayorga de Campos
Municipality of Alagón	Municipality of Medina del Campo
Municipality of Alcalá de Henares	Municipality of Morata de Jiloca
Municipality of Amusco	Municipality of Olmedo
Municipality of Aniñón	Municipality of Palencia
Municipality of Arévalo	Municipality of Sahagún
Municipality of Astudillo	Municipality of San Pedro de las Dueñas
Municipality of Aznalcázar	Municipality of Sanlúcar la Mayor
Municipality of Aznalcóllar	Municipality of Santervás de Campos
Municipality of Becerril de Campos	Municipality of Santoyo
Municipality of Belmonte de Gracián	Municipality of Seville
Municipality of Benecazón	Municipality of Támara de Campos
Municipality of Calatayud	Municipality of Tobed
Municipality of Calera de León	Municipality of Toledo
Municipality of Carrión de los Condes	Municipality of Tordesillas
Municipality of Cervera de la Cañada	Municipality of Toro
Municipality of Cisneros	Municipality of Torralba de Ribota
Municipality of Coca	Municipality of Utebo
Municipality of Daroca	Municipality of Villalón de Campos
Municipality of Fuentes de Nava	Municipality of Villalpando
Municipality of Gerena	Municipality of Villamuera de la Cueza
Municipality of Granada	Municipality of Zafra
Municipality of Guadalajara	Municipality of Saragossa

© 2018 Museum Ohne Grenzen | Museum With No Frontiers (MWNF) (texts and illustrations)
© 2018 Museum Ohne Grenzen | Museum With No Frontiers (MWNF)

ISBN 978-3-902782-15-1 (eBook)
    978-3-902782-14-4 (paperback)
All Rights Reserved.

Information: www.museumwnf.org

Museum With No Frontiers (MWNF) makes all possible efforts to ensure the accuracy of the information contained in its publications. However, MWNF cannot be held responsible for any errors, omissions or inaccuracies, and declines any responsibility in the event of an accident, of any kind, which could occur during the proposed visits.

This book was prepared between 1998 and 2001, but publication was postponed due to budgetary constraints. It has now been possible to complete the project and to publish the English version of this title, which is available also in Spanish, French and Italian. Please note that technical information such as accessibility, local contacts, possible restorations, etc., dates from the time of the preparation of the book. We therefore recommend that you check before arranging a visit.

The opinions expressed in this work do not necessarily reflect the opinions either of the European Union or of its member states.

Museum With No Frontiers
Idea and overall concept
Eva Schubert

Curatorial Committee
Gonzalo M. Borrás Gualís, Saragossa
Pedro Lavado Paradinas, Madrid
Rafael López Guzmán, Granada
M.ª Pilar Mogollón Cano-Cortés, Badajoz
Alfredo Morales Martínez, Seville
M.ª Teresa Pérez Higuera, Madrid

Museo Sin Fronteras España
Board of Directors
M.ª Ángeles Gutiérrez Fraile
M.ª Rosa García Brage
Consuelo Luca de Tena
Javier Muñiz
Gerardo Barros
Eva Schubert

Head of project
M.ª Ángeles Gutiérrez Fraile, Madrid

Catalogue

Introduction
Gonzalo M. Borrás Gualís, Saragossa

Presentation of Itineraries
Scientific Committee

With the collaboration of
Alfonso Pleguezuelo Hernández, Seville
Miguel Ángel Sorroche Cuerva, Granada

Technical texts
Sandra Stuyck Fernández Arche, Madrid

Photography
Guillermo Maestro Casado, Madrid
Miguel Rodríguez Moreno, Granada

General Map
José Antonio Dávila Buitrón, Madrid

Sketches
Sergio Viguera, Madrid

General Introduction
Islamic Art in the Mediterranean
Jamila Binous, Tunis
Mahmoud Hawari, East Jerusalem
Manuela Marín, Madrid
Gönül Öney, Izmir

Maps
Şakir Çakmak, Izmir
Ertan Das, Izmir
Yekta Demiralp, Izmir

Translation
Pauline Moran, Madrid

Copy-editor
Mandi Gomez, London

Layout and design
Christian Eckart
based on a project of
Augustina Fernández

Technical Co-ordination

Production Manager
Sandra Stuyck Fernández-Arche, Madrid

Production Assistant
Mónica E. González Medina, Madrid

International Co-ordination

General co-ordination
Eva Schubert

Scientific Committees, translations, editing and catalogue production
Sakina Missoum, Madrid

Photographic Archive
María Jesús Rubio, Madrid

Acknowledgements

Museum With No Frontiers would like to thank the owners and administrators of all the monuments included in the exhibition for their collaboration and support, as well as those public and private institutions without which this project would not have been possible.

Archdiocese of Granada
Archdiocese of Seville
Archdiocese of Toledo
Rural Development Association "Ruta del Mudéjar", Olmedo
Municipality of Alagón
Municipality of Alcalá de Henares
Municipality of Daroca
Municipality of Guadix
Municipality of Llerena
Municipality of Olmedo
Municipality of Zafra
Chapter of Gerona Cathedral
Metropolitan Council of Saragossa
Convent of Santa Clara, Astudillo
Convent of Santa Clara, Carrión de los Condes
Convent of Santa Clara, Zafra
Cortes of Aragón
Casa Ducal de Medinaceli Foundation, Seville
Euro-Arab Foundation, Granada
Nuestra Señora del Pilar Foundation, Granada
Hotel Palace of Santa Inés, Granada
Institute of Teruel Studies
Institute of Valencia de Don Juan, Madrid
Junta de Andalucía, Department of Culture
Junta de Castilla-León
Junta de Extremadura, Department of Culture and Heritage

Monastery of the Benedictine Sisters,
    San Pedro de las Dueñas
Monastery of Santa Isabel la Real, Granada
National Archaeological Museum, Madrid
Museum of Santa Cruz, Toledo
Sephardic Museum, Toledo, Ministry of Education,
    Culture and Sports
Diocese of Guadix-Baza
Diocese of Palencia
Diocese of Saragossa
Diocese of Tarazona
Diocese of Teruel and Albarrracín
Diocese of Zamora
Diocese of Saragossa
Offices of Tourism
Parish Priest of San Felix, Torralba de Ribota
Parish Priest of Santervás
Parish Priest of Santiago Apostol, Guadalajara
Parish Priest of San Miguel, Villalón
Patrimonio Nacional (National Heritage Trust)
Trustees of the Royal Alcázar, Seville
Zafra Development Plan
Royal Monastery of Nuestra Señora de Guadalupe
Senate
University of Alcalá de Henares
University of Granada

In addition, Museum With No Frontiers would like to thank the following people for their important contribution to the project:
Abigail Pereta, Museum Technician, Saragossa
Clara Gómez, Geographer, Madrid
Cristina Jular, Medievalist, Madrid
Manuela Marín, Dept of Arabic Studies, CSIC, Madrid
Mercedes García Arenal, Dept of Arabic Studies, CSIC, Madrid

Museum With No Frontiers would also like to thank
The Spanish Ministry of Foreign Affairs for demonstrating its support for the project *Islamic Art in the Mediterranean* from its inception, through the Spanish Agency for International Co-operation (AECI), along with the Spanish Embassies in the participating Mediterranean countries and the Regional Government of Tyrol (Austria) – where the MWNF pilot project was first set up – for facilitating the training of the Production Managers in charge of the technical co-ordination of the Exhibition Trails in the countries participating in the *Islamic Art in the Mediterranean* cycle.

Photographic references

See page 5 and National Library of Spain, page 76 (*Monumentos Arquitectónicos de España*, 1881)
© Chapter of Gerona Cathedral, page 99 ("Tresor de la Catedral de Gerona")
© Patrimonio Nacional (Department of National Heritage), pages 152 and 155 (Palace of Tordesillas)
Photographic Archive of the National Archaeological Museum, page 172 (Pedro I)
Historical-artistic Heritage of the Senate, page 237 (reproduction by Oronoz)
Torcuato Fandila, page 285 (Church of San Miguel, Guadix)

General Introduction "Islamic Art in the Mediterranean"
Ann & Peter Jousiffe (London), page 20 (Aleppo)
Archives of Oronoz Photographers (Madrid), page 23 (Alhambra, Granada)

Plan references

Franco, L., Penan M., and Estudio Camaleón, page 88 (Palace of the Aljafería, Saragossa).
García Guereta, R., page 105 (Tower of el Salvador, Teruel).
Borrás, G., (*Arte Mudéjar Aragonés*, 1985), page 122 (Church of the Virgin, Tobed).
Lampérez, V., page 145 (Castle of Coca, Segovia), page 147 (Chapel of la Mejorada, Olmedo),
   page 156 (Baths of the Palace of King don Pedro, Tordesillas).
Monumentos Arquitectónicos de España, 1879, pages 208 and 209 (Church of Santiago del Arrabal, Toledo).
Mogollón, M.ª P., (*Mudéjar en Extremadura*, 1987), page 216 (Royal Monastery of Nuestra Señora de Guadalupe).
Gómez Ramos, R., *Colección Arte Hispalense*, 1993), page 241 (Church of Santa Marina, Seville).
Duclos Bautista, G., (*Carpintería de lo blanco*, 1993), page 242 (Church of Santa Marina, Seville),
   page 248 (Church of Santa Catalina, Seville).
M.ª Luisa Marín Martín, pages 267 and 268 (Shrine of Castilleja de Talhara, Benecazón),
   page 271 (Shrine of Gelo, Benecazón).
Moreno Felipe, J., page 269 (Church of San Pablo, Aznalcazar).
José Luis Ramos Arcas and Juan Ramón Altozano Pérez, page 282 (Church of Jeréz del Marquesado, Granada).

General Introduction "Islamic Art in the Mediterranean"
Ettinghaussen, R. and Grabar, O. (*Arte y Arquitectura del Islam 650–1250*, 1987), page 26 (Mosque of Damascus).
Sönmez, Z., (*Baslangıcından 16. Yüzyıla Kadar Anadolu-Türk İslam Mimar sinde Sanatçıılar*, 1995),
   page 27 (Mosques of Divriği and Istanbul) and page 28 (Mosque of Sivas).
Viguera, S., (Madrid), page 28 (Types of minarets).
Ettinghaussen, R. and Grabar, O. (*Arte y Arquitectura del Islam 1250–1300*, 1987),
   page 29 (Mosque and *madrasa* Sultan Hassan).
Ettinghaussen, R. and Grabar, O., (*Arte y Arquitectura del Islam 650–1250*, 1987) page 30 (Qasr al-Khayr al-Sharqi).
Kuran, A. (*Mimar Sinan*, 1986), page 31 (Khan Sultan Aksaray).

Advice

Transliteration of the Arabic

We have retained the common spelling for Arabic words in common use and included those in the English dictionary, such as "suq". We have maintained the phonetic spelling of the words in Arabic as determined by the authors and in accordance with Syrian standards. For all other words, we have simplified the transcription. We do not transcribe the initial *hamza* but have kept the initial *'Ayn* in personal nouns, as in 'Ali, 'Abd al-Malik, etc. We did not differentiate between short and long vowels, which are written as *a*, *i*, *ou*. Some of the proper nouns are transliterated in the text according to the *Oxford Dictionary*. The transcription for the 28 Arabic consonants are provided below as well as "a" or "at" for the ta' *marbuta*.

Words in italic in the text without an accompanying translation or explanation can be found in the glossary.

ء	'	ح	h	ز	z	ط	t	ق	q	ه	h
ب	b	خ	kh	س	s	ظ	z	ك	k	و	u/w
ت	t	د	d	ش	sh	ع	'	ل	l	ي	y/i
ث	th	ذ	dh	ص	s	غ	gh	م	m		
ج	j	ر	r	ض	d	ف	f	ن	n		

The Muslim era

The Muslim era began with the exodus of the Prophet Muhammad from Mecca to Yathrib. Then the name was changed to *Madina*, "The City" or "town of the Prophet". With his small community of followers (70 people along with family members) recently converted to Islam, the Prophet undertook the *al-hijra* (literally "the emigration") and the new era began.

The date of the emigration is the first of the month of *Muharram* in year 1 of the *Hijra*, which corresponds to 16th July of the year 622 of the Christian era. The Muslim year is made up of twelve lunar months, each month having 29 or 30 days.

Thirty years form a cycle in which the 2nd, 5th, 7th, 10th, 13th, 16th, 18th, 21st, 24th, 26th and 29th are leap years having 355 days; the others are normal years with 354 days. The Muslim lunar year is 10 or 11 days shorter than the Christian solar year.

Each day begins immediately after sunset, i.e. at dusk rather than after midnight. Most Muslim countries use both the *Hijra* Calendar (which indicates all religious events) and the Christian Calendar.

Dates

Dates given are according to the *Hijra* calendar, followed by their equivalent date on the Christian calendar after an oblique stroke. The *Hijra* date is not indicated in references derived from Christian sources, European historical events, those that occurred in Europe, Christian Dynasties, those prior to the Muslim era or those after 1918, the end of Ottoman domination in Syria.

Exact correspondence between years in one calendar and another is only possible when the day and month are given. To facilitate reading, we chose to avoid intermediate years and, in the case of *Hijra* dates falling between the beginning and the end of a century, the two centuries are mentioned. Dates prior to the beginning of the Christian era are indicated with BC. To avoid confusion, the use of the abbreviation AD is used for periods beginning before the birth of Christ and finishing after his birth.

Abbreviations:
AD = in the year of our Lord; BC = before Christ; d = death; f.h. = first half; r. = reign

Practical Advice

The MWNF Exhibition Trail *MUDÉJAR ART: Islamic Aesthetics in Christian Art* is made up of 13 independent Itineraries spread over six Autonomous Regions. They can be visited in any order.

The use of road maps and town plans is recommended.

The text referring to each monument is accompanied by practical information – how to reach it, opening times, etc., which are accurate at the time of elaboration of this title (see also the note on page 4). It is important to remember that the recommended route is not always the shortest one, but invariably it is the simplest. The paragraphs on a grey background are the "landscape" options, selected for their beauty and/or cultural interest.

Churches cannot be visited during mass; during religious services, a discreet and respectful attitude is required.

Words that appear in italic in the text (except those immediately followed by an explanation) can be found in the glossary. The spellings for Muslim master craftsmen were determined by the authors themselves and reflect the spellings of the period.

Museum With No Frontiers is not responsible for any inconvenience, loss or injury caused during visits to the exhibition.

On behalf of the whole MWNF Team, I wish you an enjoyable visit to Mudéjar Spain.

Sandra Stuyck
Production Manager

Index

15 **Islamic Art in the Mediterranean**
    Jamila Binous, Mahmoud Hawari,
    Manuela Marín, Gönül Öney

35 **Historical-Artistic Introduction**
    Gonzalo M. Borrás Gualís

63 **Itinerary I** (half day)
    Daily Life and Liturgy:
    Home, Kitchen and Choir
    Mudéjar Ceramics
    Pedro Lavado Paradinas

75 **Itinerary II** (half day)
    The "Cisneros" Style
    Mudéjar Carpentry
    Pedro Lavado Paradinas

85 **Itinerary III**
    The Coronation of the Kings of Aragon
    Pedro IV
    Gonzalo M. Borrás Gualís

101 **Itinerary IV**
    Mudéjar Cities: From Islam to Christianity
    The Moorish Quarter of Teruel
    Gonzálo M. Borrás Gualís

119 **Itinerary V**
    Church-Fortresses on the Border with Castile
    Mahoma Rami, Master Craftsman
    Gonzalo M. Borrás Gualís

137 **Itinerary VI**
    Castles and Walled Cities
    Pedro Lavado Paradinas

151 **Itinerary VII** (two days)
    Daughters of Kings and Nobles:
    Through the St Clare's Convents
    Pedro I of Castille
    Pedro Lavado Paradinas

175 **Itinerary VIII**
    Consequences of the Birth of Gothic
    Cathedrals: Working with Brick
    Fairs and Markets
    Pedro Lavado Paradinas

195 **Itinerary IX**
    Traces of the Past: Churches, Synagogues
    and Palaces
    Mudéjar Plasterwork in Toledo
    María Teresa Pérez Higuera

213 **Itinerary X** (two days)
    Noble and Monastic Patronage
    Military Orders
    María Pilar Mogollón Cano-Cortés

239 **Itinerary XI**
    Temples and Palaces of Seville
    Alfredo J. Morales, Alfonso Pleguezuelo
    Nature and Architecture
    Alfonso Pleguezuelo Hernández

259 **Itinerary XII**
    The Aljarafe of Seville
    Traditional Muslim Funerary Chapels
    and Presbyteries
    Alfredo J. Morales

275 **Itinerary XIII** (two days)
    Rodrigo de Mendoza: Marquis of Zenete –
    from La Calahorra Castle to El Albaicín
    Education and Scientific Knowledge
    Rafael López Guzman, Miguel Ángel Sorroche Cuerva

301 **Glossary**

305 **Historical Personalities**

307 **Bibliographic References**

309 **Authors**

ISLAMIC DYNASTIES IN THE MEDITERRANEAN
The Umayyads | The Abbasids | The Fatimids | The Mamluks

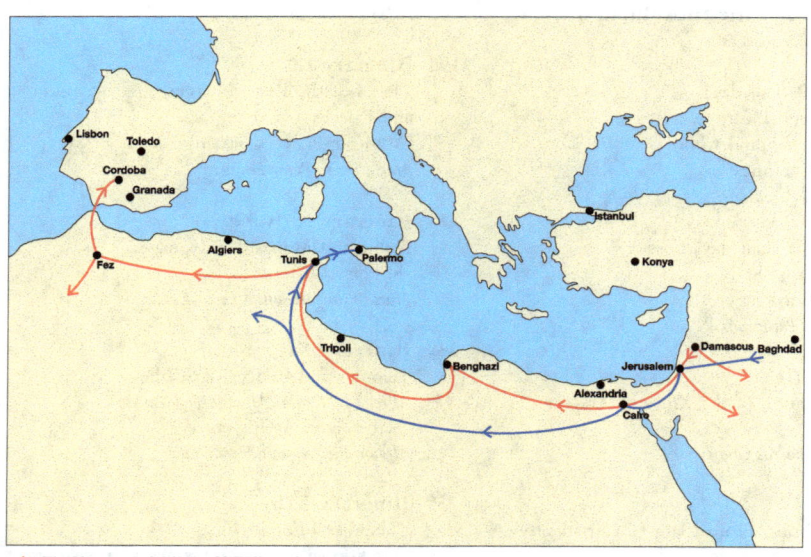

← The Umayyads (41/661-132/750)   Capital: Damascus
← The Abbasids (132/750-656/1258)   Capital: Baghdad

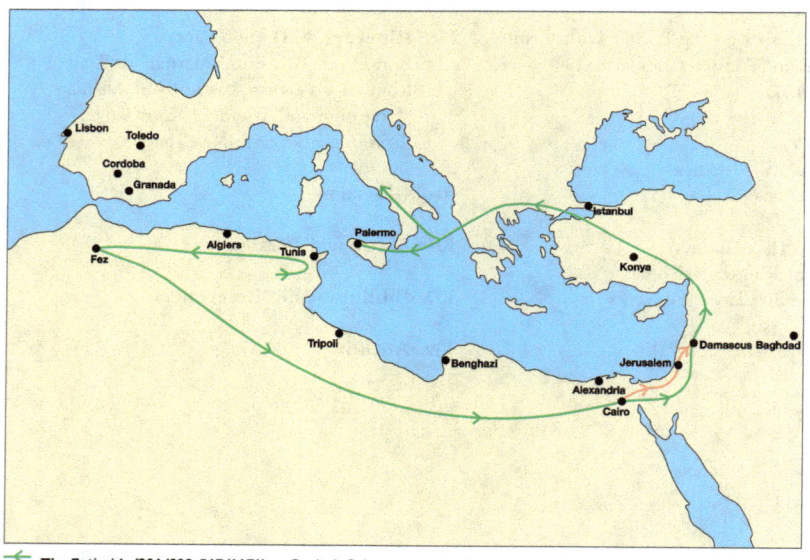

← The Fatimids (296/909-567/1171)   Capital: Cairo
← The Mamluks (648/1250-923/1517)   Capital: Cairo

ISLAMIC DYNASTIES IN THE MEDITERRANEAN
The Seljuqs | The Ottomans | The Almoravids | The Almohads

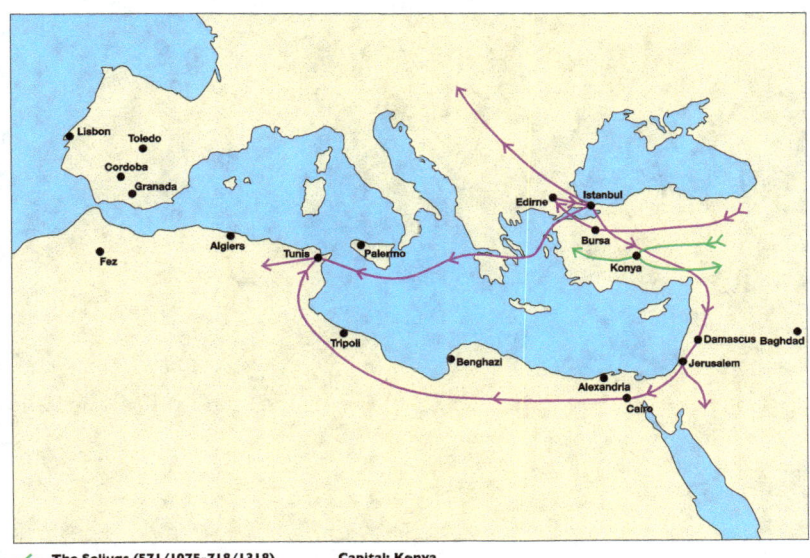

← The Seljuqs (571/1075-718/1318) Capital: Konya
← The Ottomans (699/1299-1340/1922) Capital: Istanbul

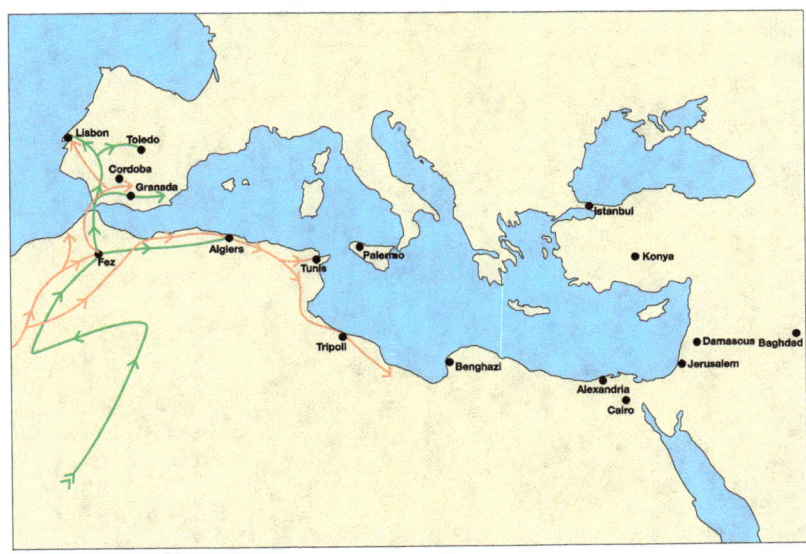

← The Almoravids (427/1036-541/1147) Capital: Marrakesh
← The Almohads (515/1121-667/1269) Capital: Marrakesh

ISLAMIC ART IN THE MEDITERRANEAN

Jamila Binous
Mahmoud Hawari
Manuela Marín
Gönül Öney

The Legacy of Islam in the Mediterranean

Since the first half of the 1st/7th century, the history of the Mediterranean Basin has belonged, in remarkably similar proportion, to two cultures, Islam and the Christian West. This extensive history of conflict and contact has created a mythology that is widely diffused in the collective imagination, a mythology based on the image of the other as the unyielding enemy, strange and alien, and as such, incomprehensible. It is of course true that battles punctuated those centuries from the time when the Muslims spilled forth from the Arabian Peninsula and took possession of the Fertile Crescent, Egypt, and later, North Africa, Sicily, and the Iberian Peninsula, penetrating into Western Europe as far as the south of France. At the beginning of the 2nd/8th century, the Mediterranean came under Islamic control.

This drive to expand, of an intensity seldom equalled in human history, was carried out in the name of a religion that considered itself then heir to its two immediate antecedents: Judaism and Christianity. It would be a gross oversimplification to explain the Islamic expansion exclusively in religious terms. One widespread image in the West presents Islam as a religion of simple dogmas adapted to the needs of the common people, spread by vulgar warriors who poured out from the desert bearing the Qur'an on the blades of their swords. This coarse image does away with the intellectual complexity of a religious message that transformed the world from the moment of its inception. It identifies this message with a military threat, and thus justifies a response on the same terms. Finally, it reduces an entire culture to only one of its elements, religion, and in doing so, deprives it of the potential for evolution and change.

The Mediterranean countries that were progressively incorporated into the Muslim world began their journeys from very different starting points. Forms of Islamic life that began to develop in each were quite logically different within the unity that resulted from their shared adhesion to the new religious dogma. It is precisely the capacity to assimilate elements of previous cultures (Hellenistic, Roman, etc.), which has been one of the defining characteristics of Islamic societies. If one restricts his observations to the geographical area of the Mediterranean, which was extremely diverse culturally at the time of the emergence of Islam, one will discern

Qusayr 'Amra, mural in the Audience Hall, Badiya of Jordan.

quickly that this initial moment does not represent a break with previous history in the least. One comes to realise that it is impossible to imagine a monolithic and immutable Islamic world, blindly following an inalterable religious message.

If anything can be singled out as the leitmotiv running through the area of the Mediterranean, it is diversity of expression combined with harmony of sentiment, a sentiment more cultural than religious. In the Iberian Peninsula – to begin with the western perimeter of the Mediterranean – the presence of Islam, initially brought about by military conquest, produced a society clearly differentiated from, but in permanent contact with Christian society. The importance of the cultural expression of this Islamic society was felt even after it ceased to exist as such, and gave rise to perhaps one of the most original components of Spanish culture, Mudéjar art. Portugal maintained strong Mozarab traditions throughout the Islamic period and there are many imprints from this time that are still clearly visible today. In Morocco and Tunisia, the legacy of al-Andalus was assimilated into the local forms and continues to be evident to this day. The western Mediterranean produced original forms of expression that reflected its conflicting and plural historical evolution.

Lodged between East and West, the Mediterranean Sea is endowed with terrestrial enclaves, such as Sicily, that represent centuries-old key historical locations. Conquered by the Arabs established in Tunisia, Sicily has continued to perpetuate the cultural and historical memory of Islam long after the Muslims ceased to have any political presence on the island. The presence of Sicilian-Norman aesthetic forms preserved in architectural monuments clearly demonstrates that the history of these regions cannot be explained without an understanding of the diversity of social, economic and cultural experiences that flourished on their soil.

In sharp contrast, then, to the immutable and constant image alluded to at the outset, the history of Mediterranean Islam is characterised by surprising diversity. It is made up of a mixture of peoples and ethnicities, deserts and fertile lands. As the major religion has been Islam since the early Middle Ages, it is also true that religious minorities have maintained a presence historically. The Classical Arabic language of the Qur'an, has coexisted side-by-side with other languages, as well as with other dialects of Arabic. Within a setting of undeniable unity (Muslim religion, Arabic language and culture), each society has evolved and responded to the challenges of history in its own characteristic manner.

The Emergence and Development of Islamic Art

Throughout these countries, with ancient and diverse civilisations, a new art permeated with images from the Islamic faith emerged at the end of the $2^{nd}/8^{th}$ century and which successfully imposed itself in a period of less than a hundred years. This art, in its own particular manner, gave rise to creations and innovations based on unifying regional formulas and architectural and decorative processes, and was simultaneously inspired by the artistic traditions that proceeded it: Greco-Roman and Byzantine, Sasanian, Visigothic, Berber or even Central Asian.

The initial aim of Islamic art was to serve the needs of religion and various aspects of socio-economic life. New buildings appeared for religious purposes such as mosques and sanctuaries. For this reason, architecture played a central role in Islamic art because a whole series of other arts are dependent on it. Apart from architecture a whole range of complimentary minor arts found their artistic expressions in a variety of materials, such as wood, pottery, metal, glass, textiles and paper. In pottery, a great variety of glaze techniques were employed and among these distinguished groups are the lustre and polychrome painted wares. Glass of great beauty was manufactured, reaching excellence with the type adorned with gold and bright enamel colours. In metalwork, the most sophisticated technique is inlaying bronze with silver or copper. High quality textiles and carpets, with geometric, animal and human designs, were made. Illuminated manuscripts with miniature painting represent a spectacular achievement in the arts of the book. These types of minor arts serve to attest the brilliance of Islamic art.

Figurative art, however, is excluded from the Islamic liturgical domain, which means it is ostracised from the central core of Islamic civilisation and that it is tolerated only at its periphery. Relief work is rare in the decoration of monuments and sculptures are almost flat. This deficit is compensated with a richness in ornamentation on the lavish carved plaster panelling, sculpted wooden panelling, wall tiling and glazed mosaics, as well as on the stalactite friezes, or *muqarnas*. Decorative elements taken from nature, such as leaves, flowers and branches, are generally stylised to the extreme and are so complicated that they rarely call to mind their sources of origin. The intertwining and combining of geometric motifs such as rhombus and etiolated polygons, form interlacing networks that completely cover the surface, resulting in shapes often called arabesques. One innovation within the decorative repertoire is the introduction of epigraphic elements in the ornamentation of monuments,

Dome of the Rock, Jerusalem.

sometimes bear their names. Islamic art is, above all, dynastic art. Each one contributed tendencies that would bring about a partial or complete renewal of artistic forms, depending on historical conditions, the prosperity enjoyed by their states, and the traditions of each people. Islamic art, in spite of its relative unity, allowed for a diversity that gave rise to different styles, each one identified with a dynasty.

The Umayyad dynasty (41/661–132/750), which transferred the capital of the caliphate to Damascus, represents a singular achievement in the history of Islam. It absorbed and incorporated the Hellenistic and Byzantine legacy in such a way that the classical tradition of the Mediterranean was recast in a new and innovative mould. Islamic art, thus, was formed in Syria, and the architecture, unmistakably Islamic due to the personality of the founders, would continue to bear a relation to Hellenistic and Byzantine art as well. The most important of these monuments are the Dome of the Rock in Jerusalem, the earliest existing monumental Islamic sanctuary, the Great Mosque of Damascus, which served as a model for later mosques, and the desert palaces of Syria, Jordan and Palestine.

When the Abbasid caliphate (132/750–656/1258) succeeded the Umayyads, the political centre of Islam was moved from the Mediterranean to Baghdad in

furniture and various objects. Muslim craftsmen made use of the beauty of Arabic calligraphy, the language of the sacred book, the Qur'an, not only for the transcription of the qur'anic verses, but in all of its variations simply as a decorative motif for the ornamentation of stucco panelling and the edges of panels.

Art was also at the service of rulers. It was for patrons that architects built palaces, mosques, schools, hospitals, bathhouses, *caravanserais* and mausoleums, which would

Mesopotamia. This factor would influence the development of Islamic civilisation and the entire range of culture, and art would bear the mark of that change. Abbasid art and architecture were influenced by three major traditions: Sassanian, Central Asian and Seljuq. Central Asian influence was already present in Sassanian architecture, but at Samarra this influence is represented by the stucco style with its arabesque ornamentation that would rapidly spread throughout the Islamic world. The influence of the Abbasid monuments can be observed in the buildings constructed during this period in the other regions of the empire, particularly Egypt and Ifriqiya. In Cairo, the Mosque of Ibn Tulun (262/876–265/879) is a masterpiece, remarkable for its plan and unity of conception. It was modelled after the Abbasid Great Mosque of Samarra, particularly its spiral minaret. In Kairouan, the capital of Ifriqiya, vassals of the Abbasid caliphs, the Aghlabids (184/800–296/909) expanded the Great Mosque of Kairouan, one of the most venerable congregational mosques in the Maghrib. Its *mihrab* was covered by ceramic tiles from Mesopotamia.

The reign of the Fatimids (297/909–567/1171) represents a remarkable period in the history of the Islamic countries of the Mediterranean: North Africa, Sicily, Egypt and Syria. Of their

Kairouan Mosque, mihrab, Tunisia.

Kairouan Mosque, minaret, Tunisia.

Citadel of Aleppo, view of the entrance, Syria.

Complex of Qaluwun, Cairo, Egypt.

architectural constructions, a few examples remain that bear witness to their past glory. In the central Maghrib the Qal'a of the Bani Hammad and the Mosque of Mahdiya; in Sicily, the Cuba (*Qubba*) and the Zisa (*al-'Aziza*) in Palermo, constructed by Fatimid craftsmen under the Norman king William II; in Cairo, the Azhar Mosque is the most prominent example of Fatimid architecture in Egypt.

The Ayyubids (567/1171–648/1250), who overthrew the Fatimid dynasty in Cairo, were important patrons of architecture. They established religious institutions *(madrasas, khanqas)* for the propagation of *Sunni* Islam, mausoleums and welfare projects, as well as awesome fortifications pertaining to the military conflict with the Crusaders. The Citadel of Aleppo in Syria is a remarkable example of their military architecture.

The Mamluks (648/1250–923/1517) successors to the Ayyubids who had successfully resisted the Crusades and the Mongols, achieved the unity of Syria and Egypt and created a formidable empire. The wealth and luxury of the Mamluk sultan's court in Cairo motivated artists and architects to achieve an extraordinarily elegant style of architecture. For the world of Islam, the Mamluk period marked a rebirth and renaissance. The enthusiasm for establishing religious foundations and reconstructing existing ones place the Mamluks among the greatest patrons of art and architecture in the history of Islam. The Mosque of Hassan (757/1356), a funerary mosque built with a cruciform plan in which the four arms of the cross were formed by four *iwans* of the building around a central courtyard was typical of the era.

Anatolia was the birthplace of two great Islamic dynasties: the Seljuqs (571/1075–718/1318), who introduced Islam to the region; and the Ottomans (699/1299–1340/1922), who brought about the end of the Byzantine Empire upon capturing Constantinople, and asserted their hegemony throughout the region.

A distinctive style of Seljuq art and architecture flourished with influences from Central Asia, Iran, Mesopotamia and Syria, which merged with elements deriving from Anatolian Christian and antiquity heritage. Konya, the new capital in Central Anatolia, as well as other cities, were enriched with buildings in the newly developed Seljuq style. Numerous mosques, *madrasas*, *turbes* and *caravanserais*, which were richly decorated by stucco and tiling with diverse figural representations, have survived to our day.

As the Seljuq emirates disintegrated and Byzantium declined, the Ottomans expanded their territory swiftly changng their capital from Iznik to Bursa and then

Selimiye Mosque, general view, Edirne, Turkey.

Tile of Kubadabad Palace, Karatay Museum, Konya, Turkey.

Great Mosque of Córdoba, mihrab, Spain.

Madinat al-Zahra', Dar al-Yund, Spain.

again to Edirne. The conquest of Constantinople in 858/1453 by Sultan Mehmet II provided the necessary impetus for the transition of an emerging state into a great empire. A superpower that extended its boundaries to Vienna including the Balkans in the West and to Iran in the East, as well as North Africa from Egypt to Algeria, turning the Eastern Mediterranean into an Ottoman sea. The race to surpass the grandeur of the inherited Byzantine churches, exemplified by the Hagia Sophia, culminated in the construction of great mosques in Istanbul. The most significant one is the Mosque of Süleymaniye, built in the $10^{th}/16^{th}$ century by the famous Ottoman architect Sinan, epitomises the climax in architectural harmony in domed buildings. Most major Ottoman mosques were part of a large building complex called *kulliye* that also consisted several *madrasa*s, a Qur'an school, a library, a hospital (*darussifa*), a hostel (*tabhane*), a public kitchen, a *caravanserai* and mausoleums (*turbe*s). From the beginning of the $12^{th}/18^{th}$ century, during the so-called Tulip Period, Ottoman architecture and decorative style reflected the influence of French Baroque and Rococo, heralding the westernisation period in arts and architecture.

Al-Andalus at the western part of the Islamic world became the cradle of a brilliant artistic and cultural expression. 'Abd al-Rahman I established an independent Umayyad caliphate (138/750–422/1031) with Córdoba as its capital. The Great Mosque of Córdoba would pioneer innovative artistic tendencies such as

Tinmal Mosque, aerial view, Morocco.

the double tiered arches with two alternating colours and panels with vegetal ornamentation which would become part of the repertoire of al-Andalus artistic forms. In the 5th/11th century, the caliphate of Córdoba broke up into a score of principalities incapable of preventing the progressive advance of the reconquest initiated by the Christian states of the Northwestern Iberian Peninsula. These petty kings, or Taifa Kings, called the Almoravids in 479/1086 and the Almohads in 540/1145, repelled the Christians and reestablished partial unity in al-Andalus.

Through their intervention in the Iberian Peninsula, the Almoravids (427/1036–541/1147) came into contact with a new civilisation and were captivated quickly by the refinement of al-Andalus art as reflected in their capital, Marrakesh, where they built a grand mosque and palaces. The influence of the architecture of Córdoba and other capitals such as Seville would be felt in all of the Almoravid monuments from Tlemcen, Algiers to Fez.

Under the rule of the Almohads (515/1121–667/1269), who expanded their hegemony as far as Tunisia, western Islamic art reached its climax. During this period, artistic creativity that originated with the Almoravid rulers was renewed and masterpieces of Islamic art were created. The Great Mosque of Seville

Ladies Tower and Gardens, Alhambra, Granada, Spain.

Mertola, general view, Portugal.

Decoration detail, Abu Inan Madrasa, Meknes, Morocco.

with its minaret the Giralda, the Kutubiya in Marrakesh, the Mosque of Hassan in Rabat and the Mosque of Tinmal high in the Atlas Mountains in Morocco are notable examples.

Upon the dissolution of the Almohad Empire, the Nasrid dynasty (629/1232–897/1492) installed itself in Granada and was to experience a period of splendour in the $8^{th}/14^{th}$ century. The civilisation of Granada would become a cultural model in future centuries in Spain (Mudéjar Art) and particularly in Morocco, where this artistic tradition enjoyed great popularity and would be preserved until the present day in the areas of architecture and decoration, music and cuisine. The famous palace and fort of *al-Hamra'* (the Alhambra) in Granada marks the crowning achievement of al-Andalus art, with all features of its artistic repertoire.

At the same time in Morocco, the Merinids (641/1243–876/1471) replaced the Almohads, while in Algeria the 'Abd al-Wadid's reigned (633/1235–922/1516), as did the Hafsids (625/1228–941/

Qal'a of the Bani Hammad, minaret, Algeria.

Sa'adian Tomb Marrakesh, Morocco.

1534) in Tunisia. The Merinids perpetuated al-Andalus art, enriching it with new features. They embellished their capital Fez with an abundance of mosques, palaces and *madrasa*s, with their clay mosaic and *zellij* panelling in the wall decorations, considered to be the most perfect works of Islamic art. The later Moroccan dynasties, the Sa'adians (933/1527–1070/1659) and the 'Alawite (1077/1659 – until the present day), carried on the artistic tradition of al-Andalus that was exiled from its native soil in 897/1492. They continued to build and decorate their monuments using the same formulas and the same decorative themes as had the preceding dynasties, adding innovative touches characteristic of their creative genius. In the early $11^{th}/17^{th}$ century, emigrants from al-Andalus (the *Moriscos*), who took up residence in the northern cities of Morocco, introduced numerous features of al-Andalus art. Today, Morocco is one of the few countries that has kept traditions of al-Andalus alive in its architecture and furniture, at the same time modernising them as they incorporated the architectural techniques and styles of the $15^{th}/20^{th}$ century.

ARCHITECTURAL SUMMARY

In general terms, Islamic architecture can be classified into two categories: religious, such as mosques, *madrasa*s, mausoleums, and secular, such as palaces, *caravanserai*s, fortifications, etc.

Religious Architecture

Mosques

The mosque for obvious reasons lies at the very heart of Islamic architecture. It is an apt symbol of the faith that it serves. That symbolic role was understood by Muslims at a very early stage, and played an important part in the creation of suitable visual markers for the building: minaret, dome, *mihrab*, *minbar*, etc.

The first mosque in Islam was the courtyard of the Prophet's house in Medina, with no architectural refinements. Early mosques built by the Muslims as their empire was expanding were simple. From these buildings developed the congregational or Friday mosque (*jami'*), essential features of which remain today unchanged for nearly 1400 years. The general plan consists of a large courtyard surrounded by arched porticoes, with more aisles or arcades on the side facing Mecca (*qibla*) than the other sides. The Great Umayyad Mosque in Damascus, which followed the plan of the Prophet's mosque, became the prototype for many mosques built in various parts of the Islamic world.

Two other types of mosques developed in Anatolia and afterwards in the Ottoman domains: the basilical and the dome types. The first type is a simple pillared hall or basilica that follows late Roman and Byzantine Syrian tradition, introduced with some modifications in the 5th/11th century. The second type, which developed during the Ottoman period, has its organisation of interior space under a single dome. The Ottoman architects in great imperial mosques created a new style of domed construction by merging the Islamic mosque tradition with that of dome building in Anatolia. The main dome rests on hexagonal support system, while lateral bays are covered by smaller domes. This emphasis on an interior space dominated by a single dome became the starting point of a style that was to be intro-

Umayyad Mosque of Damascus, Syria.

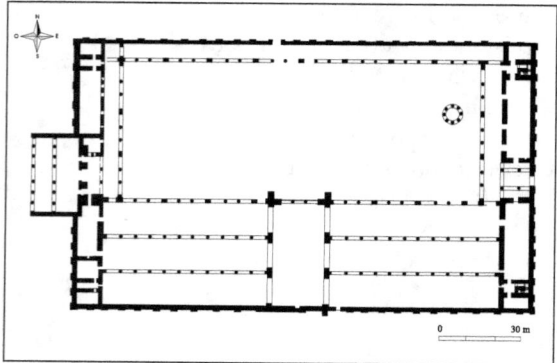

duced in the 10th/16th century. During this period, mosques became multipurpose social complexes consisting of a *zawiya*, a *madrasa*, a public kitchen, a bath, a *caravanserai* and a mausoleum of the founder. The supreme monument of this style is the Sülaymeniye Mosque in Istanbul built in 965/1557 by the great architect Sinan.

The minaret from the top of which the *muezzin* calls Muslims to prayer, is the most prominent marker of the mosque. In Syria the traditional minaret consists of a square-plan tower built of stone. In Mamluk Egypt minarets are each divided into three distinct zones: a square section at the bottom, an octagonal middle section and a circular section with a small dome on the top. Its shaft is richly decorated and the transition between each section is covered with a band of *muqarnas* decoration. Minarets in North Africa and Spain, that share the square tower form with Syria, are decorated with panels of motifs around paired sets of windows. During the Ottoman period the octagonal or cylindrical minarets replaced the square tower. Often these are tall pointed minarets and although mosques generally have only one minaret, in major cities there are two, four or even six minarets.

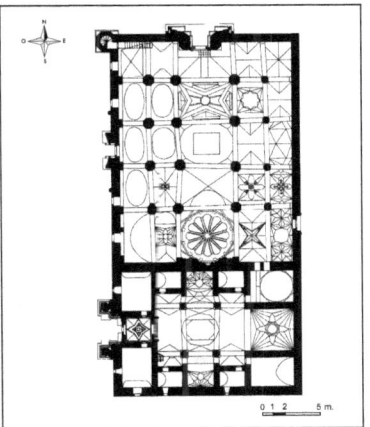

Great Mosque, Divriği, Turkey.

Madrasas

It seems likely that the Seljuqs built the first *madrasa*s in Persia in the early 5th/11th century when they were small structures with a domed courtyard and two lateral *iwan*s. A later type developed has an open courtyard with a central *iwan* and surrounded by arcades. During the 6th/12th century in

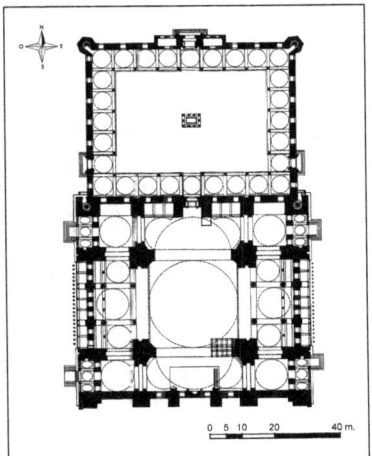

Sülaymeniye Mosque, Istanbul, Turkey.

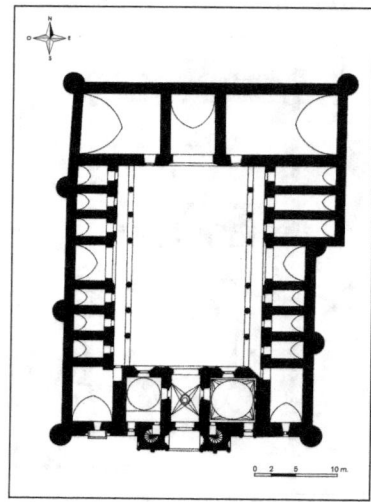

Typology of minarets.

Sivas Gök Madrasa, Turkey.

Anatolia, the *madrasa* became multifunctional and was intended to serve as a medical school, mental hospital, a hospice with a public kitchen (*imaret*) and a mausoleum. The promotion of *Sunni* (Orthodox) Islam reached a new zenith in Syria and Egypt under the Zengids and the Ayyubids (6th/12th–early 7th/13th centuries). This era witnessed the introduction of the *madrasa* established by a civic or political leader for the advancement of Islamic jurisprudence. The foundation was funded by an endowment in perpetuity (*waqf*), usually the revenues of land or property in the form of an orchard, shops in a market (*suq*), or a bathhouse (*hammam*). The *madrasa* traditionally followed a cruciform plan with a central court surrounded by four *iwan*s. Soon the *madrasa* became a dominant architectural form with mosques adopting a four-*iwan* plan. The *madrasa* gradually lost its sole religious and political function as a propaganda tool and tended to have a broader civic function, serving as a congregational mosque and a mausoleum for the benefactor.

The construction of *madrasa*s in Egypt and particularly in Cairo gathered new momentum with the coming of the Mamluks. The typical Cairene *madrasa* of this era was a multifunctional gigantic four-*iwan* structure with a stalactite (*muqarnas*) portal and splendid façades. With the advent of the Ottomans in the 10th/16th century, the joint foundation, typically a mosque-*madrasa*, became a widespread large complex that enjoyed imperial patronage. The *iwan* disappeared gradually and was replaced by a dominant dome chamber. A substantial increase in the number of domed cells used by students is a characteristic of Ottoman *madrasa*s.

One of the various building types that by virtue of their function and of their form can be related to the *madrasa* is the *khanqa*. The term indicates an institution, rather than a particular kind of building, that houses members of a Muslim mystical (*sufi*) order. Several other words used by Muslim historians as synonyms for *khanqa* include: in the Maghrib, *zawiya*; in Ottoman domain, *tekke*; and in general, *ribat*. Sufism permanently dominated the *khanqa*, which originated in eastern Persia during the 4th/10th century. In its simplest form the *khanqa* was a house where a group of pupils gathered around a master (*shaykh*), and it had the facilities for assembly, prayer and communal living. The establishment of *khanqa*s flourished under the Seljuqs during the 5th/11th and the 6th/12th centuries and benefited from the close association between *Sufism* and the *Shafi'i madhhab* (doctrine) favoured by ruling elite.

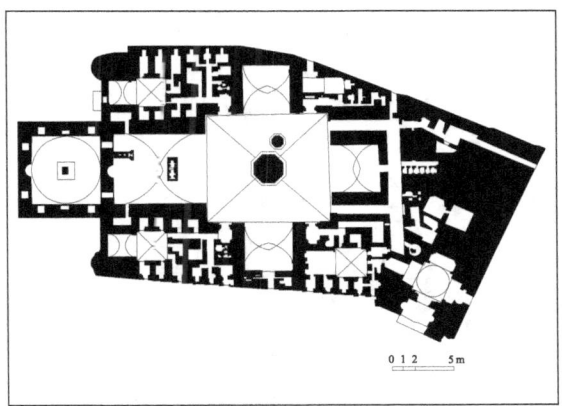

Mosque and madrasa Sultan Hassan, Cairo, Egypt.

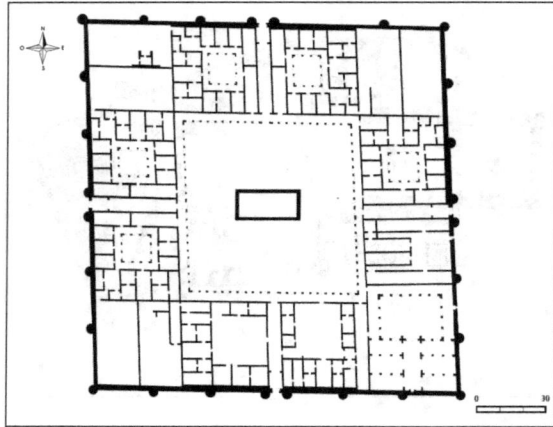

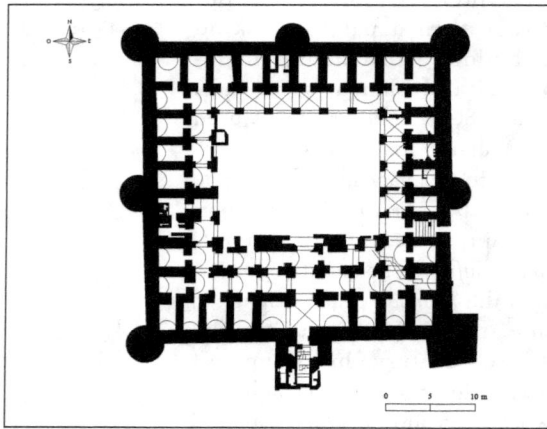

Qasr al-Khayr al-Sharqi, Syria.

Ribat of Sousse, Tunisia.

Mausoleums

The terminology of the building type of the mausoleum used in Islamic sources is varied. The standard descriptive term *turbe* refers to the function of the building as for burial. Another term is *qubba* that refers to the most identifiable, the dome, and often marks a structure commemorating biblical prophets, companions of the Prophet Muhammad and religious or military notables. The function of mausoleums is not limited simply to a place of burial and commemoration, but also plays an important role in "popular" religion. They are venerated as tombs of local saints and became places of pilgrimage. Often the structure of a mausoleum is embellished with qur'anic quotations and contains a *mihrab* within it to render it a place of prayer. In some cases the mausoleum became part of a joint foundation. Forms of medieval Islamic mausoleums are varied, but the traditional one has a domed square plan.

Secular Architecture

Palaces

The Umayyad period is characterised by sumptuous palaces and bathhouses in remote desert regions. Their basic plan is largely derived from Roman military models. Although the decoration of these structures is eclectic, they constitute the best examples of the budding Islamic decorative style. Mosaics, mural paintings, stone or stucco sculpture were used for a remarkable variety of decorations and themes. Abbasid palaces in Iraq, such as those at Samarra and Ukhaidir, follow the same plan as their Umayyad forerunners, but are marked by increase in size, the use of the great *iwan*, dome and courtyard, and the extensive use of stucco decorations. Palaces in the later Islamic period developed a distinctive style that was more decorative and less monumental. The most remarkable example of royal or princely palaces is the Alhambra. The vast area of the palace is broken up into a series of separate units: gardens, pavilions and courts. The most striking feature of Alhambra, however, is the decoration that provides an extraordinary effect in the interior of the building.

Caravanserais

A *caravanserai* generally refers to a large structure that provides a lodging place for travellers and merchants. Normally, it is a square or rectangular floor plan, with a single projecting monumental entrance and towers in the exterior walls. A central courtyard is surrounded by porticoes and rooms for lodging travellers, storing merchandise and for the stabling of animals.

The characteristic type of building has a wide range of functions since it has been described as *khan, han, funduq, ribat*. These terms may imply no more than differences in regional vocabularies rather than being distinctive functions or types. The architectural sources of the various types of *caravanserai*s are difficult to identify. Some are perhaps derived

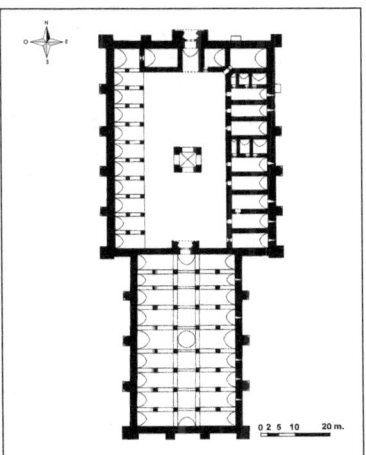

Aksaray Sultan Khan, Turkey.

from the Roman *castrum* or military camp to which the Umayyad desert palaces are related. Other types, in Mesopotamia and Persia, are associated with domestic architecture.

Urban organisation

From about the $3^{rd}/10^{th}$ century every town of any significance acquired fortified walls and towers, elaborate gates and a mighty citadel (*qal'a* or *qasba*) as seat of power. These are massive constructions built in materials characteristic of the region in which they are found; stone in Syria, Palestine and Egypt, or brick, stone and rammed earth in the Iberian Peninsula and North Africa. A unique example of military architecture is the *ribat*. Technically, this is a fortified palace designated for the temporary or permanent warriors of

Islam who committed themselves to the defence of frontiers. The *ribat* of Sousse in Tunisia bears resemblance to early Islamic palaces, but with a different interior arrangement of large halls, mosque and a minaret.

The division of the majority of Islamic cities into neighbourhoods is based on ethnic and religious affinity and it is also a system of urban organisation that facilitates the administration of the population. In the neighbourhood there is always a mosque. A bathhouse, a fountain, an oven and a group of stores are located either within or nearby. Its structure is formed by a network of streets, alleys and a collection of houses. Depending on the region and era, the home takes on diverse features governed by the historical and cultural traditions, climate and construction materials available.

The market (*suq*), which functions as the nerve-centre for local businesses, would be the most relevant characteristic of Islamic cities. Its distance from the mosque determines the spatial organisation of the markets by specialised guilds. For instance, the professions considered clean and honourable (bookmakers, perfume makers, tailors) are located in the mosque's immediate environs, and the noisy and foul-smelling crafts (blacksmith, tanning, cloth dying) are situated progressively further from it. This geographic distribution responds to imperatives that rank on strictly technical grounds.

Royal Alcázar, detail of
Patio de las Doncellas,
Seville.

HISTORICAL-ARTISTIC INTRODUCTION

Gonzalo M. Borrás Gualís

The reason Mudéjar art was chosen as the Spanish contribution to the project *Islamic Art in the Mediterranean*, among the manifold expressions of Spain's Islamic heritage, is its singular and unique character; an artistic manifestation without parallel in the rest of Islamic culture. The Mudéjar aesthetic arose out of the particular historical circumstances of Spain in the Middle Ages, a set of circumstances which did not occur in any other territory under Islamic rule. A historical explanation of these circumstances is essential in order to understand Mudéjar art and architecture.

A Brief History of Islam in Spain

The presence of Islam in Spain spans eight centuries, from 711, the date of the Muslim invasion of the Iberian Peninsula by the troops of Tariq and Musa, emissaries of the Umayyad Caliphate of Damascus, to 1492, when the capture of Granada by the Catholic Monarchs put an end to the last Nasrid sultanate.

These eight centuries of Islamic domination have left a mark of such profundity on Spanish culture that the historian Ramón Menéndez Pidal defined the role of Spain as the *"communicating link between Christianity and Islam"*.

More recently, the writer Juan Goytisolo has underlined that *"Spanish culture can be distinguished from the other cultures of the present European Community by its tinged Occidentalism"*; this Spanish "tinge" arises from a series of components and characteristics that are a direct consequence of the presence of Islam in Spanish history.

The history of al-Andalús, the name given by the Arabic chroniclers to the territory in the peninsula dominated by Islam, acquires a peculiar slant when, in the year 75, the Umayyad 'Abd al-Rahman I – a survivor of the slaughter of the Abbasids – established a kingdom in the city of Córdoba, proclaiming himself *Emir* independent of the Eastern Caliphate of Baghdad. His desire to make Córdoba the new Damascus of the West meant that Andalucían culture was imprinted with the definitive characteristics of Arabic culture. During 300 years, 8th–10th century, Córdoba was the capital of the western Umayyads and the centre for the creation and dissemination of art. Its period of maximum splendour coincided with the proclamation of 'Abd al-Rahman III as Caliph in the year 929. The Great

Church of San José, window of alminar-tower with a horseshoe arch, Granada.

Historical-Artistic Introduction

The Alhambra, view from Sacromonte, Granada.

Royal Alcázar, dado tiling in the Patio de las Doncellas, Seville.

Mosque of Córdoba (786–990) and the archaeological remains of Medina al-Zahra' (936–976), the Caliphate City of 'Abd al-Rahman III and al-Hakam II, are the most singular monuments of the Córdoban period. The integrating role played by the Umayyad Dynasty of Córdoba in al-Andalús disappeared after the collapse of the caliphate as the result of civil wars at the beginning of the 11th century, giving way to a period of political fragmentation known as the Taifa kingdoms. Some local dynasties emerged, such as the Hudids in Saragossa, the Dhu-l-Nunids in Toledo, the Abbasids in Seville and the Zirids in Granada. All of them represented a blend of political weakness with cultural and artistic splendour. One of their most outstanding testimonies is the Hudid Aljafería Palace in Saragossa.

The 11th century ended with the weight of the political scales in favour of the Christian kingdoms of the north. The clearest evidence of this change is that, in 1085, the city of Toledo, ancient capital of the Visigothic kingdom and later the Islamic capital of the Middle March territories and of the Taifa Dhu-l-Nunids, fell into the hands of Alfonso VI of Castile. The surrender of Toledo marks a decisive watershed in Spanish medieval history, for both the Muslims and the Christians.

Conscious of their political weakness, the Taifa kingdoms sought the help of the Almoravid Empire of Yusuf Ibn Tashfin, who immediately crossed over to the peninsula in the year 1086. There, Ibn Tashfin defeated the Christians in the Battle of Zallaqa and then, although not originally part of his plan, from the year 1090 onwards, he unified and brought under his control the whole territory of al-Andalús.

In this way, the period of the two Berber empires – the Almoravid and the Almohad – began, stretching across both sides of the Strait of Gibraltar, in al-Andalús and in the Maghreb. Now, the Andalucían artistic tradition, which extended throughout North Africa under Almoravid domination, took on new oriental influences. This mixture of characteristics is evident in the Great Mosque of Tlemcen or in the Qarawiyyin Mosque in Fez.

Castle, general view, Arévalo.

Still extant from the Almohad period in the city of Seville, residence of the Caliph from 1171, are the Great Mosque, from which the patio de los Naranjos (Courtyard of the Orange Trees) still survives, even if somewhat altered, and the minaret, the present Giralda. Also from this same period are other town palaces in La Buhayra and in the Real Alcázar (Royal Palace).

The domination of al-Andalús by the Almoravid and Almohad empires did not stop the territorial advance of the Christians. In 1118 the King of Aragon, Alfonso I el Batallador (the Fighter) conquered the city of Saragossa, capital of the Upper March. The cities of Tudela and Tarazona were next, conquered in 1119, and Calatayud and Daroca followed in 1120. Another important Christian advance was the total occupation of the middle valley of the River Ebro.

The Almohads also had to relinquish power and give way to the continuous advance of the Christians, above all following the Battle of the Navas de Tolosa in 1212. The breakdown of Almohad domination made reconquest of the territory of the Levant much easier, with the capture of Valencia by Jaime I el Conquistador (the Conqueror) in 1238 and the Valley of the Guadalquivir by Fernando III, which included the conquests of Córdoba in 1236 and Seville in 1248. The 8th-century history of al-Andalús is a succession of periods of concentrated political power – the Córdoban, Almoravid and Almohad periods as already mentioned – each followed by other periods of fragmentation – the *taifas*.

After the final breakdown of Almohad power, only one dynasty managed to survive, thanks to a pact with the Castilian king, and this was the Nasrids (1232–1492), who in 1237 chose Granada as their capital. The Nasrids built a new palace-city in the Alhambra on the Sabika hill, dominating the territory of Upper Andalucía. Here the art of al-Anadalús reached the zenith of expression in the monumental complexes of the Alhambra and the Generalife. In Granada, the history of al-Andalús and of Islamic art in Spain

Historical-Artistic Introduction

La Aljafería, ceiling of the Palace of the Catholic Monarchs, Saragossa.

reaches both its highest point and its end. In this way, then, for eight centuries, medieval Spain was split-up into an unequal and constantly changing balance between Christendom and Islam, two cultures in political and religious opposition. The history of military deeds has often confused and hidden far richer lessons in the history of this time about the cultural contact between Christians and Muslims. One cultural consequence of this contact is Mudéjar art.

The Mudéjar:
Between Islam and Christendom

In this context of cultural interchange, the capitulation of Toledo to Alfonso VI of Castile in 1085, and the capture of Saragossa by Alfonso I el Batallador in 1118, meant something more than just another incident in the division of the territory of the peninsula between Christians and Muslims, for they are historical events of great cultural importance. In fact, the reconquest of Toledo and Saragossa meant the beginning of a new situation for the Christians: the occupation of large urban centres within their respective territories for which they did not have any potential resettlers. From that time on, a policy of resettlement was established, and this was to be decisive in the structural formation of society in Christian medieval Spain.

The difficulty experienced by the Christian kingdoms in the north of the peninsula in repopulating the vast reconquered territories, led to a political decision that had long-lasting consequences for medieval Spain. This was the authorisation granted to the conquered Muslim population, which allowed them to remain under Christian domination in the conquered territories and to conserve the Muslim religion, the Arabic language and their own judicial system. This explains why the Mudéjars appeared on the social scene at that time; they were the Muslims permitted to remain in Christian Spain on payment of a tribute.

While Muslim domination of the Iberian Peninsula lasted, the two communities – of Christians, called *Mozárabes*, or Mozarabs, and Jews – lived as tributaries under Islamic rule, and the many Christians who converted to Islam took the name *Muladís*. Then, when the balance weighted on the Christian side, between the 11th and 12th centuries, after the capitulation of Toledo and Saragossa, it was the defeated Muslims – the Mudéjars – along with the Jews, who became the tributaries of the Christian kings. It is from this crucial moment on that the Muslims settled, not only in al-Andalús, but also on medieval Hispanic soil on the other side of the political frontier, in Christian territory. So now, there was the cultural assimilation of the conquered Muslims – the Mudéjars – within Hispanic society, while the Christians showed evident fascination for the Islamic monuments in the conquered cities.

Muslim fortresses were transformed into palaces for Christian kings, and the Great Mosques were purified and consecrated as cathedrals and churches. In parallel, the Christian kingdoms maintained close cultural relationships with the territories of still-unconquered al-Andalús and especially with the Nasrid kingdom.

All of these factors help to explain the creation and development of Mudéjar art in Christian Spain.

These social circumstances favoured the birth of Mudéjar art – defined as the result of the confluence of two artistic traditions: the Islamic and the Christian – and gave rise to a new form of artistic expression, one that markedly diverges from the two artistic styles that influenced it.

Culturally speaking, therefore, Mudéjar art belongs between Christian and Islamic art. This is why Mudéjar constitutes the most genuine artistic manifestation of Christian medieval Spain as the crucible of three cultures, and why it represents the authentic material expression of popular thought of a society in which Christians, Mudéjars and Jews lived side by side.

It is for this reason that Mudéjar ought to be appreciated as more than merely a product of Castillian exaggeration. Furthermore, it is why the sensible opinion of Marcelino Menéndez Pelayo – "*Mudéjar art is the only type of construction that is uniquely Spanish which we can be proud of*" – prevails, and why Mudéjar was considered appro-

Parish Church, detail of the tower, Utebo.

priate and decisively chosen for the International Cycle: *Islamic Art in the Mediterranean*.

Nevertheless, perhaps precisely because of its unique character, Mudéjar is the expression of Spanish art that has been interpreted in the most contradictory ways, from completely opposing positions according to the specific evaluation each historian has made of this artistic phenomenon, and according to the proportion of each of the different elements – Islamic and Christian – contained within it.

On the one side are ranged those who have classified Mudéjar as a brilliant epilogue to the history of Hispano-Muslim or Andalucían art, a final chapter which concerned itself with the survival of Islamic art in Christian territory. This historiographical approach neglects an important historical circumstance however, and this is that Mudéjar art was not created under Muslim political domination. The line between Muslim art and Mudéjar art is drawn by an important historical event: the

Historical-Artistic Introduction

Casa de Pilatos, window of the principal patio, Seville.

Christian *Reconquista*. In Mudéjar art, which developed under Christian domination, what is no longer apparent is precisely the cultural basis of Muslim art, which is to say that evidence of Mudéjar art's subjection to the political domination of Islam is absent. In the strictest sense, in fact, Mudéjar art does not belong to the Muslim artistic tradition.

On the other side are those who interpret Mudéjar art as part of Western Christian art, valuing it merely as an ornamental addition in the Islamic tradition to the Western Romanesque or Gothic styles. For this second group of historians, the Mudéjar monuments clearly belong to the Western European tradition with certain traces or influences from Islamic art. It is from this evaluation that the use of terms such as "Romanesque Mudéjar" or "Gothic Mudéjar" derive, to describe artistic manifestations whose structure and principal

always relates to Western art, with the Muslim contribution limited to the ornamental and secondary elements. This historiographic school, as will be seen later, overvalued the Christian influences and undervalued the role of the Islamic elements that make up Mudéjar art since these are not purely ornamental; and, furthermore, the ornamental characteristics of Mudéjar art do not have the same function as those in the Western European tradition.

Mudéjar art, therefore, does not belong in the strictest sense to the history of either Muslim art or Western Christian art, but rather, it represents the link between two cultures. It is a unique phenomenon in the history of Spanish art. The detailed analysis of the Muslim and Christian artistic elements that make up Mudéjar art and the different values attributed to them, which has led to the opposing attitudes described above, are probably both equally far removed from the cultural and social reality which made Mudéjar art possible. Some years ago, Fernando Chueca denounced with beautiful clairvoyance that these fragmentary analyses of Mudéjar *"only emphasise the problem, because with whatever components we choose, we find ourselves faced with the reality of a people manifesting itself in a very precise way and with great unanimity"*. Definitively, then, these extreme attitudes to an interpretation of Mudéjar art and architecture fail to recognise the most important of facts: that art, above all, is the expression of a society. Mudéjar is nothing but an artistic expression of medieval Spanish society in which Christians, Muslims and Jews lived together. This society was the result of the political pragmatism and religious tolerance of the resettlers. In a strictly orthodox context, the Christians would not have allowed the Muslims to remain, and the Muslims would not have stayed either. Without any doubt, it was a cultural anomaly, but so is Mudéjar to some extent.

It should be emphasised again, that Mudéjar is a unique artistic expression that differs from the Muslim and Christian elements that helped fashion it. In fact, it belongs *pro indiviso* to both the Islamic and Christian cultures, just as a large part of Spanish medieval history does, in fact.

The Artistic Characterisation of Mudéjar

All artistic manifestations use a formal language that requires precise definition before attributing any work to a particular style or period. In the case of Mudéjar art and architecture, the discrepancies in the analysis and evaluation of the formal elements which define it, some coming from the Islamic tradition and others from the Western tradition, have made this artistic characterisation more difficult. This, in turn, has produced some controversial discrepancies in the argument as to the Mudéjar character of certain monuments.

In relation to the stylistic content of Mudéjar art, it has progressed both by excess and by defect. In terms of excess, because of the classification of some Christian works as Mudéjar, even when certain formal traits or Islamic influences only appear in isolation or sporadically. Thus, a certain fashion for Mudéjarism has caused enormous damage to reaching a precise definition of Mudéjar art. In terms of defect also, because of the failure to recognise as such some monuments that are Mudéjar. The basis for this error on occasion has been the apparent discovery in these monuments of an excessive Islamisation, with the result that some monuments of Christian Spain were classified as Islamic. To cite but one example of this historical incongruence, Torres Balbás placed the synagogue of Santa Maria la Blanca in Toledo under the heading "Almohad art".

On other occasions, contrary to the refusal to recognise the Mudéjar character of particular monuments is the failure to record correctly the Islamic elements in Mudéjar monuments. The best known and most notable of these cases is the concentration of Mudéjar in León and Castilla la Vieja (Old Castile) from the 12th and 13th centuries, where some scholars have simply preferred to call it "brick-built Romanesque" or "brick-built architecture". In fact, Mudéjar should be characterised from a formal point of view by the conjunction of Christian and Islamic artistic elements. It was

Grange at Mirabel, doors of the Chapel of la Magdalena, Guadalupe.

Synagogue of Santa María la Blanca, capital detail, Toledo.

Church of San Miguel, detail of brick pillar, Villalón de Campos.

artistic elements one by one, instead of insisting on the characteristic synthesis of these formal Christian and Muslim elements that resulted in this new and different artistic expression that diverges from its constituent elements.

This attitude of analysis and disintegration has profoundly damaged the understanding of Mudéjar art: what art has brought together let not the historian put asunder.

An analysis of the formal elements within any artistic manifestation can be tedious and we would have disregarded it here altogether had an incorrect interpretation of the text of Amador de los Ríos not completely distorted this analysis, leading to an over-valuation of the formal elements. According to Amador de los Ríos, Mudéjar art sometimes uses *"for its principal forms those of ogival art which was flourishing at that time and as ornamental forms those of mahometan art"*. He immediately adds, however, that on other occasions it follows *"quite the opposite system"*, which is to say that the reverse happens.

It comes down to the error made by Vicente Lampérez, who was followed blindly by the majority of later historians, where he almost completely ignored the "opposite system" of Amador de los Ríos, and affirmed in general terms that Mudéjar art always utilised Christian structures and Islamic ornamentation. This is essentially a distortion, where there is also an underlying Western aesthetic prejudice that considers the structural element the principal one and the ornamental as secondary. It is from Lampérez's evaluation that the current confusion over an interpretation of what Mudéjar art comprises comes.

defined earlier as such in the seminal exhibition by Amador de los Ríos in 1859, who coined brilliant defining expressions such as *"the marriage of Christian and Arabic architecture"*, *"a singular consortium"*, or *"the prodigious fusion between the art of East and West"*.

However, since the time of Amador de los Ríos, experts have insisted on engaging in a laboratory-style dissection to quantify and evaluate the said

Because of this, any present-day analysis of the formal elements of Mudéjar art should emphasise two observations: first, that ornamentation did not constitute a secondary element in Mudéjar art, but rather it was the primordial one; secondly, that Islamic art also contributed very important structural elements to the formation and development of Mudéjar art.

With respect to the ornamentation, even though it may be unnecessary to offer a reminder of what constitutes the essential principle of all the artistic manifestations of Islam, both Islamic architecture and objects are richly decorated, whatever the scale or the material used might be. It is for this reason that Mudéjar art has preserved the most essential factor of Islamic art: decorative art.

In any analysis of Mudéjar ornamentation, identifying the formal motifs from the Islamic tradition should be a priority. These include the stylised plant motifs – *ataurique*; the geometric elements – strapwork and stars; and the Arabic epigraphic elements – *kufic* or *naskhi* script; as well as the compositional principles in Islamic ornamentation, such as repetitive rhythms, that is, the tendency to cover the surface totally with decorative elements or designs which use patterns without spatial limits.

It was precisely the enormous versatility of the Mudéjar style and its great capacity for formal assimilation – creative attitudes transmitted by Islamic art – that enabled the incorporation of a rich variety of motifs from Christian art into the ornamental repertoire of Mudéjar art and architecture. One example of this is in the Gothic naturalist flora. These ornamental motifs from the Christian tradition are used quite differently by the Mudéjar artists in their compositions, in accordance with the rhythmic system of the Islamic tradition.

The influence of Islam on Mudéjar ornamentation is not confined to ornamental elements, but affects the whole system of composition regard-

Palace of Pedro I, façade, Astudillo.

Seo or Cathedral del Salvador, detail of the ceiling of the Parroquieta, Saragossa.

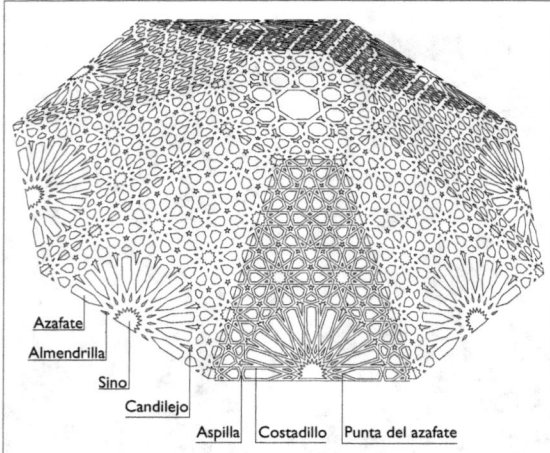

Scheme of armadura, *example of mixed knots of 10 and 20.*

less of the motifs used. The Islamic contribution to Mudéjar art cannot be dismissed as exclusively ornamental either, since it affected the structural elements considerably; what Amador de los Ríos called the "*opposite system*". Here, it will be sufficient to mention two fundamental examples of Mudéjar architectonics that come from the Muslim tradition.

In the first place, we can consider the structure of the numerous bell towers, with the main body – a minaret – and the addition of the belfry at the top; no other Mudéjar construct reflects so transparently the structure of the society that created it. In this respect, the nucleus of Mudéjar in Aragon is outstanding, evident in its bell towers – with either a square or an octagonal ground plan – that comprise two towers, one inside the other, with a staircase connecting the two. The interior tower, divided into rooms one above the other, is reminiscent of the structure of La Giralda in Seville except in the upper part or belfry, which is Christian in its typology.

Another element of Islamic origin that is a basic component of the Mudéjar architectural system are the wooden *armaduras* used in both the *par y nudillo* and *limas* roof styles. As these types of roof design are lighter – although posing a greater fire risk – they distribute the weight on the walls equally, but stylistically this means that the walls are less important in the structure as a whole and, therefore, that their joints are noticeably less articulated than in contemporary Gothic architecture. Fernando Chueca has clearly pointed out that the wooden *armaduras* were one of the most felicitous discoveries of Mudéjar architecture; there are many of them in all concentrations of Mudéjar and the tradition has survived to modern times, both in Spanish and in South American architecture.

As far as the Christian elements in Mudéjar art are concerned and frequently overvalued as they are in the traditional historiography, we must remember that the patrons of Mudéjar art were for the most part Christians and, therefore, both the architectonic functions and the subsequent typologies are Christian. As a result, there is a predominance of Christian religious architecture in the Mudéjar style, with the notable exceptions already mentioned of the Mudéjar synagogues and mosques.

If, throughout history, Islamic art has been characterised by its amazing ability to assimilate the artistic expressions of the people it dominated, therefore allowing Islamic architecture to assimilate numerous typologies and artistic forms from other cultures, it is not surprising that under Christian political domination, faced with the new situation, its adaptability became even stronger. This was possible because – from that time on – it was no longer a case of simply adapting architectonic typologies from other cultures into the architectonic functions of Islam, but rather of putting into practice the Islamic system of working according to the needs of the Christian patrons. What happened then is that the result of this work is no longer Western Christian art but, rather, Mudéjar art, because it produced a new artistic expression, a true synthesis of both Muslim and Christian artistic elements, a new aesthetic unity, as Guillermo Gustavino has argued. It is only with this global context borne in mind that any serious detailed analysis of the artistic elements of Islamic or Christian origin in Mudéjar art is possible.

The Mudéjar System of Working

The most appropriate criteria to achieve a definition of Mudéjar art is an evaluation of a combination of things: the materials used, the techniques employed by its craftsmen as well as the forms of art it gave rise to. In Mudéjar art there is a unity of materials, techniques and art forms, which – although theoretically it may be possible to analyse and evaluate them separately – in the aesthetic reality of the Mudéjar system, they are so closely united that it is impossible to separate them. It is for this reason that the basic materials – i.e. brick, plaster, wood and ceramic – as well as the techniques used, should not be isolated from the aesthetic result, both structural and ornamental, which determine their artistic dimension and transform them into works of art.

In Islamic art as well as in Mudéjar art and architecture, it is the intimate marriage of materials, techniques and art forms that create the perfection of the finished whole, and we dispose

Tower of San Martín, Teruel.

Alcázar, Sanctuary vaulting, Zafra.

Historical-Artistic Introduction

Palace of Pedro I, detail of the High Altar ceiling frieze, Tordesillas.

Detail of the Chapel of Luis de Lucena, Guadalajara.

"It is a palace in which the splendour is spread over all the ceiling, the floor and all the four walls; in the stucco and the tiles there are marvels, but the carved wood of its roof is even more wonderful."

There could hardly be a more concise and felicitous expression of the Islamic aesthetic, with regard to both the concept of the delimitation of space brought about by the ornamental surfaces and also the Unitarian and global concept of all the materials used, in this case the stucco, wood and decorative ceramics. In fact, these materials make up a perfect artistic whole, acting as a formal framework for the splendour and marvels of artistry worked upon them with various techniques. By their very nature and due to the techniques used these materials conditioned formal Islamic design following a gradual process of integration into the system, becoming a vehicle that allowed the formal elements to develop and thereby multiply themselves to infinity. The materials, which provided a surface for the ornamentation, were both interchangeable and adaptable according to the scale. The conception was a symbiosis to achieve both an aesthetic result and a system of representation. To corroborate the idea of a conceptual unity presiding over the treatment of materials in Mudéjar art, we find in the documentation the term "*manobra*" which refers to all that is required to complete a Mudéjar building. So when in the 15th century the Mudéjar master, Muça Domalich won the contract to build the chapter house in the cloisters of the convent of San Pedro Mártir in Calatayud, in the conditions it was stipulated that:

of many examples that clearly demonstrate that, in fact, they were treated as an inseparable. It will be enough to mention one example for each artistic manifestation.

For Islamic art, we can use a poem by Ibn al-Yayyab that decorates the walls of the "Torre de la Cautiva" (Captive's tower) inside the fortified precinct of the Alhambra. Transcribed and studied by María Jesús Rubiera it reads like this:

"The said Master Muça shall provide all manner of necessary things such as wood, nails, plaster, paint and all other manobra which shall be deemed for said work and all other expenses."

Here the term *"manobra"* refers not only to all the proposed materials, which were given dedicated consideration in the contracts, but also, and more generally, to everything necessary for the completion of the work, both the materials and the working of them.

It is only by considering the whole – the materials used, the techniques and art forms – that is to say the Mudéjar system of working, that incorrect interpretations can be avoided. Brick architecture is not to be confused with Mudéjar architecture; likewise with the other materials used. The use of a particular material, technique or art form, considered in isolation, does not constitute in itself a viable method for defining Mudéjar art. We must always keep in mind that we are considering a system.

Social and Economic Factors in Mudéjar Art

Many reasons have been given to explain the success of Mudéjar art, which spread quickly and profusely during the late Middle Ages and scattered monuments throughout almost the whole of Spain. There was a suggestion that there were geographic reasons for the expansion of Romanesque and Gothic architecture that relied on the use of stone, a material difficult to obtain in many parts of the Spanish territory. Another factor may have been the economic crisis and recession, which might explain the spread of a building method that

University, floor tile from the Paraninfo, *Alcalá de Henares.*

was considered cheaper to realise. A further reason could have been the existence of a workforce: the Mudéjar craftsmen were generally thought to be numerous, cheaper, quicker and more efficient. Other interpretations that emphasise the cultural aspects have mentioned the decline of the French influence on Spanish architecture to explain the success of Mudéjar. This influence was definitive throughout the 11th, 12th and

Pharmacy jar or ceramic "pot" from Paterna or Manises, Instituto Valencia de Don Juan (1425), Madrid.

Royal Alcázar, interior of the Pavilion of Carlos V, Seville.

Palace of Pedro I, High Altar ceiling, Tordesillas.

13th centuries, and is obvious in the Romanesque monuments and in the Cistercian monasteries and Gothic cathedrals of the classical period in Castile, but from the 13th century onwards it started to decline, and was replaced by the expansion of Mudéjar architecture in all its splendour.

What is certain is that contemporary researchers have failed to investigate these socio-economic factors satisfactorily, perhaps because there is not enough documentary evidence for a correct evaluation. Manuel Gómez-Moreno suggested in his time that what really happened was the competition between the two systems of working: that of the stonemasons used in Romanesque and Gothic architecture, with techniques and skills strongly influenced by the French building tradition, and that of the Mudéjar craftsmen whose materials, techniques and skills were closely linked to the Islamic building tradition. Ovidio Cuella has unearthed important information from the accounts for the work carried out on the Mudéjar Church (now demolished) of San Pedro Mártir in Calatayud (Saragossa) between 1411 and 1414. This information is extremely important when comparing the relative competitiveness of the work of the Mudéjar and masonry systems, and which in general terms considerably rectifies some of the accepted theories mentioned before. Thanks to documentary sources from Aragon, it has now been possible to affirm that the Mudéjar system at the beginning of the 15th century offered considerable specialisation in the building process. This meant that the workforces moved from place to place according to each of the basic stages of a Mudéjar building: the foundations, main brickwork, facing, and finishing in plaster. The considerable specialisation and professional expertise of the Mudéjar workforce allows us to assume that acceptable standards of production were in place which were competitive not only within the Mudéjar system itself, but also when compared to the work of stonemasons of the same period.

On the other hand, this range of professional expertise meant a considerable difference in the salaries of the workforce, which range from that of the builder to the master craftsman, Mahoma Rami in the example we are dealing with here – who received 5 daily stipends plus 2 allowances for living expenses – down to the daily wage of an apprentice. In between was a wide-ranging salary scale for all the different grades of the remaining master craftsmen and the other skilled workers. The workforce was almost exclusively Mudéjar. The participation of Christian and Jewish workers is irrelevant, but it is significant when we realise that the differences in pay scales relate not to social discrimination but rather to professional qualifications.

Although we do not have sufficient documentation available to compare costings between the two systems completely, the costs of the Mudéjar work varied considerably according to which procedure was followed: officially administered contracts, direct contract, or lowest tender. This undoubtedly influenced the quality of the finished work, but in general, if we consider the achievement of a single annual building season between spring and autumn, this system appears to be extremely efficient. In a calculation following the standards of production for Mudéjar projects, the suggestion is that it would have been possible to complete each single Mudéjar tower for the churches in Teruel in a single season.

The same efficiency, however, cannot be claimed for records pertaining to the Mudéjar craftsmen or for how much they charged. The documentation from the Royal Chancellery of Aragon gives reliable evidence of the precarity of the Mudéjar workforce, confirms that they were highly regarded, and shows that the kings encouraged their administrators to obtain them. Despite this scarcity of documentation, however, we must not forget the important role the Mudéjar workforce played, who appear in the numerous payrolls of the Aragonese master craftsmen in the 14th, 15th and 16th centuries. As far as their charges are concerned, as already mentioned, difference in salary was not due to social discrimination. Another question of considerable interest is how the practical tasks were selectively divided between the two systems, that of the stonemasons and of the Mudéjar workforce. This is verifiable with reference to the 15th century, and the answer relates more to the function of the work in question than the possible economic factors. All of these considerations, although only verifiable in 15th-century documents, undoubtedly can refer retrospectively to other centuries.

With regard to the geographic conditioning intended as a restraint on the system of the stonemasons and as a driving force for the success of

Tabernacle door from Jaén, National Archaeological Museum (57833), Madrid.

Monastery of Nuestra Señora de Guadalupe, Mudéjar Cloister or Cloister of the Miracles, Guadalupe.

Church of La Peregrina, details of the plasterwork, Sahagún.

ples of this. However just as the system of the stonemasons prevailed on many occasions over the geographical limitations, so also, and even more easily, could the Mudéjar spill over what was considered its natural territory, considering the basic materials employed by its system. As a result, it is prudent to revert to the historical reasons for an interpretation of any artistic phenomenon. As José María Azcárate has rightly noted with respect to Mudéjar art, the economic factors "*contributed to its establishment and spread*", but "*do not justify in themselves the creation of a style*".

Historical Factors of Mudéjar Art

If we accept the idea that the wisest approach to the understanding of any artistic expression is to identify the thought and the structure of the society that created it, then we will realise that this approach, which we define as "historical", will give particularly fruitful results for the appreciation of Mudéjar art.

The first factor that made possible the rise of Mudéjar art was the long-held fascination of Christian society for Islamic artefacts. Many elaborate and precious objects – ivory jars, ivory and silver caskets, bronze ewers, silks, and objects in cut glass or rock crystal – passed into the collections of the monasteries and cathedrals of the Christian kingdoms, enriching their hoard of treasures. Formed often from the spoils of war or tributes-in-kind these collections took on new functions and religious uses. It is thanks to that Christian fascination that a great number of sumptuous objects from Andalucían art were conserved. A similar phenomenon took

Mudéjar art, assessments must be made with extreme caution to avoid radical and deterministic thesis on the relationship between the geographical environment and the artistic creation. The will of the artist often overcame the geographical constraints, and in Spanish art, we can see many exam-

place in medieval Christian Europe, where the monasteries and cathedrals accumulated equally dazzling Islamic objects – the booty from the different crusades.

A gradual reconquest of Andalucían territory incorporated an enormous heritage of Islamic monuments into Christian dominions; the most outstanding were the palaces, converted into palaces for the Christian kings, and the mosques, converted into cathedrals. In this way, it was not only the population that converted to Mudéjar, but also the Islamic monuments that submitted to Christian domination too.

The local acceptance of Islamic art in Christian Spain was the first step towards the birth of Mudéjar art. Thus, if the monumental legacy of Islam in some Spanish cities many centuries after the reconquest is still considerable (e.g. among the most outstanding: Saragossa, Toledo, Córdoba, Seville and Granada), we have to make an effort to imagine what must have been, over the centuries, the monumental Islamic heritage in a great number of reconquered Spanish cities.

However, without any doubt, the factor that most influenced the formation of Mudéjar art was the historical process of the Christian reconquest (Reconquista). As noted already a precondition of the appearance of Mudéjar art was the reconquest of the territory. For very complex reasons, this was a gradual process, progressing in stages at irregular intervals between the 11th and 15th centuries.

The Reconquista interrupted the processes of Islamic art at different times in each region of Spain. As a result, the precedents of Islamic monuments in each region were different. As the formal characteristics of Islamic art had a decisive influence on the initial stages in Mudéjar art in each area, they gave it a strong personality and introduced an important element of differentiation in the vast geographical panorama of Hispanic Mudéjar. The chronology of the Reconquista, the circumstances of the resettlement, and the Islamic monumental tradition of each region are very important factors to take into consideration in the shaping of Mudéjar art in general, and of each regional nucleus of Mudéjar art in particular.

However, the appearance of Mudéjar art in each region did not follow immediately from the moment of the reconquest. Between that date and the appearance of the first Mudéjar monuments a certain amount of time passed. This time lapse reflects both the concrete difficulties the repopulation in each case faced, as well as the desire of the conquering Christians to

Church of Santa María, façade window, Sanlúcar la Mayor.

Church of Santa Marina, Sacramental Chapel arches and vaulting, Seville.

leave evidence of Western styles in the recently occupied territories. Only a complex conjunction of concurring elements – i.e. geographic, social and economic factors – can explain the successful rise and development of Mudéjar art.

In his study of the Mudéjar architecture of Seville, Diego Angulo noted a process of progressive "*Mudéjarisation*" that can also be applied to the other regional concentrations: "*at the same time as the art of the defeated Muslims developed, it also gradually distanced itself from the Christians and adopted forms and ornamentation which were more typically Muslim*".

The historical factors of Mudéjar art do not end with these considerations. We must keep in mind that Mudéjar art is a long-lasting phenomenon, more enduring than successive contemporary Western European art styles (Romanesque, Gothic and Renaissance), and also more so than the successive historical stages of Hispano-Muslim art (Taifas, Almoravid, Almohad and Nasrid), which it survived after the conquest of Granada.

For this reason, the stylistic qualities of each regional Mudéjar grouping were derived from the local Islamic precedents and also constantly in the process of enrichment within the historical context by innovations borrowed from al-Andalús and other Mudéjar centres.

Outstanding examples of this are the Mudéjar buildings of Toledo and Teruel.

In the Mudéjar art and architecture of Toledo – despite the city's early capitulation in 1085 – with local and very archaic Islamic precedents, formal influences from Almoravid and Almohad art are evident from very early on, even before the conquest of Seville in 1248. This phenomenon of a formal precociousness in the Mudéjar style of Toledo can find explanation according to the *Latin Chronicle* of Alfonso VII, which relates it to the return of a colony of Mozarabs to Toledo after the destruction of Marrakesh by the Almohads in 1147. The highly archaic Aragon precedents, however, do not explain the precociousness of Mudéjar forms in Teruel, although the characteristics of its open Moorish Quarter, inhabited mainly by immigrant Muslims from the Levant, do offer an explanation.

We should not forget that the mobility of the Mudéjar workforce, especially those affiliated to royal contracts, allowed art forms to move freely, not just between different regional Christian centres, but also between these and the Islamic territories and vice versa. This was the case with the Muslim workers from Toledo, Seville and Granada, who worked for

Pedro I of Castile in the Real Alcázar in Seville. It was also the case with Muhammad V in the Patio de los Leones (Courtyard of the Lions) in the Alhambra, who used the same formal elements on both sides of the political frontier between Christianity and Islam. The reintroduction of the unifying factors of Mudéjar art was via this route.

Identical considerations of a historical nature can be useful to analyse and evaluate the evolution of Mudéjar art and the use therein of architectonic typologies and art forms borrowed from Western Christian art.

Mudéjar Centres in the Iberian Peninsula

Although the unifying elements of Mudéjar art are unmistakeable and easily perceived by Western visitors, the different regional styles of Mudéjar in Spain offer a rich diversity as the consequence of the historical factors that prevail in each area. This variety increases the allure of our project and obliges us to define some of the distinctive formal characteristics of the principal Mudéjar concentrations – those in Aragon, León and Castilla la Vieja, Toledo, Extremadura and Seville – before we justify the itineraries chosen in each case.

One of the most outstanding formal signatures of Mudéjar art and architecture in Aragon is the importance of brick in the architecture. While brick is the basic building material of the whole work, at the same time it acts as a decorative element of prime importance, especially on the exterior. It is used to make the ornamental motifs – that stand out in relief against the background –

Taller del Moro, detail of the plasterwork, Toledo.

become more concentrated in certain areas within religious buildings, such as in the apse, bell tower and the *cimborio*.

Another unique signature is the abundant application of decorated ceramics on the exterior, made possible by the existence of many important Mudéjar potteries, such as those of Teruel or Muel. The Aragonese Mudéjar decoration was characterised by the simplicity of the strapwork, the six- and eight-pointed stars, as well as the use of the *mixtilíneo* arch, single or intersecting. The local precedents can be found in the Hudid Palace of the Aljafería, where the highly archaic formal plan denotes a relative isolation compared to the practice in use in the kingdoms of the crown of Castile.

Among the structural elements of Islamic origin in the Mudéjar centre of Aragon, the typology of the minaret —seen in the majority of the bell towers —stands out, whether these

Historical-Artistic Introduction

Cathedral of Santa María, ceiling detail, Teruel.

Church of San Martín, doorway detail, Morata de Jiloca.

are of square or octagonal ground plan. The *par y nudillo* ceiling of the cathedral in Teruel is unique in Spanish Mudéjar for its figurative decoration. Another outstanding structure of the Mudéjar style in Aragon, although this time of Christian origin, is the fortified church, which is analysed in detail in Itinerary V described in this guide.

Ever since the definition of geographical centres proposed by Vicente Lampérez at the beginning of the 20th century, the Mudéjar centres in León and Castilla la Vieja on the one hand, and Toledo on the other, have been characterised and studied separately. However, the fact that there are as many, if not more factors that unify rather than differentiate the two could help explain why so often nowadays both sets are considered as a global whole. Many researchers have argued over which of the two Mudéjar styles is earlier. The majority have decided that the Mudéjar concentration in Toledo came first, since the capitulation of the city to Alfonso VI of Castile in 1085 is the starting point for all Hispanic Mudéjar art. On the other hand, Manuel Valdés has insisted that the Mudéjar style of León is earlier, as there is documentary evidence to support the thesis that a number of Mudéjar monuments in the city of Sahagún can be dated to the 12th century. Yet, surely, a far more useful approach – rather than either of the groups basing its priorities on the precise dating of the oldest monument in each set – would be to establish the historical circumstances that allowed the earliest appearance and development of a Mudéjar style to emerge. In this sense, everything points to Toledo, because the north of the Meseta had no Islamic past and, consequently, there had never been a Christian reconquest of cities with a previous Mudéjar population. In his day, Claudio Sánchez Albornoz established the theory of the "human desert" – created in the valley of the River Duero during the high Middle Ages – a wide empty space, which acted as a frontier between al-Andalús and the small Christian kingdoms in the north of the peninsula.

It is for this reason that the Islamic monumental past of the city of Toledo not only serves as the reference and formal precedent for the Mudéjar centre to which it lends its name, but also for the Mudéjar centre of León and Castilla la Vieja, which had no history of Islamic urban precedents.

The same is true of the Mudéjar population that gradually established itself in the north of the Meseta, which then grew with the influx of Mudéjar immigrants from Toledo, as documentary evidence presented by Miguel Ángel Ladero proves. We must recognise that the Mudéjar centre of León and Castilla la Vieja, devoid of monumental urban Islamic precedents and with no autochthonous Mudéjar population, was, rather, a satellite of the centre of Toledo.

As already mentioned, the city of Toledo, once it was under Christian domination again, remained the foremost nucleus from the late 11th century onwards because of its receptiveness to the new artistic influences from al-Andalús. This was equally true for the Almoravid and Almohad influences before the conquest of Seville in 1248 and for the Nasrid influence before the conquest of Granada in 1492. The importance of the centre of Toledo – the principal crucible of Mudéjar to the north towards the valley of the River Duero and to the south towards the River Guadalquivir – was superseded only by the centre of Seville, starting with the renovations undertaken in Andalucía and in the Guadalquivir valley after the Seville earthquake of 1356. Nevertheless, the concentration of Mudéjar in León and Castilla la Vieja was distinguished by the appearance and spread of an architectural style with strong artistic personality. Its high point comes at a very early date, around 1200, and this quality lasts throughout the whole of the 13th century and the first decades of the 14th century, especially in urban centres like Sahagún, Toro, Arévalo, Olmedo or Cuéllar.

Church of San Tirso, interior view of the sanctuary, Sahagún.

Some historians have tried to deny the Mudéjar character of these artistic manifestations, preferring to call them "Romanesque brick-built architecture" or "Medieval brick-built architecture" because, in fact, the use of brick is very relevant, even if the hypertrophy of the style seen in Aragon does not occur everywhere. Itinerary VII actually draws attention to the predominance of brick in the Mudéjar of León and Castilla la Vieja. In any case, as this happens in all Mudéjar art, the material does not have a merely constructive value but also a very important decorative one. Although the formal elements – such as double semicircular arches, surrounds and courses of brickwork arranged in raked or barge course

Historical-Artistic Introduction

Mosque of Cristo de la Luz, general view, Toledo.

patterns — may be simple and make no definite reference to any particular Islamic ornamental tradition, the aesthetic result, however, is different and far removed from the Western European tradition.

In the formal characterisation of the Mudéjar centre of Toledo, some other materials and techniques and certain formal elements and architectonic typologies ought to be added to the examples already mentioned above. Among the materials used, there is a predominance of the "*aparejo toledano*" or Toledo bond, which meant that the main walls of the building were constructed on a base of masonry with edging borders and interposed brick courses. This was a construction method used in Islamic Toledo for walls, which had precedents in the area from the late Roman era, as recent archaeological excavations revealed.

This type of *aparejo toledano*-wall construction allowed bricks to be reserved for use in certain parts of a building where they also played a very important decorative role.

This is evident in the apses of churches, for example, which are faceted on multiple sides and decorated with horizontal registers of double blind arcades, as in the Mudéjar apse of the Mosque of Cristo de la Luz; and in the formal arrangement of the different parts of various church towers. One of the most emblematic ornamental motifs of the Mudéjar architecture of Toledo is the horseshoe arch framed in multifoil arches, a motif which was also common in the Mudéjar architecture of Seville, with reminiscences of the Almohad tradition.

The Mudéjar plasterwork of Toledo is outstanding for its richness and diversity from the late 12th century onwards. It has its own strong artistic personality which, on the one hand, combined and developed all the formal Andalucían traditions — Almoravid, Almohad and Nasrid — and, on the other, from the middle of the 14th century, incorporated naturalistic plant motifs of Gothic origin. This latter has allowed us to identify the presence of plasterers from Toledo in the Mudéjar palace of Pedro I in the Real Alcázar in Seville (1364–1366) and in the Chamber of the Kings in the Patio de los Leones in the Alhambra in Granada. All this provides yet more proof of the mobility of the Mudéjar workforce between royal building contracts.

Mudéjar woodwork in Toledo also developed its own personality. The wooden *armaduras*, or ceilings, in *par y nudillo* style in the Almohad tradition were widely used in the Mudéjar architecture of Toledo during the second half of the 13th century. Some of the oldest examples have survived, such as in the Church of Santiago del Arrabal or the Synagogue of Santa María la Blanca, both in the city of Toledo.

The Mudéjar art and architecture of Toledo also had its own particular structural and typological traits, which were used as models throughout the peninsula. In the mid-13th century, in the new age of the spread of Gothic architecture, the old typology of the Mudéjar churches of Toledo – the basilica ground plan with three aisles, low and dimly lit, separated by horseshoe arches – was already obsolete. In the Church of Santiago del Arrabal in Toledo, a new typology of Mudéjar church emerges; this three-nave typology is taller than the earlier model, thanks to the use of arches supported on pillars, and the naves have by *par y nudillo*-type wooden ceilings. The Christian resettlers introduced this typology to the new Mudéjar centre in Seville.

In civil architecture, Mudéjar in Toledo allowed not only all the Andalucían typologies to emerge, some of which are still conserved in the cloisters of the conventual architecture in Toledo, but also created a Toledan palace style with its own strong personality, above all in the design of its façades.

When defining the Mudéjar style in Extremadura, the traditional studies denied it any distinctive personality of its own, dividing the territory up into areas of influence of the surrounding Mudéjar types in León, Toledo and Seville. These were believed to have penetrated into Extremadura from

Church of Santa María de la Vega, apse, Toro.

Franciscan Convent of la Concepción, detail of the plasterwork in the Palace of Pedro I, Toledo.

Historical-Artistic Introduction

Church of Santiago del Arrabal, apses, Toledo.

the north, east and south respectively, each leaving its own mark according to the particular areas of influence. The most recent studies by M. P. Mogollón Cano-Cortés (Itinerary X) offer in-depth discussion about the individuality of the Mudéjar style in Extremadura and the distinctive materials and sobriety of form, upon which the monumental precedents of the Almohad domination of the region had evidently left a deep impression.

Andalucía was divided for historical reasons into two main centres of Mudéjar: Seville and Granada. The concentration of Mudéjar art and architecture in Seville comprises the territory of the lower valley of the River Guadalquivir, with the creative and originating centre in Seville being where the direct influence of the Almohad Islamic tradition is felt most strongly. Itineraries XI and XII are dedicated to these concentrations. Apart from the Mudéjar style of Seville there is also the city of Córdoba and its surroundings, where the important caliphate tradition lent the Mudéjar of the Córdoba region

its own characteristics. Among these, we can highlight the predominance of cut stonework, which is unusual in Mudéjar architecture.

In the religious Mudéjar buildings in Seville, we can distinguish two different typologies, one indigenous and the other imported. The native type reproduces the arrangement and shape of the Almohad mosques that become churches with three aisles, separated by horseshoe arches resting on pillars. This type, with low-rise naves, wooden armaduras ceilings and that are endowed with bell towers are scaled-down versions of the Giralda. The most singular example of this archetype is the Church of San Marcos in Seville. As far as civil architecture is concerned, the most successful typology is that of the Palace of Pedro I in the Real Alcázar in Seville (1364–1366), where the formal influences from the Nasrids and Toledo are evident. This palace served as a model for the noble palaces of Seville until well into the Renaissance, despite a change in aesthetic taste led by the Emperor Carlos V.

Itinerary XIII deals with what is meant exactly by the Mudéjar centre of Granada, which is not only the territory of the present-day province of Granada but once also comprised the entirety that made up the last Nasrid kingdom of Granada, that is to say, the modern provinces of Málaga, Granada, and Almería in the Penibética mountain ranges of Andalucía. Modern studies of this Mudéjar centre, dealing separately with each one of the provinces involved (the Mudéjar of Málaga, Granada and Almería), have offered a fragmentary vision of a Mudéjar centre deserving of getting back its unity. In fact, all of this territory of Granada shares some unifying factors, such as a much later Christian reconquest (between 1487 and 1492), a predominance of Nasrid Islamic precedents, as well as a brief period in which the development and proliferation of Mudéjar art is significant. All of these common factors, which in themselves provide ample reason to talk of a unity, should be privileged with a more general consideration compared with the differentiating elements and based on the particular circumstances of the process of resettlement.

Lastly, and with respect to certain Mudéjar elements which enrich the monumental heritage in the Canary Islands or Hispano-America, it should be clear that in those contexts we cannot talk of Mudéjar in the strict sense, but rather of "Mudéjar reminiscences", or, if we prefer, isolated formal Mudéjar elements. These do not constitute a system as such, but are more correctly just instances of an integration of a system or style into a more general adoption of Spanish art and architecture in these areas. This is because the formation, development and expansion of Mudéjar art implies a territorial and historical context, namely medieval Christian Spain, and its limits cannot be changed arbitrarily, unless in an attempt to change the nature of this artistic movement.

Purpose of the project

The 13 itineraries selected for the *Mudéjar Art* Exhibition Trail and related thematic guide aim to present the vast panorama of Mudéjar art and architecture that is present in almost the whole of the peninsula. They are evenly divided between the principal regional centres in Spain — Aragon, León and Castilla la Vieja, Toledo, Extremadura and Andalucía.

Although initially there might seem to be an excessive number of itineraries, the rich variety and widespread distribution of Mudéjar monuments, as well as the fact that in the majority of cases they do not belong to important monumental complexes, makes a more limited selection almost impossible. The 13 itineraries offer a sufficient and very representative demonstration of Spanish Mudéjar. To avoid confusion the itineraries only visit Mudéjar monuments, leaving to one side the already well-known great Islamic monuments of Spain that were the precedent and stimulus for the creation of Mudéjar art in cities such as Saragossa, Toledo, Córdoba, Seville and Granada.

Itinerary I, a half day, introduces us to daily life and monastic liturgy via

College of the Humanities, gallery of the patio, Guadalupe.

Royal Alcázar, arcades of Patio de las Doncellas, Seville.

two museums in Madrid, the National Archaeological Museum and the Museum of Valencia de Don Juan, where a rich, but little-known collection of Mudéjar furniture, ceramics and carpets are kept.

Itinerary II, from Alcalá de Henares to Guadalajara, has as its own particular leitmotif – a splendid manifestation of late Mudéjar art – what is called "Cisneros style", taking its name from the famous founder and *maecenas*.

In the three one-day itineraries dedicated to Mudéjar art and architecture in Aragon, the first (Itinerary III) is essentially through the city of Saragossa. Following the route of the coronation of the kings of Aragon, it starts from the Mudéjar rooms in the Royal Aljafería Palace and ends in the Seo, or Cathedral, of San Salvador.

Itinerary IV visits two Mudéjar cities, Teruel and Daroca, which for historical reasons are very different, since Teruel was a Christian foundation and Daroca was a resettled Islamic city. These differing circumstances had clear repercussions in each city.

Itinerary V takes us to the valleys of the Rivers Jalón and Jiloca, in the lands of the former region of Calatayud, in order to demonstrate the unique character of multifunctional architecture – half-religious, half-military – of the fortified churches. Two of the most notable examples of this kind are the churches of Tobed and Torralba de Ribota, built during the Frontier War between Aragon and Castile.

Three itineraries cover the wide and varied territory of the Mudéjar of León and Castilla la Vieja:

Itinerary VI is through one of the areas that is Mudéjar by antonomasia – Moraña – with its centre in Arévalo. This time the visits are to walled-city complexes such as Madrigal de las Altas Torres and Mudéjar castles such as Coca.

Itinerary VII, two days, is through the Tierra de Campos, one of the most outstanding areas of the Mudéjar style. The unifying theme of this itinerary are the convents of the Order of the Poor Clares, where the daughters of kings and nobles were professed. Outstanding among these is the Convent of Santa Clara de Astudillo, built over the foundations of the Mudéjar Palace of King Pedro I.

Itinerary VIII allows an appreciation of brick, used as the dominant building material in Mudéjar architecture. We shall visit some outstanding Mudéjar areas such as Sahagún, in the area of León, or Toro, near Zamora. The main concentration of Mudéjar in the Toledo area, which is delimited by the present-day autonomous communities of Madrid and Castilla-La Mancha, is divided into three itineraries. The Madrid- and Cisneros-style routes, already mentioned, are only half days.

Itinerary IX is dedicated exclusively to the city of Toledo, capital of its own Mudéjar style, which shows very clearly the close relationship between the three cultures that coexisted in it: Christian, Jewish and Islamic. Following the traces of Mudéjar through churches, synagogues and palaces, we shall see monuments that share a common layout and structure that is independent of whoever commissioned the building or founded it.

Itinerary X, two days, takes us through the lands of Cáceres and Badajoz. There, we can see the strong, sober personality of the Mudéjar style in Extremadura, largely conditioned by the Almohad precedents in the area. The highlight of the visit is the Monastery of Guadalupe, a World Heritage Site, which is a place of pilgrimage, a monastery, a fort, a palace and a royal pantheon all rolled into one, which also has a beautiful Mudéjar cloister.

In the last three itineraries the intention is to offer a concentrated synthesis of the richness and diversity of Mudéjar in Andalucía, where, for historical reasons, we must clearly differentiate between two areas: Andalucía Baja (lower) and Andalucía Penibética (in the Penibética mountain range).

Andalucía Baja, in the valley of the River Guadalquivir, conquered from 1248 onwards, has a main Mudéjar focus found in and around the city of Seville.

Itinerary XI visits the Mudéjar palaces and churches in the city of Seville, among these is a monument of the first order: the Palace of King Pedro I in the Real Alcázar.

Itinerary XII takes us back out to the countryside, to a region where the perfume of the Almohad Islamic tradition still lingers: the Aljarafe, a Christian territory in the Valley of the Guadalquivir, centred on Sanlúcar la Mayor.

The panorama of Mudéjar art closes with an itinerary dedicated to the Andalucía Penibética, the mountainous area that includes the present-day provinces of Málaga, Granada and Almería, which the Christians did not conquer until 1487 and 1492, and consequently show a later Mudéjar style.

Itinerary XIII is devoted to the Mudéjar ceilings in the parishes of Granada, in the areas mentioned above, built after the Christian conquest.

Church of Santiago, interior, Guadix.

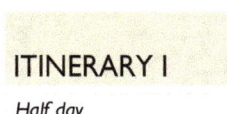

ITINERARY I

Half day

Daily Life and Liturgy: Home, Kitchen and Choir

Pedro Lavado Paradinas

I.I MADRID
   I.1.a National Archaeological Museum
   I.1.b Institute of Valencia de Don Juan

Mudéjar Ceramics

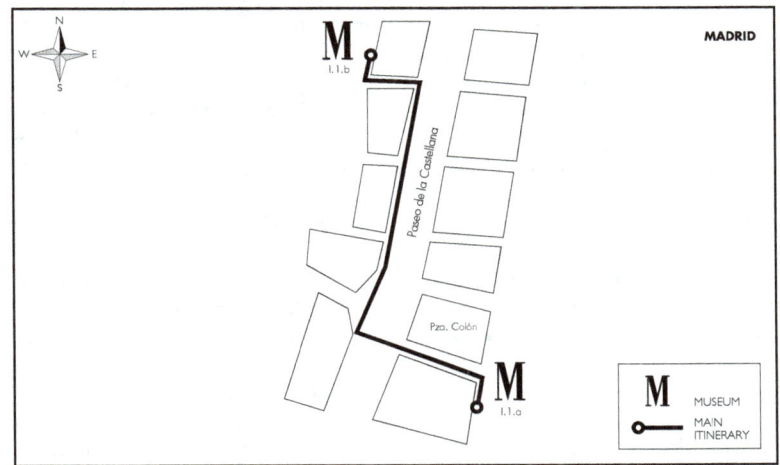

Detail of the Almirante carpet, Institute of Valencia de Don Juan (3859), Madrid.

ITINERARY I   Daily Life and Liturgy: Home, Kitchen and Choir

Detail of the Choir Stalls from Astudillo, National Archaeological Museum (60542), Madrid.

The Mudéjar style was not only employed in the context of religious architecture as one might suppose from the many buildings of this type that are preserved in Spain. The same simple materials, bricks, cob walls, wood and plaster, all of which were materials used in the construction of churches and convents, were also used in the construction of different kinds of civil and military architecture too. The development of this utilitarian architecture was influenced to great extent by several considerations: the need to economise on materials and to be able to obtain the necessary supplies from those available locally; to avoid costly transportation and expensive specialised workers, such as stonemasons.

This same humble vocation explains how Mudéjar art and architecture was employed to satisfy the needs of the lower economic strata of the population, and how it left its mark on objects of everyday use in the late medieval and early Renaissance periods.

Let us try to imagine what daily life was like at that time. Houses, palaces and convents were built to provide the basic necessities of their inhabitants. The daily life of women was divided between domestic work – cooking, sewing, the care of children and the sick, and the management of servants – and other more creative leisure activities such as reading or playing games and music. The daily life of women in the convents was much the same, though the timetable that was set by the divine office ordered the day, spent in prayer, the offices and singing in the choir, in meditation, walking and recreation in the cloister, working in the fields and in the convent, and of course to attend liturgy in the church.

The life of women centred on the estrado, or raised wooden dais, heated by hot air from the straw burning in the *gloria* or hypocaust underneath. Carpets, rugs, cushions, chests, chairs and tables were in their places alongside the implements of domestic work: the spinning wheel, distaff, pin cushion and other sewing equipment. The miniatures in the Books of Hours show different episodes of daily life and it is thanks to these that we can imagine what the most common activities were for both men and women.

The bare walls were hung with tapestries, *guadamecíes* and Cordóban leather hangings. Around the base of the ceiling, there ran a broad *arrocabe*, or plasterwork frieze, polychrome, and carved or moulded. In the lower part, there would be a dado of ceramic tiles, combining different shapes and geometric designs. Terracotta tiles would cover the floor, interspersed with *olambrillas* decorated with hunting scenes and animal motifs.

The door and window openings, which were framed in carved wood, and which closed with shutters decorated with cloth or parchment folds cut out in ogee shapes, gradually took on the new Renaissance designs. The fireplaces were plaster, adorned with a coat of arms and figurative decorations. The sparsely furnished living rooms and sleeping quarters provided different spaces for sleeping and eating. There would have been pallets of

Detail of a beam from Curiel de los Ajos, National Archaeological Museum (50742), Madrid.

ITINERARY 1   Daily Life and Liturgy: Home, Kitchen and Choir
Madrid

Choir Stalls from Astudillo, National Archaeological Museum (60542), Madrid.

Choir Stalls from Gradefes, National Archaeological Museum (50548), Madrid.

pots, cauldrons, pans, bowls, soup bowls, jugs, cups, plates, pitchers, carving dishes and ewers, and basins for washing or shaving.

Daily life in the house was very similar to the life women led in convents or palaces, and fortunately, evidence for this assertion lays in the many preserved objects from convents. At most, often all that is left of the palaces and houses are remnants of the floors, ceilings or fireplaces: occasionally a door or window frame with its plasterwork still intact survives; less is left of the carpentry work that screened the widows. However, in the convent interiors, a rich source of historical evidence still exists that relates not so much in the objects but more in the way of life and customs. This evidence takes us back centuries: apothecary jars, adorned with coats of arms and labelled with the names of their contents, bread moulds, pieces of the dowry and ceramics belonging to some of the nuns and abbesses, chamber pots and washbasins, cloths, covers, rugs, trays, games, boxes, chests and writing desks. The artefacts represent a whole world, in which the forms and designs of the Hispanic Muslims survive in the dignified simplicity of everyday objects.

straw and wool, with rugs and other coverings, which served as decoration during the day and warmed the tired bones of their owners by night.

In the kitchen, a rich variety of pottery and ceramic objects were used for water, lighting and cooking. There were metal objects too: charcoal burners, heaters, mortars and oil lamps. There was a whole range of ceramic utensils for cooking – heating, frying, roasting – serving, carving, washing and adorning: stew pots, soup

1.1 MADRID

The itinerary of Mudéjar art in Madrid contains two must-see visits: the National Archaeological Museum and the Institute of Valencia de Don Juan. In these two museums, there are numerous first-class exhibits in the Mudéjar style. Some Mudéjar artefacts are also to be found in the

ITINERARY I   Daily Life and Liturgy: Home, Kitchen and Choir
Madrid

National Museum of Decorative Arts (Montalbán Street, 12), especially ceramics, leather and wooden furniture, and in several of the churches in the city. The Church of San Nicolás de los Servitas (Plaza de San Nicolás, 1) still has its brick tower, plasterwork remnants and the 16th-century ceiling. There are other important remains of brick towers in the Church of San Pedro el Viejo (Costanilla de San Pedro Street, 1) and in the Chapel of the Carabanchel Cemetery, both of which bear some resemblance to the Mudéjar style of Toledo.

I.1.a National Archaeological Museum

Situated on Serrano Street, 13. Entrance fee, except on Saturday after 14.30. Opening hours: 09.30–20.30, Sunday and public holidays from 09.30–14.30. Closed Mondays.

The Mudéjar collection in the National Archaeological Museum is partly the consequence of some of the curators' efforts made at the end of the 19th century, the results of which were published in the pages of the *Museo Español de Antigüedades (Spanish Museum of Antiquities)* (1872–1880). Some of the names linked to this publication – José and Rodrigo Amador de los Ríos, Manuel de Assas and Juan de Dios de la Rada y Delgado, among others – not only defined the constants of the Hispano-Muslim style, but also studied and dated, in many cases for the first time, some of the most representative works of Spanish Mudéjar. In fact, many works exhibited in this museum are very similar to other

Door from the Church of San Pedro in Daroca, National Archaeological Museum (50513), Madrid.

pieces of the same type and age, which are conserved in the Museums of Valencia de Don Juan and the *Arqueológico Provincial* (Provincial Archaeological Museum) in Toledo. We get the impression that many findings and acquisitions were divided into three lots, one for each of these museums. This is the case with some of the carpentry, such as the two armoires of Santa Úrsula of Toledo, which are conserved in the National Archaeological Museum and in the Institute of Valencia de Don Juan respectively, or with a large part of the collection of Mudéjar corbels and beams kept in the three museums.

Choir Stalls

Exhibited in the National Archaeological Museum are two fine examples of Mudéjar choir stalls: one from the Convent of the Poor Clares in Astudillo (Palencia) made in around 1356, and the other from the Cistercian Monastery of Santa María in Gradefes (León), from the 13th century. The former shows the royal coat of arms of Castile and León,

ITINERARY I *Daily Life and Liturgy: Home, Kitchen and Choir*
Madrid

Tabernacle door from Jaén. National Archaeological Museum (57833), Madrid.

surrounded by firé shovels or *padillas*, the emblem of the foundress doña María de Padilla, the mistress, later the wife of King Pedro I (Peter I) of Castile. The latter shows the coat of arms of León, where the workmanship and polychromy eloquently show the Hispano-Muslim influence on the carpentry of León. Both of these choir stalls are made of pine, which is painted in red, blue, white and a greenish tone. The stalls from Astudillo are full height, their roof system comprising multifoil arches that finish in eaves, supported on corbels that represent the heads of animals, with risers in between showing coats of arms and plant motifs. In the half-height example from Gradafes the heraldic decorations appear on the choir stall seat backs, while the carving of the dividing cross bars and their supports is of very fine Islamic craftsmanship that includes *ataurique* and columns with stylised plant motifs. Multifoil curved lobed arches of the purest Almohad influence, separate the three seats.

Doors

This enormous door, which once belonged to the church of San Pedro in Daroca (Saragossa), is among the most outstanding pieces of Mudéjar furniture in the National Archaeological Museum. The door's background of polychrome themes and fine metalwork in part tones down the abstraction that characterises Hispano-Muslim art, but at the same time includes religious talismans to prevent the evil eye and ensure the protection of the Almighty. Three other doors are also of great interest: two are tabernacle doors in the Mudéjar style, which bear relation to similar examples conserved in Jaén. One of these is from Jaén Cathedral and has a border round the edge with a Eucharistic inscription in praise of the Holy Sacrament, which bears comparison to that in the Chapel of La Concepción in the Church of San Andrés in Jaén. The other door belonged to the Cathedral Archive in Jaén, and its inscription alludes to the Passion of Christ. Both are from the 16th century and come from a workshop in Andalucía responsible for a number of other works of interest, such as doors, ceilings and pulpits, all of which are evident throughout Jaén. The third door is from León, and its decoration of an anagram of Christ in Latin and Greek alongside other Gothic motifs, dates it to the end of the 15th century.

I.1.b **Institute of Valencia de Don Juan**

Situated on Fortuny, 43. Visits by prior arrangement only (Mon, Wed, Fri mornings). Tel: 91 3081848.

The Museum at the Institute of Valencia de Don Juan has outstanding collections that include Iberian and Celtic jewels, objects in jet from Santiago de Compostela, medieval pendants and enamels, and an extraordinary collection of ceramics covering the whole of the Islamic world, but its important collection of Mudéjar pieces should not be missed on a visit to Madrid. The Institute of Valencia de Don Juan was founded in 1916 by the politician and collector Guillermo Joaquín de Osma in memory of his wife, Adela Crooke, the 23rd Countess of Valencia de Don Juan. Sr. Osma and his wife were passionate *cognoscenti* of the industrial arts in Spain, and it is thanks to them that this fabulous collection was formed, specialising in Oriental and Hispano-Muslim art. This museum is to be found in the Calle Fortuny in central Madrid, in an interesting neo-Nasrid building with neo-Mudéjar elements on the facades, elevations and ceilings. Craftsmen from across the Andalucían world took part in its construction, creating tiling, ceramics, taraceas and metalwork, and skilfully integrating the contents into their surroundings.

Armoire of Santa Úrsula, Institute of Valencia de Don Juan (49013), Madrid.

***Armoire* (cupboard) of St Úrsula**
(Reg. no. 49013)
One of the most outstanding Mudéjar pieces in the Institute of Valencia de Don Juan is this superb cupboard or *armoire* from the sacristy of the Convent of St Úrsula in Toledo, the twin of the one conserved in the National Archaeological Museum in Madrid. This *armoire*, which is more than 2.5 m. high and 1.5 m. wide, has three horizontal compartments with small doors. On the inside, the shelves adopt roof forms with painted and epigraphic decoration, which repeats the word "*prosperidad*" (prosperity). The locks, handles and geometric strapwork decorations are metal as is usual in the Islamic typology, and

ITINERARY 1   Daily Life and Liturgy: Home, Kitchen and Choir
Madrid

Almirante carpet, Institute of Valencia de Don Juan (3859), Madrid.

Albufera plate, Institute of Valencia de Don Juan (183), Madrid.

the *armoire* has parallels with some of those that appear in the illuminated miniatures of the Cantigas or Canticles of Alfonso X el Sabio (the Wise) (1221–1284).

The Admiral's Carpet – Almirante rug (Reg. no. 3859)
The Museum of Valencia de Don Juan has one of the world's finest collections of Hispano-Muslim textiles and some first-class Oriental examples too. Outstanding among the former is one of the carpets of the "Admiral series". This rug is associated with the Franco de Guzmán family from Villafuerte de Esgueva (Valladolid) due to its heraldic devices, since the coats of arms it shows are the same as those on the wooden ceiling from the Parish Church of the same city, conserved in the building of the Diputación Provincial (County Council) of Valladolid.
In the same area of interest are also fragments of Nasrid textiles reused in the Christian world as, for example, a chasuble, which is very similar to another of the same type in Burgos Cathedral.

Ceramics from Paterna and Manises

Among the Museum of Valencia de Don Juan's most remarkable collections are perhaps those of Mudéjar ceramics, a perfectly chosen and catalogued selection comprising many different pieces and typologies. From potteries in Paterna and Manises (both in Valencia), the ceramics, and Teruel and Muel (Saragossa) and can be dated from the end of the 13th century up to the 17th century, at a time when the colouring of the metal oxides becomes more coppery and where the decoration is developing into naturalistic themes. The collection of Hispano-Moorish ceramics from Manises, which contains an outstanding plate depicting a duck-shooting scene in the Albufera (lagoon) in Valencia, is one of the most important.

Also represented in this museum are ceramics in the *cuerda seca* and *cuenca o arista* styles. They are engraved or moulded, and were produced in Seville or Toledo between the 13th and 16th centuries. A superb collection of glazed tiling covers several of the walls, some of which are the best known of their genre for their richness and variety of themes and designs.

MUDÉJAR CERAMICS

Pedro Lavado Paradinas

Ceramic jug or "pitxer" from Paterna, Institute of Valencia de Don Juan (1425), Madrid.

The heir to Hispano-Muslim ceramics, Mudéjar ceramics are definable by both their uses and ornamentation. Possibly the rejection of precious metal objects, so frequent in Persian and Byzantine cultures, made the Hispano-Muslim ceramicists turn very early on to the use of metallic lustres and glazes, which, although it could not exactly replace the earlier pieces, at least equalled them in beauty and decoration.

During the Middle Ages, the pottery – originally called *Malica* because it was thought to come from Malaga – flooded the European markets, especially in Italy where the Romanesque towers of innumerable buildings were decorated with medallions (known as *baccini* in Italy) from the Spanish Levante. Later, with the arrival of the Italian Renaissance glazed earthenware, the Spanish ceramics were relegated, and some authors, such as Felipe de Guevara (died c.1564), openly despised them.

In Mudéjar ceramics there are numerous pieces moulded "al fresco", with designs based on Muslim motifs and other epigraphic or heraldic work. They are often large-scale, worked without the wheel and in various pieces by the *urdido* or warp method. This was used for vats, baptismal fonts, and well or cistern copings. There were potteries in Toledo, Córdoba, Seville and Granada. Sometimes the pottery was glazed in green and white, with other colours such as black, or the same green, applied to outline and fill-in. The fonts and wells appeared in the 14th century, the same as the vats. Gradually, the ornamental motifs started to include Christian themes and Gothic lettering.

Although little is known about Mudéjar baptismal fonts, they are attributed to Toledo. There must have been a pottery near the capital because of the tonalities of the clays used. Christian themes such as crosses – both fleur-de-lis and patriarchal – are incorporated as are abbreviations of the name of Christ (JHS) or simply Gothic floral motifs. All of this co-exists, in some cases, with interesting themes peculiar to the Muslim world: the hands of Fátima and eyes to keep away the evil eye, and sometimes the name and signature of the potter is written: *"Abrayn García, who sold this for VII reals in 1508"*. This wording on the font in Camarenilla in Toledo identifies one of the most accomplished potters of the time, who was also the artist of the font conserved in the Hispanic Society of New York. There must have been other centres producing baptismal fonts in Saragossa and Seville, where some singular pieces have also survived, although they are of a different type.

The green and purple ceramics (copper and manganese), which were of some importance in al-Andalús, were more widely used during the Mudéjar period. The ceramics of Paterna, which derive from the caliphate ceramics of the 11th century, reached their height towards the end of the 14th century and the beginning of the 15th century. In 1383, Francisco Eximenis mentions Paterna and Cárcer as the two centres where "*common earthenware is made*", but he considered it coarse compared to the very fine work of Manises.

In the ceramics from Paterna, figurative motifs of animals and people cover the surface area completely. The background decoration is produced with stannic oxide, giving it a whitish tone, with figures drawn on to it in the green of the copper and the purplish black of the manganese.

The typology of the vessels goes from the kitchen to the table: jugs, plates and bowls, of all sizes, small, large, deep or shallow. In the same shapes and colours are the ceramics from Teruel, where the potteries were active during the same period (end of the 14th and the beginning of the 15th centuries), but which probably reached their height in the first third of the 16th century, verified by the fact that they are mentioned by the historian Marineo Sículo (1460–1533).

Documentation about the potteries of Manises exists from the middle of the 14th century. The decorative themes with metallic lustres appear earlier than the above-mentioned green shades from Paterna, or the blue from Manises. Such was the reputation of Manises that it inherited the appellation or trademark of "*opere de Malíca, sive de Valencia*" ("Malica work, or better said Valencia"). The use of a stannic oxide base produced a cleaner blending of the colours, and meant that the potters could abandon the old *engobe* technique.

A piece of lustreware ceramic required three firings. The first firing eliminated moisture and dried the piece out. The second firing, called *gran fuego*, or great fire, was at a temperature of more than 1000°C, giving the piece its green or bluish tones. The third firing, after application of the metallic oxide, was at a lower temperature in a reducing kiln, to fix the metallic tones.

Knowledge of this technique for the painting and firing of lusterware is thanks to a description left by the archer Enrique Cock, who accompanied King Filipe II on a journey to Muel (Saragossa) in the 16th century. The lustreware and the blue-and-white ware from Manises survived widely until well into the 17th century. It is represented in the historical and religious paintings of the time in the houses and tables of biblical personages, which although obviously an anachronism, is also evidence of the prestige this pottery had acquired.

ITINERARY II

Half day

The "Cisneros" Style

Pedro Lavado Paradinas

II.1 ALCALÁ DE HENARES
   II.1.a University
   II.1.b Oidor Chapel (optional)

II.2 GUADALAJARA
   II.2.a Church of Santiago Apóstol
   II.2.b Sister Cathedral (optional)
   II.2.c Chapel of Luis de Lucena (optional)

Mudéjar Carpentry

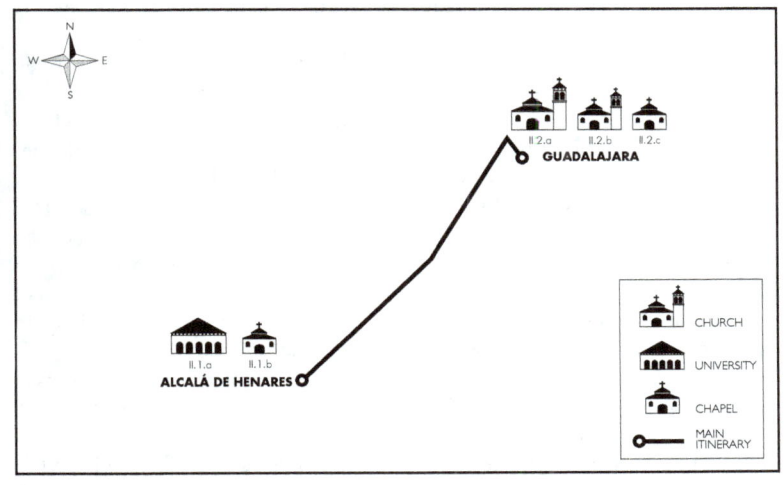

University, ceiling of the auditorium detail, Alcalá de Henares.

ITINERARY II The *"Cisneros" Style*

Staircase of the Archbishop's Palace, Alcalá de Henares, "Monumentos Arquitectónicos de España", 1881, National Library, Madrid.

At the end of the 15th century to the beginning of the 16th century, the Gothic style, which was already in its last stages, joined with Mudéjar art to create a courtly art. It was the era of the Catholic Monarchs. The reconquest had ended and Granada had fallen into the hands of Castile and Aragon. These two crowns, linked in the personae of their sovereigns, began a new undertaking. Their political project did not take long to spill out over national frontiers, and the products of their commerce arrived from all sides. The combined policy of Isabella and Fernando along with the other principal European states, contributed effectively to keeping up an active interchange. Artists and architects from other countries started to arrive in the Iberian Peninsula, aware that there was a demand for their knowledge and skills. What was shortly to develop in Spain was one of the most outstanding growth periods of its history.

In the artistic sphere, the new phenomenon of hybridisation appeared. Mudéjar had arisen in the late medieval Spanish world, when the forms and designs of the Romanesque and Gothic were blended with the craftsmanship of the *Moriscos*, workmen, who used new techniques and materials. Now the architectonic forms of Central European Gothic and the ornamental variants of Flamboyant Gothic blended again, this time with the multicoloured and geometric decoration of Mudéjar. Immediately afterwards, the forms from across the sea and from Italy would bring into contact the classical geometries and the new Vitruvian, or Serlian designs, with the geometry of Islam.

The result was a formal prodigy of the imagination. The masonry walls are pierced with traceries, the ribbed vaulting is open to the stars, the eaves are clustered with corbels, pommels, arches, *muqarnas* and other Mudéjar devices, and the interiors are completely covered with plasterwork, wood and ceramics, in which geometry, epigraphy and heraldic symbols appear on a background of naturalistic plant motifs. A horror of empty space is once again evident on every surface.

The Gothic architecture of the Catholic Monarchs flourished abundantly in the final years of the 15th century. Churches, chapels, hospitals, palaces and castles, all were seduced by the Gothic-Mudéjar forms, which, in the hands of artists such as Juan Guas, Enrique Egas and Simon of Cologne, combined Gothic structures and Hispano-Muslim ornamentation. This hybrid is known as *"estilo Isabel"* or the Isabelline style, perhaps because there are so many examples of it in Castile. The intense architectonic activity in Castile at the time amply justifies what the popular verses *"Coplas del Provincial"* say in the voice of the common people. They were fed up with paying taxes to finance Isabella's adventures in war and in America (administered by her treasurer Chacón) and also the cathedrals, churches and convents which Fray Alonso de Cartagena, the Bishop of Burgos (nicknamed "Friar Mortar"), never stopped building: *"Between the Queen, Chacón and Friar Mortar, the Court has had to ask for quarter"*.

Others preferred to call the style that emerged "Gothic-Mudéjar", but as time passed and the patrons changed — as in the case of Cardinal Francisco Jiménez de Cisneros (1436–1517) and his "Cisneros" style, some models and designs gave way to the fashions of the Italian Renaissance and with that came the style of the *"Morisco Renascent"*. Heirs to the Mudéjar tradition — in which plaster is the predominant material — are the masters of the Corral de Villapando School, who left in their work in Valladolid, Palencia and Zamora a curious repertory of ribbed vaulting and decoration as a forerunner of the Renaissance.

The activity carried out by Cisneros as Archbishop of Toledo and Regent (1495–1517) was of great importance throughout the archdiocese, which witnessed a unique flurry of construction. Through his intermediary Pedro Gumiel, the architect of the Cardinal's projects, Cisneros controlled and supervised all the building in the early decades of the 16th century. This explains the many similarities between what was produced by the workshops of the carpenters and plasterers set up in, or near Toledo, Alcalá and possibly Guadalajara. Along the route, which joined the Archbishop's see to the most important towns in the direction of Saragossa and up to the borders of the bishopric of Siguenza, the activity of these workshops and the Mudéjar themes in the carpentry, construction and plasterwork is evident. All of this lasted until the second half of the 16th century, when the construction of El Escorial opened the doors to new artists and influences from Italy, which without competition of any sort quickly dominated the scene.

The Cisneros period saw a resurge of Mudéjarism thanks to the large number of *Morisco* artists who immigrated to Castile after the fall of Granada. New types of decoration and ceiling structures show clear parallels with examples of these in Granada, which allows us to suppose that it was the workers and artists from there who brought the new forms to Castile. The use of brick spread widely from the nucleus in Toledo. The building techniques of Toledo masonry, with horizontal courses of brickwork are common in the work of this period. Many books and other objects of the *Moriscos* from Granada were set on a pyre in 1499; an act carried out without pity, in the presence of Cisneros, who, however, had saved the medical treatises. Nevertheless, the Cardinal himself made use of a walking stick of

Chapel of Luis de Lucena, general view, Guadalajara.

ITINERARY II The "Cisneros" Style
Alcalá de Heneras

University, Chapel of San Ildefonso, Alcalá de Henares.

carved wood, today conserved in the convent of San Juan de la Penitencia in Alcalá de Henares. From the inscription on it, it would appear that the stick belonged to one of the last rulers of Granada, perhaps a *qadi* or judge.

The cutlery used by the Cardinal, conserved in the Convent of San Antonio in Toledo, is another treasure of *Morisco* or Nasrid art. If the books were set alight while the *objets d'art* were not, it was because a book was perceived simply as a doctrine whereas the objects had monetary value and purpose.

II.1 ALCALÁ DE HENARES

The Renaissance precinct of Alcalá de Henares is contained within the medieval town centre, around which a wall was built in the 14th century by Don Pedro Tenorio Bishop of Toledo (1367–1399). This meant abandoning the remains of the ancient Roman Township in the valley of the River Henares. Today, the remains of the medieval settlement can be found on a nearby hill. This is where the Muslims took refuge after they were expelled from the city in 1088, and where they lasted out until 1118; in the same place, there had also been a prehistoric settlement. Bishop Tenorio, whom Pérez del Pulgar described as "*most obstinate and rigorous*", had the bounds of the city built with stout walls of Toledo masonry with square towers on the outside. In this way, he fortified the road from Toledo to Alcalá, which passed through Canales, Yepes and Santorcaz.

ITINERARY II *The "Cisneros" Style*
Alcalá de Heneras

The obstinate prelate started the work on the Archbishop's Palace. We only have a few photographic images of it from the end of the 19th century and the drawings and engravings collected in *Monumentos Arquitectónicos de España* (Madrid, 1859–1880). Following the Disentailment of Mendizabal the palace was semi-abandoned, although at the end of the 19th century the architect Urquijo and the painter Laredo restored it. In 1939, during the Civil War, it burned to the ground. Some of its rooms, such as the anteroom of the Councils, had a notable eight-sided ceiling with tie beams and plasterwork in all the spans.

Other successors of Tenorio extended his work: Pedro de Luna (1404–1414), Sancho de Rojas (1415–1422) and Juan Martínez Contreras (1422–1434) under whose governance Pope Martin V raised Alcalá to the status of the Primate See. The Bishops Alonso III of Fonseca (1475–1534), and Sandoval, whose coats of arms appear in several places, continued the work. There are several wooden ceilings from the Renaissance period, such as that over the staircase.

II.1.a University

Car parking recommended in the Plaza de Cervantes or in the car park in the Paseo de los Aguadores. Entrance fee. Guided tours: 11.30, 12.30, 13.30, 16.30, 17.30 (also 18.30 in summer). Sat, Sun and public holidays: 11.00, 11.45, 12.30, 13.15, 14.00, 16.00, 16.45, 17.30, 18.15, 19.00 (also 20.00 in summer).

The University of Alcalá de Henares is the principal foundation of Cisneros (1498), which opened its doors to students on 25th July 1508, replacing the earlier brick building with a stone edifice *(En luteam olim, marmoream nunc / Here [what was] in another time made by clay now [is] of stone)*. In the interior, there are two areas where the *Morisco* workmanship is evident. One is the *Paraninfo*, or auditorium, used for academic ceremonies. Pedro de Villarroel, Gutiérrez de Cárdenas and Andrés de Zamora built the *Paraninfo* between 1516 and 1520, along with the stucco craftsmen Bartolomé Aguilar, Hernando de Sahagún and Pedro de Villarroel, and the painters, Diego López and Alonso Sánchez. The coffered ceiling, with six-pointed star ornamentation in red, blue and gold, rests on a plasterwork gallery with spans and panels of *grutesco* decoration. The floors and tiered seats are decorated with ceramics.

The other area where the Mudéjar workmanship is evident is in the Chapel of San Ildefonso. This church has a single Gothic nave, crowned by an eight-sided ceiling above the boundary walls, whitewashed, and decorated in plasterwork with Gothic and plateresque motifs. The sanctuary has a ceiling of the same type inlaid with *ataujía* or fillets of precious metals. Both are the work of Alonso de Quevedo, a carpenter from Alcalá, who left two documented and valued works from the beginning of the 16th century.

University, floor tile from the auditorium, Alcalá de Henares.

ITINERARY II   *The "Cisneros" Style*
Guadalajara

Church of Santiago Apóstol, interior, Guadalajara.

II.1.b **Oider Chapel** (optional)

From the Plaza de San Diego, after leaving the University, go along calle Bustamante to the Plaza de Cervantes. The Chapel is at the far end beside the church, and the Town Council use it for temporary exhibitions. Opening hours: Consult the Tourist Office. Tel: 91 889 2694.

The Oidor (the Judge) Chapel was founded by don Pedro Díaz de Toledo, Bishop of Málaga (1487) and Hearing Judge of King Don Juan II, as a burial place for himself and his family. A semicircular *arco angrelado*, or cusped arch, gives access to the chapel from what was formerly the Church of Santa María, now demolished almost

without trace. Both the arch and frieze are decorated with plasterwork and clerestory, with inscriptions on the *arrocabe* and blind arcades, and the timber ceiling is worked in *par y nudillo*.

Other *Morisco* work can be found in convents established in these early years of the 16th century in Alcalá, as for example in Santa Úrsula or Santa Catalina. Much less remains of houses such as those of the Lizana or Criado families or of the Hospital of Antezana, where the late 15th-century eaves can still be seen.

II.2 GUADALAJARA

Parking recommended near the Palacio del Infantado, where the Museum and Tourist Office are situated, and then to follow the itinerary on foot.

II.2.a **Church of Santiago Apóstol**

Follow calle Miguel Fluiters and then turn left into calle Teniente Figueroa. Former Convent of Santa Clara. Open all day.

The Church of Santa Clara (St Clare), or to use the old name, of Santiago (St James the Apostle), is perhaps one of the most interesting in Guadalajara because of what has survived of it. Founded by Doña Berenguela, daughter of Alfonso X el Sabio, some improvements were made to the convent later by the Infanta Isabel, daughter of Sancho IV, and her governess Doña María Fernández Coronel; and as these two latter acquired some houses in 1299, their work started on the convent between 1305 and 1309. The convent church

ITINERARY II   The *"Cisneros" Style*
Guadalajara

was already finished for the funeral of Don Alonso Fernández Coronel in 1339; a Gothic design with a polygonal ground plan in brick, with large windows, and eaves with concave mouldings. The nave is covered with a *par y nudillo* ceiling of 14th-century Toledo work and the walls are decorated with plasterwork similar to that used in the Tránsito Synagogue in Toledo. There are three aisles, separated by octagonal brick pillars, and two chapels: the burial chapel of Don Diego García on the Epistle side and the chapel reserved for the Zuñiga family on the Gospel side. The former dates from 1452, while the latter is of a later date.

II.2.b **Sister Cathedral** (optional)

Situated in calle Santiago. Follow calle Teniente Figueroa down to the Sister Cathedral or Parish of Santa María la Mayor (The Cathedral of Guadalajara is in Siguenza). Recently restored. The bell tower and the structure above the vaulting, where the Mudéjar artesonado is conserved, may be visited on request. Apply to the Parish. Opening hours: 10.00–13.00 and 18.30–20.15.

Nearby is the Sister Cathedral, known as Santa María la Mayor (St Mary Major), la Blanca, or de la Fuente. This building must have been finished by the 15th century, and its doorways, with voussoirs, which show the influence of Granada in the cutting of the bricks, were to have an effect on the other churches of the area, such as those in Pozo de Guadalajara and Aldeanueva de Guadalajara. The timber roof survives under the plaster vaulting, and some plasterwork was revealed recently. A portico was added in the 16th century.

II.2.c **Chapel of Luis de Lucena** (optional)

Opposite the Sister Cathedral, in the cuesta de San Miguel. For opening hours, consult the Tourist Office. Tel: 949 211626.

The Chapel of Luis de Lucena is one of the most outstanding examples of building from the beginning of the 16th century. In it, we can see the artistic and iconographic ideas of one of the least well-known Spanish humanists, Luis de Lucena. The building was joined to the church of San Miguel del Monte (St Michael of the Mount), which was lost in the 19th century. It has a single nave with groined vaulting, where the lunettes represent different iconographic themes of the Renaissance, painted by some of the Italian painters who worked on the Palace of the Infantado. The building is brick with turreted forms at the corners and in the centre of the sides, which have flat arches set into solid walls. The upper part is decorated with trimmed bricks in the eaves and the mouldings. An inscription from 1540 on the windows and on one of the towers mentions the Psalm of David: *"Better to linger by the threshold of God's House than to live in the courts of the wicked."* The upper storey, suggested from the outside by a line of windows with false arches in projecting brick, was a library, while the lower floor was the chapel and burial place.

There is also the interesting neo-Mudéjar Church of Santa María Micaela (St Mary Michael), built under the auspices of the Duchess of Seville at the end of the 19th century, which is worth a visit. If the church is closed, telephone the Parish: 949 230433.

MUDÉJAR CARPENTRY

Pedro Lavado Paradinas

We know a lot about the work produced by carpenters in the 16th century for the Archdiocese of Toledo through logbooks and inspection books. The former, a record of the orders and the payments made for the works, and the latter, used by the overseers or architects, which the Toledo bishopric sent to visit the works, record the problems and incidents that arose.

Until recently, the belief was that most of the works depended on the architects, with many attributed to Pedro de Gumiel. The reading of the *Libro de Fábrica*, or the Logbook, from the Parish of Nuestra Señora de la Asunción, in Moratilla de los Meleros in Guadalajara, dating from 1515 to 1517, revealed the existence of a carpenter called Alonso de Quevedo. Immediately de Quevedo could be placed in relation to other very similar works, such as the Chapel of San Ildefonso in Alcalá de Henares, to which Cisneros added the University. Then it was demonstrated that what had originally simply been a stylistic appreciation was not only documented in Moratilla, but also in Alcalá. In this way, one of the most important names in the carpentry repertoire of Alcalá at the beginning of the 16th century was brought to light, to which others such as Pedro de los Nesperales and Joan de Ortega were added, both of whom were from Alcalá, and active between 1564 and 1566. A fourth master carpenter, Pedro de la Riba or de Arriba, from El Molar, Madrid, worked in his village in 1534 in the Church of San Bernabé de Valdenuño Fernández, Guadalajara, between 1544 and 1548, and in San Miguel de Alovera, Guadalajara, in 1569. The list of carpenters continues throughout the 16th century and into the beginning of the next. Some of them may have been of *Morisco* origin. This is the case of Juan Pérez de Escobedo, who worked on the *armadura* of the nave of Santa María de la Almudena, in Talamanca de Jarama, Madrid, in 1605 and on the choir of Casar de Talamanca, Guadalajara, between 1600 and 1602, where he had an assistant by the name of Andrés de la Hoz. One visit of 1596 mentions the *Moriscos* in that village. Could Andrés de la Hoz have been one of them?

Moriscos, or Christians, all of them used the techniques of Mudéjar carpentry, so that up to a certain point any doubts as to the racial or religious origins of certain craftsmen is no longer important.

Cathedral of Santa María, ceiling detail, scene of carpenters building an armadura de par y nudillo, Teruel.

ITINERARY III

The Coronation of the Kings of Aragon

Gonzalo M. Borrás Gualís

III.1 SARAGOSSA
    III.1.a La Aljafería
    III.1.b Church and Bell Tower of San Pablo
    III.1.c Cathedral of San Salvador
    III.1.d Church and Bell Tower of Santa María Magdalena (optional)
    III.1.e Church and Bell Tower of San Miguel de los Navarros (optional)
    III.1.f Church and Bell Tower of San Gil (optional)

III.2 UTEBO
    III.2.a Church and Bell Tower

III.3 ALAGÓN
    III.3.a Church and Bell Tower of San Pedro

Pedro IV

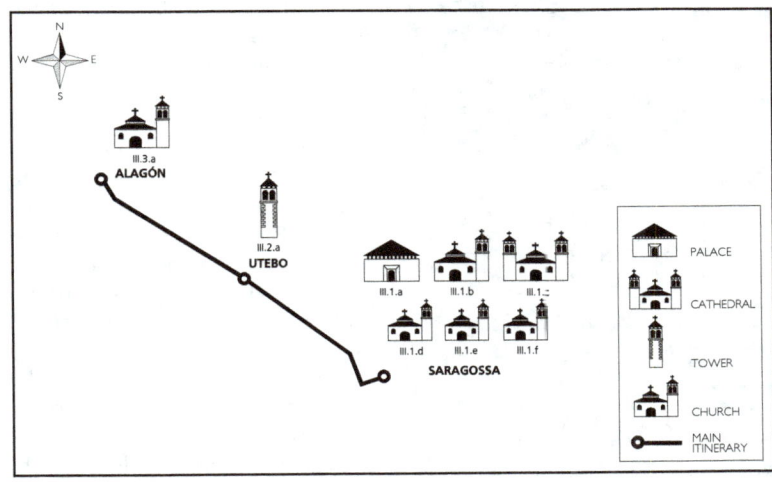

La Aljafería, Palace of the Catholic Monarchs, detail of the coffered ceiling in the Throne Room, Saragossa.

ITINERARY III The Coronation of the Kings of Aragon

The city of Saragossa, where the Kings of Aragon were crowned in the Cathedral of San Salvador, was the creative centre of the Mudéjar style in Aragon and responsible for the dissemination of the style, thanks above all to the royal patronage it enjoyed. This unique style was developed in the first place in Aljafería Palace, an Islamic palace from the 11th century, which after the conquest of the city by Alfonso I el Batallador (the Fighter) in the year 1118, was converted into a palace for the Kings of Aragon. It was during this conservation project that Mudéjar rooms were added, worked by Muslim master craftsmen. The Kings of Aragon, who also possessed royal palaces in Barcelona, Mallorca and Valencia, had a special fondness for the palace in Saragossa, which in the documents issued by the Royal Chancellery are always referred to as "*dilectissima Aliaferia*". The aesthetic fascination for this palace with its intertwined arcades of carved plasterwork and slender alabaster capitals probably explains why the palace was often used as a royal residence, for example, on occasion of the coronation at the beginning of each reign or when the court, which in the Middle Ages moved around, met in the city of Saragossa.

The royal coronation was both a liturgical and a state ceremony, which gave great solemnity to the accession of the new king to the throne of Aragon and implied the acceptance of the person of the king by those present. After Pedro II was crowned in Rome in 1205, the ceremony, attended by representatives of all the crown territories of Aragon, was held in the Cathedral of San Salvador in Saragossa, since the city was the capital of the realm and the principal seat of the crown. With Alfonso III (1285), the rite was structured according to a strict protocol, which included the anointing and coronation of the king, the receiving of the Order of Knighthood by the king and the taking of the mutual oath between the king and his kingdom.

At sunset on the eve of the coronation, the festivities commenced with a cavalcade that set off from the Aljafería Palace and processed through Saragossa to the cathedral, along the streets bright with lights and loud with the rapturous rejoicing of the people. The procession included representatives of all the Estates of the different possessions of the crown solemnly summoned by the king and arranged in rigorous order of rank.

La Aljafería, Palace of the Catholic Monarchs, detail of the coffered ceiling in the Throne Room, Saragossa.

The king rode last, wearing his most splendid robes, while the people acclaimed him, crying "Aragon, Aragon!"

Arriving at the Cathedral, the King passed the night in armed vigil. The following morning, during the solemn Mass, the principal ceremony took place before the High Altar of the Cathedral: the anointing of the king by the officiating archbishop. Then the king himself placed the sword in the scabbard, but from the time of Alfonso IV (1327) onwards, the king also placed the crown on his own head and took up the sceptre without the intervention of the archbishop, a departure from tradition that significantly reduced the role of the prelate. After the liturgical ceremony, the procession returned to the palace in the same order, although the king, now crowned, also carried the rest of the regalia. A "political banquet" then took place at the palace – so-called because its intention was to exalt the institution of the monarchy before its subjects – where the king sat at a higher level than the rest of the guests. The chronicles mention the provisional installation of dais and awnings in the patio of Santa Isabel for these celebrations; the most important nobles of the court held the ancient offices of the royal household, those of steward, chamberlain, cup-bearer and cellarer. For several days afterwards, the king invited subjects who wished to eat at his table. There was bull fighting in front of palace, in an enclosure *"with much music and many people and riders who goaded the bulls with their lances"*.

This complex ceremony is described with the title "*Coronación de los reyes de Aragón*" (The Coronation of the Kings of Aragon) in one of the most famous books by the chronicler from Aragon, Jerónimo de Blancas, written in 1583 and published in 1641.

Our itinerary through the Mudéjar area of Saragossa follows the same route as the Coronation procession. The visit begins in the Mudéjar rooms and the apartments of the Catholic Monarchs in the Aljafería Palace complex, providing excellent examples of royal patronage. Then it continues through the busy district of San Pablo, with its Mudéjar church and tower, finishing in the Cathedral of San Salvador where there are magnificent testimonies to the patronage of the archbishops and popes. The visitor can continue to the eastern part of the city, visiting the bustling Mudéjar parishes of La Magdalena, San Miguel de los Navarros and San Gil.

During these visits, we will see how the Mudéjar system of working satisfied the need both for civil architec-

Seo or Cathedral of San Salvador, night-time view of the cimborrio, Saragossa.

ITINERARY III The Coronation of the Kings of Aragon
Saragossa

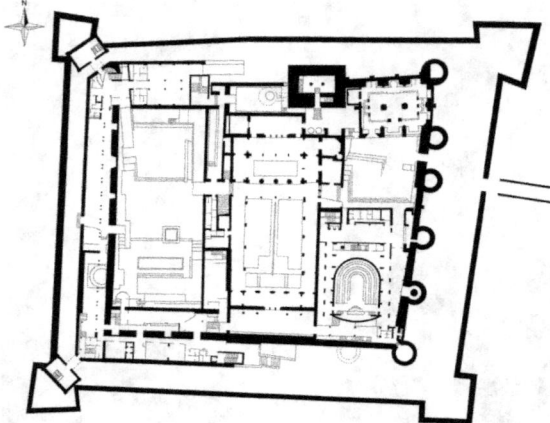

La Aljafería, Mudéjar Palace, ground plan, Saragossa.

ture (palaces and great houses) and religious buildings (cathedrals, chapels and parish churches). We will learn how these building projects converted the capital of the kingdom during the late Middle Ages into a Mudéjar city par excellence, and how Saragossa became a model for other Mudéjar cities in Aragon, such as Borja, Tarazona, Calatayud, Daroca or Teruel.

The spread of these models into the rural areas can be studied by visiting the towns of Utebo and Alagón to the north-west of the city, as each of these has a really outstanding Mudéjar monument.

III.I SARAGOSSA

III.1.a La Aljafería

Entrance in Avenida de los Diputados. Part of the monumental complex is at present the seat of the Parliament of Aragon. Entrance fee. Guided tours available. Opening hours: 15 Apr–15 Oct 10.00–14.00 and 16.30–20.00. Rest of the year: 10.00–14.00 and 16.00–18.30 (except Thurs and Fri mornings, groups only); Sun and public holidays: 10.00–14.00.

The Mudéjar Palace

From an artistic point of view, the Aljafería Palace complex divides into two different parts:

First, there is the Islamic Hudid palace dating from the 11th century, which belongs to the *taifa* period, and which is the main nucleus and oldest part of the monument. King Alfonso I el Batallador (the fighter) took possession of it on 18th December 1118, the same day as he conquered the city of Saragossa, and converted it into a Christian royal palace. In the centuries that followed, the Kings of Aragon continued to use the apartments of the old Islamic fortress, modifying parts of them.

Secondly, there is the Mudéjar palace itself, that is to say the whole complex of new apartments and official outbuildings constructed by order of the Christian kings, especially during the reign of Pedro IV (1336–1387).

The gradual transformation of the Islamic palace on the one hand, and the construction of new Mudéjar areas on the other, was the result of the painstaking diligence shown by the Kings of Aragon to preserve the palace, to which surviving documents testify. To this end, they appointed Muslim craftsmen from the Bellito family in the 13th century, and craftsmen from the Gali family during the period of the Catholic Monarchs. In this way, to accommodate and serve the needs of the kings, transformation of the Islamic palace gradually introduced new systems of ornamentation to the walls (e.g. the Gothic mural paintings that decorate the north

ITINERARY III *The Coronction of the Kings of Aragon*
Saragossa

portico of the Islamic palace). At the same time, use continued of the north chamber of the Islamic palace as the throne room and the western apartment as the royal bedchamber.

It was not long before the crown required extensions to the existing buildings. From 1371 onwards two new floors were built above the three existing floors of the Torre del Trovador (Troubadour's Tower), which is mentioned in Christian royal documents as the Torre Mayor (Great Tower), Torre Maestra (Main Tower) and Torre del Homenaje (the Keep). While the lower three floors of this tower with rectangular ground plan were pre-Hudid and Hudid from the Islamic period, both of the new floors are Mudéjar.

The reign of Pedro IV is undoubtedly the most notable for new building activity and includes the outstanding example of the Mudéjar chapel of San Martín, dated between 1338 and 1339. Built adjoining the north-east corner of the Islamic wall, this chapel, built on a rectangular ground plan, has two naves each of three spans. These spans with ribbed vaults conserve the remains of the original Mudéjar *agramilado* decoration, painted to look like brick. The chapel underwent an in-depth transformation in 1772; then, between 1947 and 1982, before its conversion into the library of the Parliament of Aragon, its original shape was restored in a process directed by the architect Francisco Iñiguez.

The entrance to the chapel is from the Patio of San Martín through a beautiful Mudéjar door, which can be dated to the early 15th century and, therefore, is later than the chapel itself. The door is set into a basket-handle arch, its tympanum decorated with *mixtilíneos* and a modern relief that represents St Martín sharing his cloak with the beggar, framed within a pointed arch. This composition is contained within the rectangular surround of an *alfiz* decorated with Mudéjar work and the arms of the Kings of Aragon in the *albanegas* on each side.

Another chapel, also built by Pedro IV, known as the chapel of San Jorge and situated in the southern hall of the Hudid palace, was demolished in 1866. Conserved fragments of a Mudéjar rosette from there are in the National Archaeological Museum in Madrid.

However, the most ambitious and large-scale additions to the Mudéjar

La Aljafería, Mudéjar Palace, doorway of San Martín, Saragossa.

ITINERARY III   The Coronation of the Kings of Aragon
Saragossa

palace were those Pedro IV began in 1354, which lasted some 10 years. This was an official building of such proportions that the royal documentation mentioned it as *"the building of a new palace"*. This new Mudéjar palace of Pedro IV respected the Islamic complex on the north side (portico, chamber and possibly upper floor) and added two large rooms to it, one on the ground floor and another on the upper floor, and built other apartments on the upper floor, over the Islamic portico and the wings.

This part, the Mudéjar palace of Pedro IV, has suffered more damage than the rest of the monumental complex. It had already seen extensive alterations at the time of the Catholic Monarchs when only the walls and two windows of the Mudéjar palace were respected. In the tracery of these two windows, the new formal language of the Gothic from the Spanish Levante is evident, as is the plant motif decoration of the *ataurique*, which created its own school, and spread throughout Aragon in the mid-14th century.

Similarly, the Mudéjar palace was almost ignored and relegated as part of the restorations carried out by the architect Francisco Iñiguez, who centred his attention as a matter of priority on the weakened structure of the Islamic palace and then on the Palace of the Catholic Monarchs. The restoration of the Mudéjar apartment of Santa Isabel, situated over the Hudid mosque, was precisely in response to the need – a priority for Iñiguez – to replace the Mudéjar cupola of the mosque, which obliged him to eliminate the room of the Catholic Monarchs. This part of the Mudéjar palace is an outstanding recovery from the most recent restoration, carried out in 1978, under the technical direction of the architects Luis Franco and Mariano Pemán.

The Palace of the Catholic Monarchs

In the 15th century, following a period when the Islamic and Mudéjar complex of the Aljafería Palace was largely abandoned as a result of the long absence of Alfonso V el Magnánimo (the Magnanimous, 1416–1458), the situation then changed during the reign of the Catholic Monarchs (1479–1504). During their reign, work began again to transform and extend the complex considerably, which in fact led to the building of a new palace. As suggested by recent studies, among the possible motives of the Catholic Kings in commissioning this new work, the decision to set up the Court of the Inquisition in the Aljafería Palace may have played a part, whereby the great Mudéjar chamber on the upper floor became the session room of the Holy Office.

Whatever purpose the palace served, there were also other architectonic reasons that were decisive in the planning of the new works. In spite of the important transformations and extensions carried out during the Middle Ages, mentioned above in the context of the Mudéjar palace, the Aljafería reached the Modern Age with some basic deficiencies.

The first was that a satisfactory solution had yet to be found to the problem of reaching the upper floor from the lower level. It could still only be reached by means of the old and narrow steep stairway attached to the west of the Islamic portico and chamber on the north side, or, alternatively,

ITINERARY III *The Coronation of the Kings of Aragon*
Saragossa

through the Torre del Trovador, where the third Islamic floor had communicated with the new Mudéjar chamber built by Pedro IV. Possibly, there was still some other way of reaching and circulating between the lower and upper floors, but in any case, even the two principal access routes were old – from Islamic times – and did not allow an easy through-flow.

It is hardly surprising therefore, that work on the new palace of the Catholic Monarchs – carried out principally between 1488 and 1493 under the direction of the Muslim master Farax Gali – included the addition of a great staircase of majestic volumes to the west of the Islamic patio. This provided easy access from the lower to the upper floor of the palace for the first time in its history. The flat ceiling of this staircase, with exposed beams and infill arches in between, was decorated with painted motifs that were both heraldic (the yoke and fasces) and also bore the first Renaissance *grutescos* of Aragonese art.

Another problem was the lack of natural light, which made all the principal rooms of the Islamic and Mudéjar palace appear quite gloomy. The desire for more natural light, therefore, was decisive in the plan of the new palace of the Catholic Kings, which took the upper floor, with the principal bays facing east and south, three rooms opening onto the Patio of San Martín and the gallery and principal chamber opening onto the Patio of Santa Isabel. In pursuit of more light, it seems there was no hesitation in destroying parts of both the Islamic palace (the cupola of the mosque was demolished on this occasion) and Mudéjar palace. The latter was in fact the most affected

La Aljafería, Palace of the Catholic Monarchs, staircase, Saragossa.

zone of all those giving onto the Patio of Santa Isabel, which was partially replaced, and then to some degree integrated into the new construction. The action of the Catholic Monarchs not only solved these deficiencies satisfactorily but it also marked out a convincing route according to protocol by which to reach the new throne room on the upper floor. This route, which heightened the formal value of the completed work, started at the outer door of the entrance, where a new gate concealed an older horseshoe arch, and continued through the recently designed patios of San Martín and Santa Isabel until it reached the new monumental staircase.

The most impressive chamber of the new palace is the *Aula Regia* or Throne Room; its magnificent *artesonado* was contracted on 23rd April 1493 to the Muslim master craftsmen Farax Gali, Mahoma Palacio and Brahem Mofferiz. A Latin inscription, duplicated for ornamental reasons, runs in Gothic letters round the base of the Mudéjar ceiling. Translated it reads: *"Ferdinand, King of Spain, Sicily, Corsica and the Balearics, the best of princes, prudent, brave, pious, firm, just and fortunate, and Isabel the Queen, above all women in piety and greatness of spirit, celebrated spouses, all-victorious with the help of Christ, after freeing Andalucía from the Moors, expelling the fierce and ancient enemy, took care to do this work in the year of grace 1492."*

Among the many notable items of artistic interest that deserve special mention in the palace of the Catholic Monarchs is the decoration of the great windows of the monumental staircase, which are worked in plaster, and the decoration of the doors and windows of the throne room. These decorative motifs, which include heraldic subjects, provide a magnificent formal repertory of the truly exuberant style known as *Reyes Católicos* (Catholic Monarchs). This decoration was undoubtedly carried out by Mudéjar plasterers who worked *de aljez*, providing yet another example of the versatility of the Mudéjar craftsmen and of their ability to absorb foreign artistic modes.

In relation to Mudéjar carpentry, in addition to the *artesonado* ceiling in the throne room mentioned above, are three notable *taujels*, or flat ornamental ceilings, in the three rooms that give onto the San Martín patio. During the restoration of the cupola of the mosque by architect Francisco Iñiguez, the *taujel* corresponding to the most northerly of these rooms was moved to another room nearby. In addition to the painted decoration of the beams and arches over the staircase already described above, and those above the gallery outside the throne room, all mainly restored by Iñiguez, it is also worth mentioning the origin and fate of the tiled floors in these rooms. These floors, created from tiles made by the Mudéjar tile works in Muel (Saragossa), were part of the 1978 restoration works on the palace carried out by the architects Luis Franco and Mariano Pemán.

As frequently happens, the royal works left a long trail of influence. The Mudéjar palace of Pedro IV in the Aljafería was the mirror that reflected all the official buildings of the Aragonese nobility of the second half of the 14th century, and in the same way, the new building of the Catholic Monarchs became the formal model for civil architecture in Saragossa in the first half of the 16th century.

III.1.b **Church and Bell Tower of San Pablo**

In the calle San Pablo, 44. Turn east out of the Palace, towards the Seo, crossing through the busy district of San Pablo. Mass hours: 09.30 and 19.00. Sundays and feast days: 10.00, 11.00, 12.00, 13.00 and 19.00 (20.00 in summer). Best time to visit is just before, or after, Mass.

The district of San Pablo, founded by Christians and located between the Aljafería Palace and the medieval market, is the result of the city's expansion to the West, outside the Roman walls, when a community of farmers settled there in the 12th and 13th centuries. Crossed by longitudinal

ITINERARY III   *The Coronation of the Kings of Aragon*
Saragossa

streets running east to west, the two main streets, named after San Blas and San Pablo, adjoin the site of the Mudéjar church to the north and south, whose very high octagonal bell tower dominates the whole district.

After the reconquest of the city, a small church was constructed in the Romanesque style, dedicated to San Blas, but nothing remains of it today. The present Mudéjar church, dedicated to San Pablo, was built in two stages: the first, from 1284 onwards, with a single nave and a polygonal, five-sided apse. Ribbed vaulting covers all four bays of the nave and there are side chapels between the buttresses. Very early on, as the population in this busy district increased, the church with its single nave church proved too small. Thus, from 1389 onwards, a project began to enlarge the church to three naves, with the primitive side chapels used to form the communicating arches between them. These side aisles of different widths enclosed the old church at the sanctuary end in the form of an ambulatory, and at the foot as a cloister that imprisoned the octagonal bell tower inside it.

The tower belongs to the first Mudéjar period and dates to probably around 1300. What attracts attention here is that although the shape of it is an octagonal prism, inspired by the stone Gothic towers of the kingdom of Aragon, its internal structure is that of an Almohad minaret: it has two towers, one inside the other, separated by a stair ramp, and the interior tower is divided into chambers one above the other as far up as the belfry. The decorative brickwork in relief is concentrated on the upper part of the tower to ensure it was visible above the level of the medieval

buildings of the town surrounding it, which were lower than at present. In it, there are notably some very old ornamental motifs with precedents in the Islamic Aljafería Palace, such as the interlaced semicircular arches and the branched crosses, which form a diamond-shaped network.

Parish Church of San Pablo, bell tower, Saragossa.

III.1.c Cathedral of San Salvador

Continue towards the east, passing the market and follow the ancient decumanus *of the Roman city, and take calle Manifestación and then calle Espoz y Mina. Opening hours: 10.00–13.30 and 17.00–18.30. Closed Mon. The* Parroquieta *is an independent church inside the Cathedral. Mass time: 18.00.*

ITINERARY III   *The Coronation of the Kings of Aragon*
Saragossa

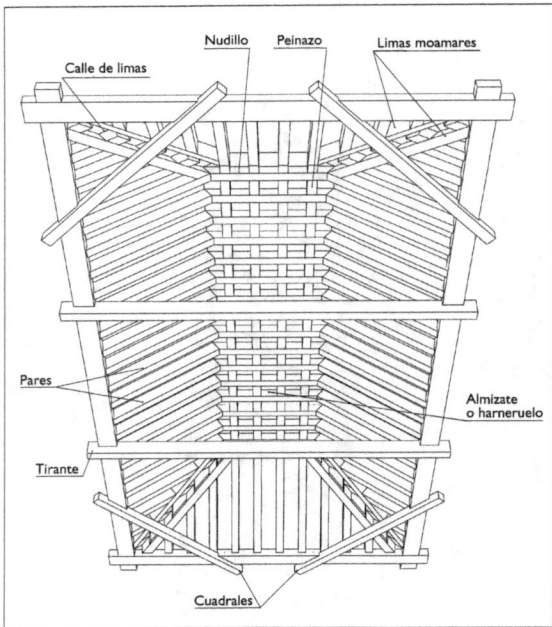

Schemes of armaduras de limas moamares.

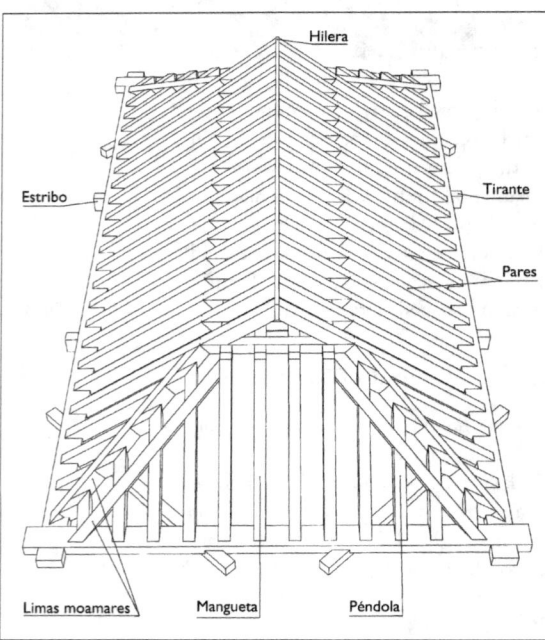

Erected on the same site as the Roman Forum and the Great Mosque, the Cathedral of San Salvador was built in various stages and in different artistic styles, and it is this diversity that provides its main interest.

Mudéjar art is well represented in three parts of the Cathedral, all of them situated at the sanctuary end: the present *Parroquieta* of San Miguel, the upper part of the three apses and the *cimborrio*.

The present *Parroquieta* or Parish Chapel of San Miguel, rectangular, and joined to the apses of the cathedral on the west side, is in fact the memorial chapel commissioned by the archbishop of Saragossa, don Lope Fernández de Luna, which was built during the years 1374 to 1379 by the master workmen Garcí and Lope Sánchez from Seville. The outside wall is very interesting, magnificently decorated with brickwork in relief in the Aragon tradition and with vitrified ceramics worked with the *alicer* technique, in which one can see in the small pointed areas different motifs, some of which are local traditional ones and others from the traditional repertoire of Seville. In the interior, apart from the magnificent Gothic alabaster tomb by the sculptor Pere Moragues, above all, it is worth noting the exquisite Mudéjar ceiling, an octagonal *armadura de limas moamares* in the Sevillian tradition.

Outside once again, the three 12th-century Romanesque apses, worked in cut-stone masonry, had become too small as the cathedral gained height during the Gothic period. In addition, the extremely high *cimborrio*, built by the Archbishop don Lope Fernández de Luna, whose memorial chapel is mentioned above, collapsed, as the result of having no

ITINERARY III   The Coronation of the Kings of Aragon
Saragossa

resistance on the side of the apses. Don Pedro Martínez de Luna, one of the popes of Avignon under the name of Benedict XIII (1394–1422 or 1423), took charge of raising the apses and rebuilding the *cimborrio*. The three Mudéjar apses constructed on a Romanesque base of stone and reaching a considerable height gave the whole complex the air of a military fortress. There were three usable walkways, one above the other, which are identifiable by their parapets decorated with pointed merlons in the Almohad tradition. The master of works of the apses built between 1404 and 1408 was the famous Muslim master Mahoma Ramí, who, as we shall see later, worked for the Papa Luna in other areas of Aragon.

The reason for raising the apses was to serve as counter-resistance on the side of the apses for the *cimborrio* or cupola above the transept, which had collapsed. The second *cimborrio* rebuilt by Benedict XIII also collapsed, although not completely, since in the interior the coat of arms of the pope is still visible in the upper part of the supporting arches. In this way, then, the existing *cimborrio*, built from 1520 at the height of the Renaissance under the direction of the master Juan Lucas, known with the pseudonym "Botero", is in fact the third lantern-tower. Its design served as a model for the Mudéjar *cimborrio* in the cathedrals in Teruel (1538) and Tarazona (1543) by the same master. If we look at it from the inside, we can see how the Hispano-Muslim tradition survived in the interlaced arches that form eight-pointed stars, which provided an efficient system of vaulting that was already in use at the time of al-Hakam II (961–976) in the Great

La Seo or Cathedral de San Salvador, exterior wall of the Parroquieta de San Miguel, Saragossa.

Mosque in Córdoba. As we leave the cathedral in Saragossa, as one would hope, it is as well to appreciate that the Mudéjar works we have just seen, which the archbishops and Pope Benedict XIII encouraged, served as a model and example of more modest ecclesiastical patronage. Thus, they constitute, along with the royal patronage in the Aljafería, the real basis for the success and spread of Mudéjar art and architecture in the former kingdom of Aragon.

III.1.d **Church and Bell Tower of Santa María Magdalena** (optional)

Plaza de la Magdalena at the end of the calle Mayor. Opening hours: 17.30–20.00, Sun: 10.00–13.00 and 18.00–20.00.

The Mudéjar building of the Parish Church of Santa María Magdalena has a single nave with a polygonal and seven-sided apse. As is usual in Mudéjar architecture it has no buttresses, so that the smooth face of the apse allowed for brickwork decoration in relief without the visual break that buttressing would have caused. Under the windows of the apse are large panels with interlaced *mixtilineos* arches, and, above the windows, other panels with branched crosses, which form a diamond-shaped honeycomb.

A Baroque renovation of between 1727 and 1730 inverted the orientation of the church, turning the apse into the gable end and opening up an entrance door in the new façade. This transformation also affected the interior of the church, although it respected the vaulting of the sanctuary and the three aisles of the nave. At the foot of the church, in calle Mayor, there is the magnificent bell tower of the Magdalena. This tower, built on a square ground plan, is a copy of the towers of San Martín and el Salvador in the city of Teruel, which it resembles both in its interior, in the form of a minaret, like the Giralda in Seville, and also because of the decoration on the outside of brickwork in relief and enamelled ceramics. The extensive alteration to the belfry of the tower was to suit Baroque taste between 1678 and 1695. The present tower is the result of a restoration carried out by the architect Francisco Iñiguez in 1970.

III.1.e Church and Bell Tower of San Miguel de los Navarros (optional)

Plaza de San Miguel, 52. Follow calle del Coso and turn left into calle Espartero. Opening hours: 11.00–13.00 and 17.00–21.00, Sun 10.00–13.00.

The Mudéjar Church of San Miguel de los Navarros dates from the 14th century. It has a single nave with three spans and a five-sided polygonal apse without buttresses. There are side chapels on both sides of the nave and there is an adjoining bell tower on the north side. A Baroque renovation carried out between 1666 and 1669 by the master Juan de la Marca affected the doorway and the interior, adding a lower side aisle and a choir at the end. In the Mudéjar work, the heraldic decoration of the apses is notable, based on large fleur-de-lis intersecting crosses, which also appear in the Mudéjar churches of Herrera de los Navarros and Azuara, both in the Saragossa area. The decoration of the tower is also interesting, with its large panels of intersecting *mixtilineos* arches, and diamond shapes. According to documentary evidence, the masters Esteban and Pascual Ferriz built the tower in 1396.

III.1.f Church and Bell Tower of San Gil (optional)

Calle Don Jaime I, 15. Take calle del Cosso to Plaza de España. Then turn right. Opening hours: 07.00–09.00, 12.00–13.30, 17.30–21.00. The whole of Monday is dedicated to the worship of St Nicholas.

The Baroque transformations carried out between 1719 and 1725 by the masters Manuel Sanclemente and Blas Ximénez affected the original Mudéjar building here more than in the case of Santa María Magdalena or of San Miguel de los Navarros mentioned above. So much so, in fact, that the original Mudéjar traces in the monument can only be distinguished from the outside.

ITINERARY III *The Coronation of the Kings of Aragon*
Utebo

The Mudéjar building was a typical fortified church (a typology visited in the next itinerary and analysed in depth). The most interesting feature of what remains is the bell tower, built on a rectangular ground plan and profusely decorated in brickwork in relief, and already mentioned in the chronicles of 1356. The rubble used for the shafts and capitals of the columns of the belfry, both here in this tower and in the Magdalena already mentioned above, was probably from the Great Mosque of the city. The architect Joaquín Soro restored the tower in 1999.

III.2 **UTEBO**

III.2.a **Church and Bell Tower**

Utebo is 14 km from Saragossa on the N 232. Mass hours are at 20.00. Sun: 12.00. If the church is closed, apply to the Parish house next to the church.

Utebo is near Saragossa as its name suggests, deriving from *octavum*, the eighth milestone on the route from Caesaraugusta (Saragossa) to Asturica (Astorga). Adjoined at the foot of the Parish Church of Utebo, is the extraordinary Mudéjar bell tower of the former kingdom of Aragon.
The tower has two sections, the lower of which is square and the upper octagonal, giving a "mixed" volume, which became widespread during the modern era from the time of the Catholic Monarchs onwards. Complementing its brick decoration in relief is a profuse application of Mudéjar tiles produced in the potteries of Muel (Saragossa). The shiny effect of *azulejos* tiles provides the structure its nickname "Tower of mirrors". According to a long inscription written across the tiles in a frieze, which divides the two areas of the lower and square part of the tower, works were complete by 1544, and the master of works was Alonso de Leznes. Since its construction was late, at the height of the Renaissance, the tower can be considered the swansong of Mudéjar art in Aragon at least as far as bell towers are concerned. As to its considerable vitality, it was in use up until the beginning of the 17th century

Parish church, bell tower, Utebo.

ITINERARY III   *The Coronation of the Kings of Aragon*
Alagón

Church and tower of San Pedro, arch plasterwork detail, Chapel of the Virgin del Carmen, Alagón.

On a hill dominating the town of Alagón where there is also the Church of Nuestra Señora del Castillo, the Parish Church of San Pedro is of a typical Mudéjar shape: a single nave covered with ribbed vaulting, a polygonal apse without buttressing and chapels on both sides of the nave. Built at the beginning of the 14th century, the church has an outstanding octagonal tower, which is structured like a minaret and exceptionally beautiful. The reduced proportions of this tower contrasts with the higher contemporary towers of the Parish Churches of San Pablo de Saragossa and Santa María de Tauste (a village that belongs to the district of the *Cinco Villas* or Five Towns, near Alagón).

Above the Mudéjar building, constructed as some time well into the 16th century, a continuous gallery of double horseshoe arches served to ventilate the vaulted areas, a style which had strong links to both the religious and civil architecture of Aragon.

If we go inside, we can see some of the entrance arches to the side chapels, decorated with carved plasterwork. Especially interesting is the former chapel of the Virgin del Carmen, which can be dated to the early years of the 16th century, and which has since been converted into the entrance porch. In this archway are perfectly combined plant motifs from the Gothic repertoire, decoration with *grutescos* from the Renaissance period, and strapwork and six-point stars of Muslim origin. This versatility, the assimilation and integration of all kinds of different motifs, is one of the essential characteristics of Mudéjar decoration.

when the *Moriscos* were expelled from Spain by the decree of Felipe III (1609 and 1610).

In the interior of the church, the restoration of the tiled *cuenca o arista*, covering the lower part of the walls of the old nave, was based on the few original traces which had survived.

III.3 **ALAGÓN**

III.3.a **Church and Bell Tower of San Pedro**

The monument is 15 km from the preceding one on the N 232. Recently restored. Opening hours: Sun only 10.00–13.00.

PEDRO IV

Gonzalo M. Borrás Gualís

The reign of Pedro IV is one of the longest in the history of the crown of Aragon, exceeded only by that of Jaime I, a century earlier. In fact, the reign of Pedro IV lasted for 51 years, between 1336 on his proclamation, and 1387 when he died. Proclaimed king on the death of his father, Alfonso IV el Benigno (the Mild), Pedro IV was only 16 years old; at his death, he was 67. He was succeeded by his two sons, Juan I and Martin I el Humano (the Humane), and in 1410 the dynasty ended.

Brave and steadfast, although of violent and choleric temper, Pedro IV consolidated the power of the crown of Aragon in the Mediterranean. A great man of letters and patron of the arts, he sponsored many architectural projects, especially in the city of Barcelona, where he had the Salón del Tinell built in the main royal palace.

As far as Mudéjar art is concerned, Pedro IV dedicated particular attention to the Aljafería Palace in Saragossa. He remodelled and decorated some rooms of the old Islamic palace, especially in the north chamber, where he used the western alcove as his bedchamber. He rebuilt the main towers of the fortified Islamic complex and built the new Mudéjar Chapels of San Martín (1338) and San Jorge (1358). He improved the defences and the fosse, because of the frontier wars with Castile, and extended the whole complex considerably with new Mudéjar rooms from 1354 onwards. Finally, from 1371, he added new floors to the Torre del Trovador. It is not surprising, then, that the chronicles refer to the Aljafería palace as a new building.

Thanks to royal documentation transcribed and published by José María Madurell, we know that King Pedro IV paid constant attention to making improvements in the Aljafería Palace in Saragossa. We also know that the renovations he made acted as a stimulus for the spread of the Mudéjar style throughout the whole of the kingdom of Aragon in the mid-14th century.

Sculpture of Pedro IV, by Jaume Cascalls, Museum of the Cathedral, Gerona.

ITINERARY IV

Mudéjar Cities:
From Islam to Christianity

Gonzalo M. Borrás Gualís

IV.1 TERUEL
- IV.1.a Medieval City
- IV.1.b Tower of el Salvador
- IV.1.c Church and Tower of San Pedro
- IV.1.d Cathedral of Santa María
- IV.1.e Tower of San Martín

IV.2 DAROCA
- IV.2.a Medieval City
- IV.2.b Apse of San Juan de la Cuesta
- IV.2.c Tower of Santo Domingo de Silos
- IV.2.d Main Residence of Pope Benedict XIII

The Moorish Quarter of Teruel

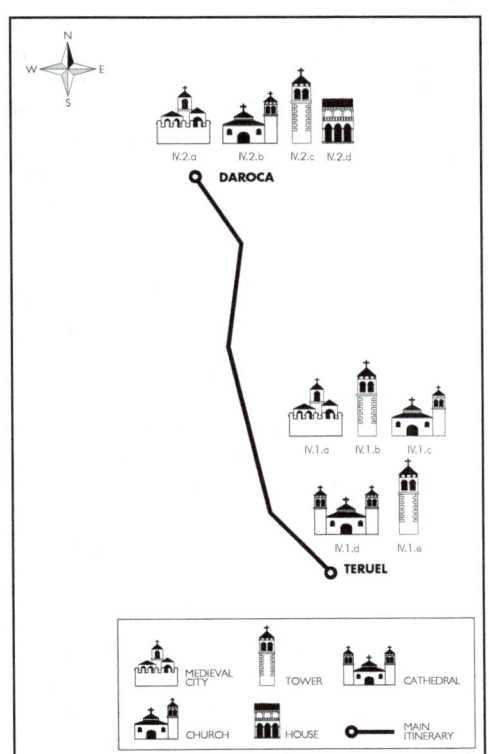

Cathedral of Santa María, general view of the cimborrio, *Teruel.*

ITINERARY IV   Mudéjar Cities: From Islam to Christianity

Church of San Pedro, detail of the apse turrets, Teruel.

Scheme of an alfarje.

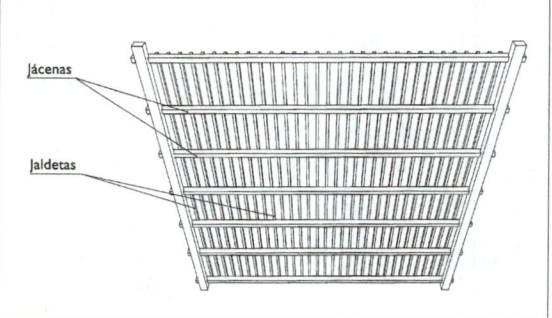

This itinerary encompasses two of the great Mudéjar cities of Aragon – two border towns on the frontier of Islam – to introduce two medieval urban systems of different origins: on the one hand the fairly regular grid of the city of Teruel, a Christian foundation and, on the other, the irregular plan of the city of Daroca, an Islamic foundation. In the former, the Mudéjar towers of the parish churches seem perfectly integrated into the streets that run under them. In the latter the irregularity of the streets that crisscross the medina persists on the south side of the hill of San Cristóbal, while those in the district built round the calle Mayor, which grew up in a deep gully after the Christian occupation, are regular in their layout.

There are three essential values in the Mudéjar art and architecture of Teruel, which UNESCO declared a World Heritage Site. First, the Mudéjar ceramics from Teruel represent the continuation of the caliphate production in green and purple and in addition to their use in crockery they were used as an ornamental element in the architecture as well. Second, the open character of the Mudéjar style of Teruel, which took on the artistic innovations from the south, became one of the main centres of the renewed Mudéjar style in Aragon. Finally, the figurative decoration on the ceiling of Teruel Cathedral is a unique feature in Spanish Mudéjar, and a splendid graphic testimony to the life of the different medieval social classes and Estates – the nobles, the clergy and the people – and of their different activities.

In the visit to Daroca, Mudéjar art appears as an alternative system to the Romanesque art of the conquerors,

ITINERARY IV Mudéjar Cities: From Islam to Christianity
Teruel

of which there are splendid examples such as the old Collegiate Church of Santa María de los Corporales. The spread of the Romanesque came up against serious difficulties in the area, because of the shortage of suitable stone in the valley of the River Ebro. This meant that the Christians had to interrupt some of their building projects and continue them in the Mudéjar style, as can be seen in the apse of the Church of San Juan de la Cuesta or in the Tower of Santo Domingo de Silos. However, the principal houses of Benedict XIII (who was Pope in Avignon between 1394 and 1422 or 1423) in the calle Mayor, with their *alfarjes* and the plasterwork of the windows of the interior patio, constitute the most important civil Mudéjar monument of Aragon, at present in private hands.

IV.1 TERUEL

IV.1.a Medieval City

Stroll through the old part of the city. Originally designed for military use, the Medieval City stands on a tableland for the obvious strategic advantage this elevated position allowed it.

The name Teruel derives from the toponym *Tirwal*, quoted in Arabic sources, and which refers to a watchtower or military fort, since no evidence of a *medina* in the strict sense exists. This is why the medievalist Antonio Gargallo didn't hesitate in making his deduction that the city of Teruel was entirely refounded by Alfonso II (King of Aragon between 1162 and 1196). After the conquest of the highlands in the south of Aragon in 1171, the monarch decided to establish a nucleus of a Christian population in the border territory there, as an outpost against the power of the Almohads, who remained intact in the city of Valencia. In the same year, he granted the population its *fuero* or municipal code of laws. The historical circumstances surrounding the foundation of the city are reflected in both the urban plan and in the social structure of its medieval population. The medieval precinct, perched on a high spur surrounded by deep ravines on the left bank of the River Turia, conforms to the model of the Ideal Christian Town, promoted from that time on

Tower of Santo Domingo de Silos and Apse of San Juan de la Cuesta, seen from the castle, Daroca.

Teruel

by the crown of Aragon in the resettlement of the whole of the Levant region of the peninsula. The city's regular ground plan forms a walled rectangle: the four main gates, situated centrally on the sides and facing the four cardinal points, were given the names of Daroca (to the north), Saragossa (to the east), Valencia (to the south) and Guadalviar (to the west). Although now only the first of these has survived, we know that the main streets began at the gates and then crossed perpendicularly in the centre, where they open into the Plaza Mayor or del Mercado (Market Square) — now called *Plaza del Torico* (Square of the Bull).

The integration of the medieval religious architecture with its churches and towers into the urban plan is equally complete. Out of the nine parishes that divide the city, the main Parish Church, dedicated to Santa María (now the Cathedral named Santa María de Mediavilla), was centrally located in the city, while the other eight are at the sides, four to the north and four to the south.

One of the peculiar aspects of the town plan of Teruel is its church towers, which supported by great pointed arches, allow the street traffic to pass along below; it also means that the Mudéjar bell towers, as well as having a religious use, also had an important function as watchtowers.

Since there had not previously been a Muslim city here, there had not been an *aljama* either, nor a closed area for the Moorish Quarter. The particular character of the Moorish Quarter in Teruel derives primarily from the fact that it was inhabited initially by Muslim immigrants, originally prisoners, who arrived after the reconquest of Valencia and who bought themselves out of captivity by working. Afterwards, from 1285 onwards, other immigrants joined them during a campaign of Mudéjar resettlement proposed by King Pedro III. For this reason, the Mudéjars were not confined to a closed Moorish Quarter as was the usual practice, but enjoyed an open regime where they were scattered throughout the city, although they tended to be concentrated more in the northern part, near the Daroca Gate. Coming as they did from outside, the Muslims in Teruel introduced the formal innovations of Mudéjar art into the city. Scenes of knights on horseback, tournaments and hunting scenes represented on the ceiling of the Cathedral reflect the political and social importance of the knights in this frontier town. Their all-important role, decisive in the reconquest of the Levant, contributed to the creation of a militarised society the paintings on the ceiling describe proudly.

IV.1.b Tower of el Salvador

In the calle del Salvador. From the Plaza del Torico take calle del Salvador. It is still in use as the belfry of the church and since its restoration in 1993, has been open to the public. Opening hours: 11.00–14.00 and 17.00–20.00 (extended in Holy Week and summer). It may be possible to arrange visits outside this timetable, for example, on a moonlit night. Tel: 978 602061.

The medieval precinct is accessible from the west along the calle del Salvador, where the gate of Guadalviar used to be; very near the exact spot of the former gate, the street passes under the Mudéjar Tower of el Salvador, which towers over it, guarding it, giving its name to this stretch of street as far as the Plaza Mayor.

Only the tower is left of the medieval Parish Church of el Salvador, since the present church was rebuilt in the Baroque style after the original one collapsed on 24th May 1677.

The date of the Tower of el Salvador is not documented, although its formal characteristics, which are very similar to the Tower of San Martín (1315–1316), date it to the same period. In any case, this date does not contradict the documented fact published by Alberto López Polo. This shows that on 11th April 1277 the Bishop of Saragossa don Pedro Garcés authorised the Prebendary of the Parish of el Salvador, the *mosén*, or bursar Monsignor Pedro Navarrete, to obtain funding from the whole diocese for the building of the church and its bell tower. An inscription cut in the stone that reinforces the base of the tower, informs us that this work of reinforcement was achieved in 1650. Restoration of the tower has occurred at various times in the 20th century; the last time was in 1992, by the architects Antonio Pérez and José María Sanz.

The interior of the Tower of el Salvador has been organised for visitors, and is, therefore, the most appropriate one to ascend as far as the belfry to examine its internal structure, which is similar to that of the *alminares* in the Almohad era. The building has two towers, an exterior one of brick and another interior one of plaster masonry, with the stairway between the two. The interior tower is divided vertically into three chambers, the lowest with a roof of ribbed vaulting and the other two covered with

Tower of San Martín, cross section, Teruel.

pointed barrel vaulting. At the top is the belfry.

A number of special features confirm the highly developed late character of this tower. It is the latest of all the extant towers in Teruel; in fact, if the short-lived Tower of San Juan – also known as la Fermosa (the Fair), built in 1343–44 – is left aside, as it was destroyed in 1366 when Castilian troops occupied the city during the *Guerra de los dos Pedros* (The War of the two Peters).

Mudéjar Cities: From Islam to Christianity
Teruel

Tower of el Salvador, Teruel.

IV.1.c Church and Tower of San Pedro

In calle M. Abad. From the Plaza del Torico take calle Hartzenbusch. Interior closed for restoration.

Older than the present church building, the Tower of San Pedro adjoins the main façade. Its construction, which can be dated to the middle of the 13th century, was the last in the first phase of Romanesque building in this parish and is the only one to have survived.

The typology and decoration of the Tower of San Pedro has always linked it to the Tower of Santa María, which according to the account of the judges of the city of Teruel was constructed between 1257 and 1258. The dendrochronological analyses dated the Tower of San Pedro to 1240, so that some scholars defend its chronological precedence over Santa María.

In the year 1795, the original structure of the belfry of San Pedro was infilled, to enable it to support a sober neoclassical finial on the top. After the Civil War of 1936–1939, the architect Manuel Lorente Junquera removed the neoclassical addition to restore the original belfry. Antonio Pérez and José María Sanz restored the tower again in 1994.

The supporting arch that makes up the lower part of this tower, which also allows the street to pass underneath it, has a simple ribbed vaulting roof, rather than the pointed barrel vaulting of the other arches. Greater artistic maturity is also observable in the decorative system, where the great ornamental stretches of brickwork in relief are progressively larger. This is true both of the panels of interlaced *arcos mixtilíneos* and of the series of four-strand knots forming eight-pointed stars combined with crosses. The zigzag bands even double up to give them more emphasis. Apart from that, the ceramics follow the formal tendency of the Tower of San Martín, that is to say, with a greater variety of pieces of smaller format, and a wider colour range.

This tower, just like others in Teruel, is built upon a pointed arch – here with a double border – which allows the street traffic to pass below it. It shares at least three characteristics with the Tower of Santa María: the design of the interior in the Christian tradition, consisting of only one tower divided into floors; the ornamental system, with the outstanding feature of the frieze of interlaced semicircular arches, the precedent for which can be found in the Islamic façade of the mosque of the Aljafería in Saragossa; and in the application of Mudéjar ceramics in the green and manganese version.

One of the most interesting elements in the decoration of the tower is the series of capitals in worked stone. Mariano Navarro Aranda drew attention to one of these in 1953 that represents a *jamsa* or hand of Fatima. This theme, which symbolises the five basic precepts of Islam and the protection against evil, was introduced by the Almohads, according to Juan Antonio Souto, and is found in the *sgraffito* ceramics of the first half of the 13th century as well.

The existing Mudéjar structure of the Church of San Pedro replaced an earlier one dating to the Romanesque period. It is to the present building that documentary sources dug up by Alberto López Polo undoubtedly refers; that is, to its construction in 1319, the obligation to build a cloister on the part of Francisco Sánchez Muñoz in 1383, and to the consecration of the church in 1392.

All of this information agrees with the structural and formal characteristics of the present Church of San Pedro, which follows the typology of the Mudéjar fortified church established in the Parish Church of Montalbán (Teruel), especially in the apse area. The apse is a seven-sided polygon with chapels between the buttresses and with the characteristic tribune above the chapels. The outside of the apse of San Pedro is richly decorated, with panels of brickwork in relief and buttresses, which take the form of octagonal turrets that are more slender and developed than those of the Parish

Church and tower of San Pedro, detail of the tower, Teruel.

Church of Montalbán which they imitate.

Both the church interior and cloister were subjected to Modernist reform in the first decade of the 20th century, in which the architect Pablo Monguió Segura and the artist and decorator Salvador Gisbert took part. Their work profoundly modified the whole complex and conservation of the original decoration was limited to the area hidden by the main retable. At present, a vast project is under way to restore the monument.

IV.1.d **Cathedral of Santa María**

In the Plaza de la Cathedral. Opening hours: 11.00–14.00 and 16.00–20.00. Guided tours available, including access to the recently restored ceiling.

ITINERARY IV   Mudéjar Cities: From Islam to Christianity

Teruel

Cathedral of Santa María, general view of the ceiling, Teruel.

Santa María is near the Plaza Mayor in the city centre, as is reflected in its earlier name of Santa María de Mediavilla. The temple only acquired the status of a Cathedral in 1587, the date when the Diocese of Teruel was created.

The Tower of Santa María was built, by all accounts, between 1257 and 1258. Like San Pedro, it is the oldest part of the whole complex and ended an era of Romanesque building during the first half of the 13th century. In this case, however, the three aisles from the Romanesque period were not demolished, but consolidated. This reduced the number of wall arches separating the naves by half and raised the height of the walls, which form the three existing aisles, the central one of which is covered with the famous Mudéjar ceiling. Dendrochronolgical analyses dated the tower to 1250, which coincides with the documented date. Along with the Tower of San Pedro from the same period, it is the oldest example of a Mudéjar tower in Teruel. Its most singular element is the pointed arch in the lower part beneath which the street passes, a formula that has many precedents in the architecture of the time, including that of Italy. In this way, the bell towers have been integrated into the town plan perfectly. There are also outstanding ornamental elements of Islamic provenance, indicated earlier in the Tower of San Pedro, that is to say the interlaced semicircular arches and the ceramics in green and manganese applied as architectonic decoration in the different forms of tiles, discs or plates and shafts.

The interior of the Cathedral has a wooden ceiling that covers the central nave: it is a unique work of Mudéjar art, both in its construction and in its decoration. In it two traditions, the Islamic and the Christian come together and are fused into a new artistic manifestation. It has been called the Sistine Chapel of Mudéjar art. Although we do not have documentary references to verify the date when it was made, all the indications point to the last quarter of the 13th century. During the Spanish Civil War, a bomb destroyed the last section at the foot of the church. Later, between 1943 and 1945, restorers from the Official Department of Regiones Devastadas (Devastated Areas) restored it inappropriately. Finally, between 1996 and 1999, and

under the direction of the Instituto del Patrimonio Histórico Español (Spanish Historical Heritage Institute), an extraordinary labour of study, cleaning, consolidation and treatment of the ceiling was carried out.
Structurally, this consists of an *armadura de par y nudillo* with double anchor ties following the tradition of Almohad carpentry. It is not very common to find *armaduras* of this type, and as old as this, conserved, although there are some examples from the same period in the city of Toledo (the Church of Santiago del Arrabal and the Synagogue of Santa María la Blanca). In the case of Teruel Cathedral, where the naves had been raised without the necessary buttressing to allow for the possibility of vaulting, this solution for the roof is a very adequate one, since the structure distributes the load equally on the walls.

The artistic interest of the ornamentation of this ceiling is even more important, with geometric, plant and, above all, figurative motifs that offer an unequalled repertoire of images. Applied with distemper onto the wood and in the Gothic linear style, the sacred images – including an outstanding cycle of the Passion – are in a minority, with the profane images – representing the different social classes of the town and their activities – in the majority. To be noted are the knightly scenes of cavalcades, tournaments and hunting, and the different trades and activities of the carpenters, artists and musicians. Other images, allegorical or symbolic, are from the figurative tradition of the bestiaries or related to literary themes. However, in the spatial distribution of the images, there is no apparent coherent

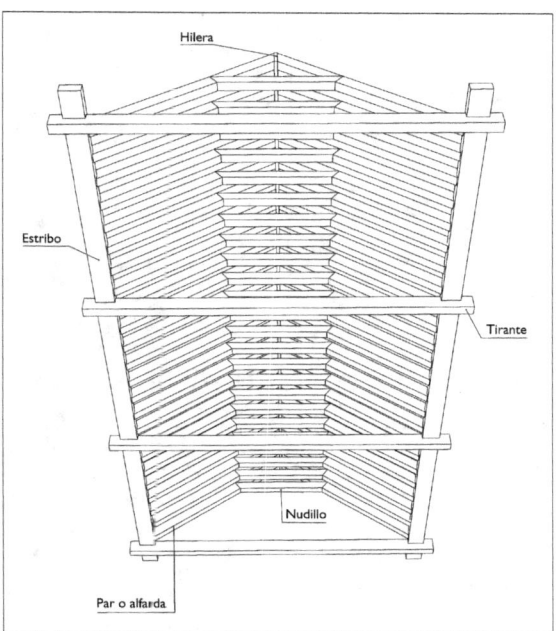

Schemes of armadura de par y nudillo.

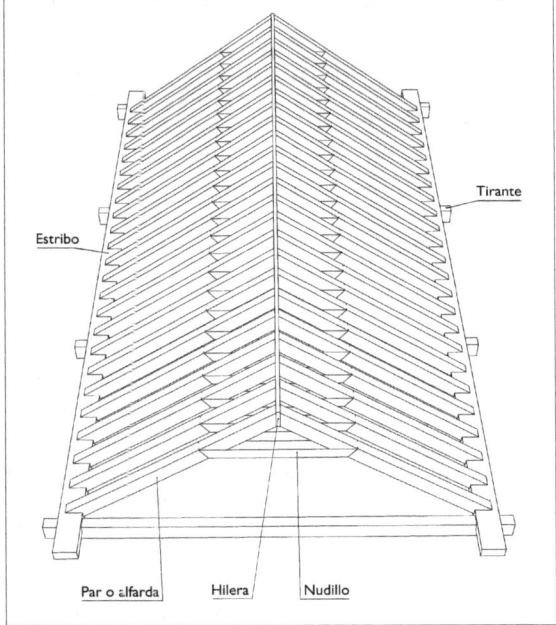

ITINERARY IV *Mudéjar Cities: From Islam to Christianity*

Teruel

Tower of San Martín, detail, Teruel.

and installed in 1536, resulted in the building of the new *cimborrio*. Designed by the master Juan Lucas (also known as "Botero"), it was built in 1538 under the direction of Martín de Montalbán. This *cimborrio* in Teruel Cathedral is the second oldest in Aragon, second only to that in Seo in Saragossa whose structure of Islamic origin it reproduces, even if on the exterior the new formal elements of the Renaissance are more evident, such as the medallions with busts in relief.

Note the Neo-Mudéjar door of the Cathedral and of other buildings in the same style, and the stairs leading to the station.

IV.1.e Tower of San Martín

In the Plaza Pérez Prado. From the Cathedral, take calle de Temprado or Calle de los Amantes. Opening hours: Holy Week and 15 May–12 October 11.00–14.00 and 17.00–20.00. For other opening hours, contact the Tourist Office. Tel: 978 6022799.

order and scholars are still discussing its function and significance. A global evaluation of this work cannot ignore the historical perspective that made it possible, that is to say, the city and the society of Teruel in around 1285. After the raising of the naves and the installation of the Mudéjar ceiling, work continued on the Cathedral towards the head, and the transept and apses were built in 1335. The evident need for better illumination of the new retable of the high altar in more modern times, exquisitely sculptured in natural coloured wood by the sculptor Gabriel Joly,

To the north of the Cathedral very near the Daroca Gate and towering over the longitudinal street of los Amantes, is the Mudéjar Tower of San Martín. Just as in the case of the Tower of el Salvador, it is the only Mudéjar vestige of the parish of the same name, after the church underwent a complete transformation in the Baroque era.

This tower was built between 1315 and 1316, according to the record of the judges of the city of Teruel. Data published by José María Cuadrado shows that the French engineer and architect Quinto Pierres Vedel oversaw the repairs between 1549 and 1551, which is the earliest intervention known to have taken place in any of the Mudéjar churches in Teruel. His intervention consisted largely of building a sloping wall of cut stone at the base of the tower to act as a prop. At the same time, some houses that belonged to the Monastery of the Santisima Trinidad were required, which freed the tower from the adjoining buildings and allowed the construction of a square in front of it, which is a modern planning concept. In the 20th century it has been subject to various restorations, including the outstanding work of Ricardo García Guereta in 1926.

The Tower of San Martín, on the one hand, is loyal to the Teruel system of an open arch at ground level to allow the street to run through below it. On the other hand, it introduces an important structural novelty: that of the Almohad *alminar* already seen in the Tower of el Salvador, and which differentiates it from the old model used in the Towers of Santa María and San Pedro. Also of great importance are the innovations in the decoration above all the brickwork in relief, where the Almohad influence is very evident in the design. In addition, the ceramic decoration signifies an important advance over the previous stage, whereby there is an increase in the chromatic range and variety of the pieces, and a reduction in the size of the pieces used.

As Francisco Íñiguez reminds us, these towers are nothing else but an Islamic *laminar*, with the addition of a Christian belfry. The Tower of San Martín is undoubtedly the most successful model, although it has the congenital defect that there was no adequate solution for the roof of the belfry, which is anyway a foreign element in the Mudéjar work system.

La Laguna de Gallocanta
23 km from Daroca, situated at the bottom of a large depression formed by a tectonic movement, the Gallocanta Lake is one of the largest in the peninsula, with a surface area of more than 1,000 hectares. The area has been declared a Wetland of International Interest and an Area of Special Interest for Bird life. From mid-February to mid-March concentrations of cranes, which may contain over 20,000 birds can be seen, although they can frequently be observed from mid-October onwards. The best places to watch the birds are the hides around the lake. Taking binoculars is recommended. There is a Visitor Centre and The Bird life Museum of Gallocanta.

IV.2 DAROCA

IV.2.a Medieval City

97 km on the N 234. The monuments in the Medieval City are signposted. The Tourist Office organises free guided tours. Tel: 976 800129.

The city of Daroca is lodged between the ridges of San Cristóbal to the north and San Jorge to the south, and is surrounded by 4 km of walls that are for the main part adobe, faced with brick. A deep ravine, the present-day calle Mayor, runs across it from east to west – or from the Puerta Alta (Upper Gate) to the Puerta Baja (Lower Gate). Arabs from Yemen founded Daroca at the end

Daroca

of the 8th century and built a castle on the ridge of San Cristóbal. In the 9th century, there was already a small but busy *medina* on the slope on the south side of the ridge. The structure of this Islamic *medina* is still preserved with its two principal streets, Grajera and Valiente at the top, and a series of small streets, which cross, sloping steeply with terraces of houses.

Daroca, just like Calatayud, was reconquered by Alfonso I el Batallador in 1120, as a result of the Battle of Cutanda, and it also became the capital of the local community.

Its historical importance (in addition to the miracle of the holy altar cloths, the relics of which are kept in the Collegiate Church of Santa María) dates from 1366, when King Pedro IV granted it city status in recognition of how its inhabitants had defended it against the Castilian troops in the frontier war. From that moment on – until the end of the 16th century – the city became an important commercial and artistic centre, so that it is not surprising to find that the Aragon Pope Benedict XIII had his principal house built there, probably with the intention of living in Daroca, before he decided definitively in favour of Peñiscola.

During the medieval Christian era, the urban development of Daroca reached the area of the ravine, and the district called la Franquería grew up on both sides, the forerunner of the present calle Mayor. The unusual width of this medieval street is due to the floodwaters that frequently turned it into a fast-flowing torrent; then, in the mid-16th century, the French engineer Quinto Pierres Vedel directed the construction of a mine, which hollowed out the ridge of San Jorge, diverting the rainwater before it reached the city. To the north of the calle Mayor, between the puerta Alta and the former Church of San Pedro, at the foot of the castle, there is the Jewish Quarter around the present-day plaza del Barrio Nuevo (New District), while the Moorish Quarter was to the south of the present calle del Rey, near the puerta Baja.

In the spectacular complex of the walled precinct, which is outstanding from the viewpoint of urban planning, is the Puerta Baja or Lower Gate. Although fairly well preserved, built of cut stone between two of the wall turrets, following the late Gothic typology of the city gates in the kingdom of Aragon, its final form today is the consequence of remodelling in the time of the Emperor Carlos V (1516–1556).

IV.2.b Apse of San Juan de la Cuesta

Plaza de San Juan. The church is not in use. For opening hours, contact the Tourist Office.

Situated in the plaza of the same name, the Church of San Juan de la Cuesta attracts interest for two reasons: there was a change in the materials used and in the work system applied, both of which came about after an interruption to the works. The apse, which can be dated to the mid-13th century, was begun in the Romanesque style in well-worked stone and a series of courses were laid in this material. After the interruption, work continued in brick. This phenomenon should not be evaluated simply as a change of material, but should also be regarded

Daroca

Apse of San Juan de la Cuesta, general view, Daroca.

as a change in the whole system of work, as also happened in other monuments in the peninsula, such as the Church of San Tirso in Sahagún (León). That is to say, the second phase of the building did not merely complete the projected Romanesque apse in brick, but rather, with the change of system, new ornamental elements appeared, such as the window apertures within multifoil arches, which have precedents in traditional Islamic construction. This is a good example to illustrate how Mudéjar is an alternative construction system to stonemasonry, in which the materials, the constructive techniques and the formal elements make up an indivisible whole.

IV.2.c **Tower of Santo Domingo de Silos**

Plaza de Santo Domingo. The interior (which is not Mudéjar) is not open to the public.

All that is left of the original church is the apse and this tower, the lower part of which is built of stone and can be dated to the mid-13th century. At that same time, the building of the tower was interrupted, and it was later continued in accordance with the Mudéjar work system. This example is even more definitive – if that is possible – than the previous one of the apse of San Juan de la Cuesta, in demonstrating that it was not only a change in the materials used, but also in the entire artistic system.

The internal structure of this tower is completely within the Christian tradition; the lower part, of stone blocks, consists only of an internal nucleus of a spiral staircase, while the rest, of brick, is two-storeys high covered with simple ribbed vaulting, which allowed insertion of similar window apertures in each of the four sides. Communication from the lower floor to the upper floor was by means of a

Daroca

Tower of Santo Domingo de Silos, general view, Daroca.

spiral staircase in one of the corners. From the viewpoint of the formal Islamic precedents, the most interesting apertures are those on the lower floor, formed by twin *arcos mixtilineos* echoed by multifoil arches and contained within a squared frame. These latter arches, and the bricks of the lintels laid in barge course, are reminiscent of the solutions used in the Mudéjar architecture of León.

As a support for the roof overhang, roll-shaped modillions worked in stone were used, a formal element of the Córdoba tradition widespread throughout the peninsula, but uncommon in the Mudéjar style in Aragon. The use of discs or plates of vitrified ceramics below the eaves are also very early. Along with the ceramic applications (already noted in relation to the Towers of Santa María and San Pedro in Teruel), these discs are among the oldest in the Mudéjar architecture of Aragon.

IV.2.d Main Residence of Benedict XIII

In Calle Mayor 77. Also known as the Casa de los Luna (The House of the Luna Family).

In the medieval period, the city of Daroca offered some outstanding examples of Mudéjar religious architecture, which have now disappeared. Among these was the Church of San Pedro – its door is conserved in the National Archaeological Museum in Madrid – or the Church of Santiago, whose splendid tower was demolished in 1913. Nevertheless, the principal objective of this visit, as well as the route through the town commented on above, is a unique work of Mudéjar civil architecture in the calle Mayor. This building is of maximum interest since there are so few examples of Mudéjar civil architecture to have survived to the present day.

ITINERARY IV   *Mudéjar Cities: From Islam to Christianity*
Daroca

Although relatively transformed and adapted at present to the needs of a dwelling, this Mudéjar house in Daroca presents the building of the greatest interest among all the Mudéjar civil architecture in Aragon, after the disappearance of Casa de la Diputación del Reino in the city of Saragossa, which also dated from the 15th century. Pope Benedict XIII ordered the house in Daroca to be built in around 1411, probably under the direction of the Mudéjar master craftsman Mahoma Rami, and its structural reform took place at the end of the 16th century.

Fortunately, interpreting its original plan and structure is possible, in spite of the transformations and renovations carried out in order to adapt it to the needs of modern dwellings. The house has three storeys: the ground floor at street level, the main floor and the attics. On the outside of the ground floor, which was high enough to allow an entresol, there are interesting overhanging eaves resting on wooden corbels. These served to support the principal floor, and still have their painted decoration with different heraldic motifs that María Dolores Peréz González has studied. Preserved on one side of the interior on the ground floor is the original system of supports for the upper floor, with a triple arch and pillars upon which the *alfarjes* rest, while on the other side, this system was replaced at the end of the 16th century by an annulated column and lintel. Flanked by this system of supports, at the back, a small interior patio opens up, at the end of which there are rooms with pointed barrel vaulting, which were used as stables and cellars.

The *alfarjes* ceiling on the ground floor represents an outstanding example that corresponds to a space that may have been a chapel. In one part of the main floor, the well-preserved *alfarjes* inform us of the measurements of the principal rooms that gave onto the street; on one of the beams, the coats of arms of the pope stand out, with the inscription *"Benedictus"*. On the main floor, the treatment of the windows, which give onto the interior patio, is worth noting. They are decorated profusely with carved plasterwork, in which ornamental elements of traditional Islamic design are combined with flamboyant Gothic traceries, intensely worked in rosettes, in the style that Mohama Rami made fashionable in the Seo in Saragossa between 1403 and 1409. The structural and ornamental interest in this Mudéjar house from the early 15th century is altogether exceptional, and its recovery as a monument should be a mandatory objective, if, as hoped, the whole of the remains of Mudéjar Aragon is to be named a World Heritage Site by the UNESCC.

Principal house of Benedict XIII, window plasterwork, Daroca.

115

THE MOORISH QUARTER IN TERUEL

Gonzalo M. Borrás Gualís

Moorish Quarter of Teruel, calle San Blas, Teruel.

The Mudéjar minorities, in the same way as the Jews, belonged to the royal domains and were organised into groups belonging to each mosque, independent of the Council, with their own authorities and legal system and under the immediate jurisdiction of the bailiff or representative of the Royal Authority, who protected them and looked after the interests of the crown.

In Teruel, on the other hand, the reconquest and subsequent re-population of the territory had its own particular characteristics. Here there were no capitulation treaties with the conquered, and, as a result, none of the former Mudéjar population remained, so that in contrast to the usual pattern of events under these circumstances, the Moorish Quarter grew up gradually.

The first stage was at its height during the reconquest of Valencia in 1238, and was made up of Muslim prisoners of war who obtained their freedom or redemption by paying a certain sum of money. The freed Muslims formed the first Mudéjar community in Teruel, and its existence is recorded in the Municipal Byelaws of 1258.

After the Christian conquest of the Andalucían cities, and due to the difficulties they had in resettling them, the Christian monarchs came to an agreement with the Mudéjar population to ensure that they would remain. In the case of Saragossa, after the conquest by Alfonso I in 1118, the Mudéjar population who wished to remain were given a year to relocate to a district outside the walls; this is how the closed Moorish Quarter was created, which is a characteristic element in Mudéjar urban planning.

The Mudéjar population in Teruel continued to grow, and in 1278, King Pedro III ordered his bailiff Aaron Abinafia to move the Mudéjar population to a district outside the walls, in accordance with the practice already mentioned. This intention was opposed by the Council of Teruel, probably to avoid the over depopulation of the town centre.

The privilege granted by the same king, Pedro III, on 2nd March 1285, was decisive and transcendental in the formation process of the Moorish Quarter in Teruel and in the requests from numerous potential Mudéjar immigrants from elsewhere who wanted to settle in it. To encourage Mudéjar immigration to Teruel and to ensure that successful settlement, the royal privilege authorised them to acquire rural properties and to pay only half the rates or tax normally levied on land.

As a result of all of this, in the city of Teruel a closed Moorish Quarter was not formed outside the walls, but instead the Mudéjar population established itself above all in the north of the city, between the Daroca Gate and the Church of San Martín. Although this was where the Moorish Quarter was officially, some of the Mudéjar population lived scattered in other areas of the city and even occupied shops and houses in the Plaza Mayor or in the Plaza del Mercado.

The productive activities of the Mudéjar population were no different from the rest of Teruel's citizens, since they worked above all in agriculture, in sheep farming and in crafts, where they were outstanding in the building trades, the making of tiles and bricks and the production of ceramics.

Undoubtedly, the immigrant Mudéjar population from the lands of the Levante and from the south were responsible for introducing the formal innovations, both structural and ornamental, into the Mudéjar art of Teruel. To cite an example, on 8th April 1306 the master tile-makers from Teruel, Abdulhaziz de Bocayren (a common name from the Levante) and his son Abdomalich, were exempted from all kinds of taxes as compensation for the tiling work they had already carried out and were to continue to do, for the royal building projects.

ITINERARY V

Church-Fortresses on the Border with Castile

Gonzalo M. Borrás Gualís

V.1 TOBED
V.1.a Church of the Virgin

V.2 BELMONTE DE GRACIÁN (optional)
V.2.a Tower of the Parish Church

V.3 MALUENDA
V.3.a Church of Santa María
V.3.b Church of Santas Justa y Rufina

V.4 MORATA DE JILOCA
V.4.a Church of San Martín

V.5 CALATAYUD
V.5.a Church and Tower of San Pedro de los Francos
V.5.b Church and Tower of San Andrés
V.5.c Collegiate Church and Tower of Santa María

V.6 TORRALBA DE RIBOTA
V.6.a Church of San Félix

V.7 ANIÑÓN
V.7.a West Wall of the Church and Mudéjar Tower

V.8 CERVERA DE LA CAÑADA
V.8.a Church-Fortress of Santa Tecla

Mahoma Rami, Master Craftsman

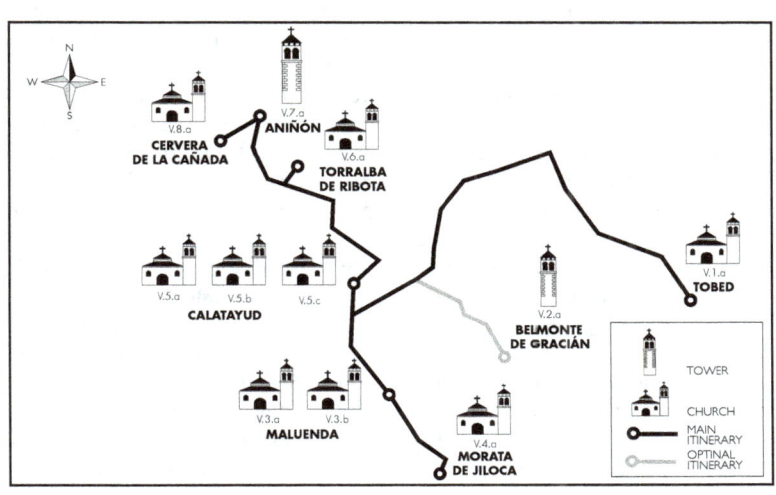

Church of the Virgin, façade and tower, Tobed.

ITINERARY V   Church-Fortresses on the Border with Castile

Parish Church, general view, Aniñón.

This itinerary takes us through the province of Saragossa, through valleys carved out in between the hills. This is an ancient fruit-growing area, documented at least since the 15th century. The valley of the River Jalón — the largest tributary of the River Ebro on the right-hand bank — is the most important Mudéjar area in Aragon. Various minor tributaries such as the Rivers Grío, Perejiles, Jiloca or Ribota, which flow into it, are included in this itinerary, as well as the Jalón itself. These lands of the ancient community of Calatayud had large Mudéjar and Morisco populations before their eviction in the 17th century, a historical circumstance which no doubt explains the density of Mudéjar monuments in these valleys to the south of the River Ebro. The objective of this itinerary is to present Mudéjar as a valley culture, developing as one main theme and two complementary themes. The main theme, approached from the beginning with the Church of the Virgin in Tobed, forms the backbone of the whole itinerary. The purpose of it is to examine in depth a unique architectural typology, a genuine creation of Mudéjar art in Aragon: the fortified church. This formal model has no equal in Spain. Although we frequently find churches that had a defensive function, there is no other case where there is a similarly crystallised architectonic solution equivalent to that of the Mudéjar in Aragon. This constructive typology integrates in a particularly effective way the forms and structures of a church in the interior with a fortress on the exterior.

Two factors can be pinpointed, which, from a historical point of view allows an explanation of the creation of this architectonic typology. The first is the important role that the Military Orders played in the Christian repopulation of the territory of Aragon. In this particular case, it was the Military Order of the Holy Sepulchre, which established its main base in the territory of Calatayud, to which Tobed belongs.

As we know, the singular Will and Testament of King Alfonso I el Batallador (1134) bequeathed the Kingdom of Aragon to the Military Orders, and in compensation for the annulment of this they were given important lands in Aragonese territory. The Knights of the Military Orders that were established in Aragon – the Knights Hospitallers, Templars, Knights of the Holy Sepulchre, of Santiago (St James) and of Calatrava – were the lords of important estates. They encouraged Mudéjar architecture in their domains, following the example of the kings, Pope Benedict XIII and the archbishops, as already seen in the previous itinerary. It seems reasonable, therefore, that the Military Orders should have been the patrons of architecture, which exactly fitted the double function of the Knights – as monks and as soldiers. An example of this is the work undertaken by the Order of the Holy Sepulchre in the Church of the Virgin in Tobed.

As well as this historical factor, there is another equally important reason for the creation of the Mudéjar model of the fortified church. This was the fierce Frontier War that Pedro I of Castile (Pedro the Cruel) and Pedro IV of Aragon (Pedro the Ceremonious) waged against each other, with the first skirmishes starting in 1356 lasting for 13 years. Between 1357 and 1366, Aragon was at times in an utterly chaotic situation, and on more than one occasion, it seemed that the Castilians were certain to gain a definitive victory. The war affected especially the cities of Calatayud and Tarazona. The Military Order of the Holy Sepulchre of Calatayud took an active part in the war, resisting the Castilian troops in the Castle of Nuevalos. In reprisal, when Pedro I took the city of Calatayud in 1362, he razed

Church of San Martín, general view, Morata de Jiloca.

ITINERARY V Church-Fortresses on the Border with Castile

Tobed

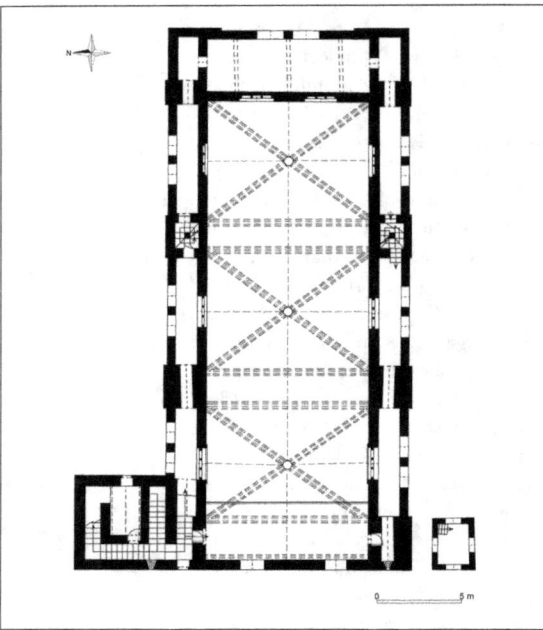

Parish Church, general view, Aniñón.

both the castle and the archives of the Military Order of the Holy Sepulchre to the ground.

Today, after five centuries of territorial unity in Spain achieved by the Catholic Monarchs in 1492, it is difficult to imagine these lands of the ancient community of Calatayud as frontier territory with Castile. However, the conception and development of the Mudéjar fortified church in the territory of Aragon coincides with the historical moment of the war with Castile and is the result of the impression that it left in the collective consciousness.

The other two motives to consider during this itinerary are equally interesting, although complementary. One of them emphasises the authority of the Muslim masters of works, some of whose names have survived to the present day in monumental inscriptions, which from the viewpoint of artistic prestige and social consideration makes them equivalent to Christian artists. This is the case for Yuçaf Adolmalih, a name conserved in an inscription painted under the Mudéjar ceiling of the choir of the Church of Santa María de Maluenda. It goes also for the famous master of works of Benedict XIII, the Muslim Mahoma Rami, whose name is found on an inscription carved in plaster on the railing of the choir of the Church of Santa Tecla in Cervera de la Cañada. The second of the two complementary objectives is to underline the harmony between the Oriental and Occidental artistic languages in the churches in this area, between the Mudéjar interiors and the splendid altarpieces of Gothic art. This is what happens, among many other cases, in the Churches of Santas Justa y Rufino in Maluenda, of San Martín in Morata de Jiloca and of San Félix in Torralba de Ribota, all of them in the province of Saragossa.

V.I TOBED

V.1.a Church of the Virgin

Visits can be arranged through the Town Hall. Tel: 976 629101.

This church shows two different stages of building. The first began on 1st April 1356, at the beginning of the frontier war with Castile, when the Prior of the Holy Sepulchre in Calatayud was Fray Domingo Martínez de Algaraví and his commander in Tobed was Fray Juan Domingo. In this first stage, the chancel and the first two sections of the nave were built. The work must have been finished three years later, since on 3rd June 1359 the Archbishop of Saragossa, don Lope Fernández de Luna, gave his arbitral verdict against the pretensions of the Episcopal jurisdiction of Tarazona in favour of the Priors of the Holy Sepulchre of Calatayud. The sentence adjudicated to the latter the ownership of the church built in Tobed and the altars built in its sanctuary in honour of the Virgin, St John the Baptist and St Mary Magdalen and the corresponding income from them.

The last part of the foot of the church was built in the second stage, which was started in 1394, the year when Pope Benedict XIII was elected, and his arms decorate the keystone of the vault in this section and the ceiling of the upper choir. From the formal characteristics of this last part, it can be supposed that Mahoma Rami was the master craftsman. The chronology of this last part is corroborated by the information that on 8th August 1385 the Canons of the Holy Sepulchre of Calatayud decided to dedicate all the income and donations from the sanctuary of Tobed to the finishing of the building, since *"the work is not yet completed in its building"*.

The church's magnificent west façade and end wall was hidden partially until 1984 by the Town Hall building, which adjoined it. The present state of the façade, which is comparable in its decoration of brick and applied ceramics only to the exterior wall of the *parroquieta* of San Miguel in the Seo in Saragossa, is the result of the restoration begun in 1985 by the architect Úrsula Heredia.

The Church of the Virgin in Tobed is the best example of the architectonic model of the fortified church in Aragon. The building has one single nave with a rectangular chancel and triple chapels at the head. The nave

Church of the Virgin, upper arches of the apse, Tobed.

has three sections, all covered with simple ribbed vaulting, alternating with other shorter spans, which are covered with pointed barrel vaulting and counterbalanced on the outside by buttress towers. Between these at ground level, the side chapels, three on each side of the nave, are covered with pointed barrel vaulting. Above the side chapels and the three chapels at the head of the chancel is a gallery or tribune that opens to the outside through pointed arcades to form a passage similar to a military parapet, which is accessible from the interior of the church through the buttress towers.

Structurally speaking, this is a very solid building, perfectly reinforced both lengthwise and crosswise by the pointed barrel vaulting, which is linked together by the buttressing towers. The interior area has a unity that conserves the original Mudéjar decoration. This, seen in the painted brick design and the painting on the walls, in the vaulting and plasterwork on the windows and *oculos* – not forgetting the decorated wood of the keystones of the vaults and that of the *alfarje*, or flat wooden ceiling of the upper choir, at the end of the nave. With this profusion of ornamental elements, an effect is achieved of Mudéjar interior space that has altered very little over the years.

This same spatial effect can be perceived in the other Mudéjar interiors in this itinerary.

From the outside, in contrast to the decorative interior, the building has a compact and unornamented appearance – except for the west façade, built in the second phase as we saw above, when the war with Castile had already been forgotten – which gives it an extreme military air. This military appearance is emphasised by the buttress towers, four on each side of the nave, and by the open passageway with pointed arches between the towers, like a parapet or sentry walkway, which, from the outside, appears more appropriate for a fortress than for a church.

To judge from the successful spread of this model throughout the whole of Aragon, represented so magnificently in the Church in Tobed, and which will be found throughout the itinerary, it was seen as a satisfactory way to solve the technical and functional problems of architecture at the time.

V.2 BELMONTE DE GRACIÁN (optional)

V.2.a Tower of the Parish Church

26 km on the A1505. If the church is closed, contact D. Leoncio. Tel: 976 892093.

The Parish Church of Belmonte de Gracián is a magnificent example of a five-sided Mudéjar apse, without buttresses, profusely decorated with brickwork in relief, forming a diamond shaped network. The church is late Mudéjar, from the beginning of the 17th century. Building was interrupted after the construction of the apse and the rest of the building continued in a Classical Occidental language.

Nevertheless, the objective of our stop is not this apse, but something much older; the square-based 14th-century tower that stands somewhat separated from the church itself,

V.3 MALUENDA

The village of Maluenda had three extremely beautiful Mudéjar churches, built at the same time (in the last decades of the 14th and the early 15th centuries), which form a group with its own powerful artistic personality. This is due in part to the material used – puddle or gypsum mortar – obtained directly from the hills, which dominate the valley. The Church of San Miguel, perched on high, is at present not consecrated and in ruins, but the other two (Santa María and Santas Justa y Rufina), situated at opposite ends of the village, are still intact and in use.

V.3.a Church of Santa María

14 km on the A 504 until the N-II and then turn on to the N 234. Visits can be arranged through the Town Hall. Tel: 976 893007.

This church has one single nave, with a polygonal, seven-sided apse and three sections covered with ribbed vaulting, side chapels between the

on the south side. This tower comprises two parts, the lower with an internal structure of an *alminar* and the upper completely hollow part, which is the belfry. The materials used in this tower are rubble and plasterwork in the lower part, and brick and applied ceramics in the upper section.

From its ornamental characteristics, the tower can be related to the Tower of the Church of Santa María in Ateca and to the no longer extant Tower of the Church of Santa María in Maluenda. Together, these comprise an autochthonous group with its own strong personality, especially because of the presence of a herringbone pattern, an ornamental motif seldom used. The tower in Belmonte also shares other decorative elements with the one in Ateca, such as the series of interlaced pointed arches or the use of applied ceramics both in the form of discs or bowls and of shafts.

The volumetry of this Mudéjar tower with two parts one over the other, the upper one of smaller proportions, has reminded some historians of the *alminares* there used to be in the area although here the second part corresponds to the design and function of the Christian bell tower. As in many other cases in Aragon, this is not a former and re-converted *alminar*, since the reconquest of the valley of the River Ebro was very early – in this area of Calatayud and Daroca it was in 1120 – but rather Christian bell towers built by Muslim craftsmen following the tradition of the *alminares* of the area. In fact, Mudéjar art is nothing else but the survival of the Islamic artistic tradition in Christian Spain.

Church of Santa María, detail of the Choir ceiling, Maluenda.

ITINERARY V *Church-Fortresses on the Border with Castile*

Maluenda

Church of Santas Justa y Rufina, Chapel of the Rosary plasterwork arch, Maluenda.

master who made it, Yuçaf Aldolmalih, who belonged to a Mudéjar family from Calatayud, and who added an inscription in Arabic with a shahada or Islamic profession of faith. This inscription in Maluenda, according to the translation of Professor Fernando de la Granja reads: *"There is no god but the one God (and) Mahomet is the messenger of God. There is not ... except God"*. This is a unique and extremely eloquent example of the social condition of the Mudéjar masters of works, some of whom were alfaquíes or Muslim Doctors of Law.

V.3.b Church of Santas Justa y Rufina

Visits can be arranged through the town Hall.

Very similar to the Church of Santa María, although it has a west front that emulates European Gothic, flanked on high by two towers, the work on this church was not completed until the year 1413, according to the inscription under the choir loft, at the foot of the nave. In the interior, there are two notable works in carved plaster: the pulpit, which is contemporary with the building of the church, and the archway at the entrance to the Rosary Chapel, which is from the early Renaissance period. The magnificent altarpiece over the high altar, dedicated to the saints who gave the church its name, and painted by Domingo Ram and Juan Rius between 1475 and 1477, is perhaps the most successful example in the whole of Aragon of the integration of Mudéjar space and Gothic painting.

buttresses and a choir loft at the foot. Just as in the Church of San Pedro de los Francos in Calatayud, so in the west façade of Santa María there is also a Gothic-style portal, built of ashlars, in perfect harmony with the rest of the Mudéjar complex. To the right of the façade is the Mudéjar tower, its lower part screening the façade, a late work from the second half of the 16th century.

The most outstanding aspect of the interior is the Mudéjar *alfarje*, which covers the upper choir at the foot, is a flat wooden ceiling with exposed beams, decorated with plant and heraldic motifs. An inscription painted beneath it conserves the name of the

ITINERARY V Church-Fortresses on the Border with Castile
Morata de Jiloca

V.4 MORATA DE JILOCA

V.4.a Church of San Martín

13 km on the N 234. Visits can be arranged through the Town Hall. Tel: 976 894022.

Although we lack any documentary information in relation to the building stages of this parish church, a formal analysis allows us to differentiate between two different phases. The first stage occurred in around 1400, when the main Mudéjar building was constructed, including the great, decorated monumental façade. The second stage took place 200 years later at the beginning of the 17th century, when the change in the orientation and in the head of the church were carried out, and the upper gallery of double semicircular arches which crowns the monument was built.

The most interesting thing about the Church of San Martín is that although it still corresponds to the model of the fortified church, its structure was completely hidden and masked by the exuberant decoration of the exterior. Once the difficult times of the war with Castile had passed, the exterior of the church abandoned the sober, austere character of this model to glory in its ornamentation of brickwork in relief and glazed ceramics on the whole of the side wall. There are only a few similar examples, such as the wall of the *Parroquieta* of the Seo in Saragossa and the west front of the Church of the Virgin in Tobed.

In this church in Morata de Jiloca the doorway is outstanding above all, with its tympanum dedicated to the titular saint (St Martin on horseback, dividing his cloak to share it with the beggar). In it, there is a splendid integration of Oriental and Occidental forms, with the archivolts enclosed in an *alfiz* with *arcos mixtilíneos*, in the most felicitous combination of a Gothic portico and the façade of a *mihrab*.

A recent restoration has recovered the original orientation of the church, restored the triple chapel of the chancel, which corresponds to the singular architectonic typology of the fortified church, and installed a beautiful Gothic altarpiece painting, which came from a shrine in the area.

Church of San Martín, doorway, Morata de Jiloca.

ITINERARY V   Church-Fortresses on the Border with Castile

Calatayud

Church and tower of San Pedro de los Francos, details of the façade with eaves, Calatayud.

V.5 CALATAYUD

The city of Calatayud was founded by the Muslims about 5 km upstream of the River Jalón, on the site of the Ibero-Roman ruins of the ancient city of Bilbilis. Although tradition holds that the founding of Calatayud occurred at the time of the Muslim conquest, in around 862, we have no information about the reconstruction carried out by the *emir* from Córdoba, Muhammad I in his main castle, to use it as a base for the military control of the rebellious Banu Qasi of Saragossa. In 1120, only two years after Saragossa, the city came under Christian domination, and the resettlers installed themselves at the foot of the five promontories overlooked by the great Muslim castle from the 9th and 10th centuries. The medieval centuries saw the building of numerous parishes in the Mudéjar style, some of which have disappeared, such as the Churches of San Martín and San Pedro Mártir, this latter demolished in 1856. In spite of such unfortunate losses, the itinerary through the city still allows a glimpse at the splendour of its Mudéjar past.

V.5.a Church and Tower of San Pedro de los Francos

22 km on the N234. In calle de la Rúa, 16. At present, the church is under restoration.

This church takes its name from the Franks of Bigorre in Gascony who had collaborated with King Alfonso I (1104–1134) in the conquest of the city and then settled in it, taking advantage of the decree of 1131. In this church, and in that of San Andrés, the Council held its meetings until the Town Hall was built during the Renaissance. The Aragon parliament was held under its roof in 1411, which preceded the famous agreement of Caspe, which in June 1412 gave the crown of Aragon to don Fernando, Infante of Castile.

The present building, with its three aisles, is earlier than the war with Castile, and its tower served during the war as *atalaya* or a watchtower. The top of the Mudéjar tower, which was leaning over at a considerable angle, was lopped off in 1840 on account of the presence in the city of the royal party who were staying in the Palace of the Baron of Wersage, just opposite. This amputation of the monument ensured that the governing Queen, Maria Cristina, lost no sleep. It is also missing its original Mudéjar cloister.

As well as its magnificent broad projecting eaves, which protect the great monumental façade, in the interior of the church there is a notable organ casing from the late 15th century, a unique and extraordinarily high-quality work of Mudéjar carpentry from Calatayud.

V.5.b Church and Tower of San Andrés

Plaza de San Andrés. Guided tours arranged by the Tourist Office. Tel: 976 886322.

Historically this has been the rival Parish Church of Santa María and the building has undergone recent restoration. It was just about to disappear, like other Mudéjar churches in Calatayud, because of the decision of the Town Council of 10th March 1870, a decision fortunately overturned by the Diputación Provincial of Saragossa.

In the church, there is evidence of two different construction stages; one that took place in the 14th century and the other in the 16th century, at the sanctuary end. The nave and two side aisles are the oldest and most interesting parts, with the central nave higher than the others and all roofed with ribbed vaulting, displaying great simplicity and purity of structure.

The Mudéjar tower, which stands out above the whole complex, is octagonal in ground plan, and situated at the south-west corner of the church; its ground floor is used as the baptistery. A decision to build a tower was made on 2nd February 1508, following the design and shape of the Tower of Santa María, in the rival parish. However, the Tower of San Andrés turned out to be more slender and delicate, not only because its proportions are smaller but also because of some of its decorative elements, which give it an Oriental air: intimate and withdrawn.

Church of San Andrés, tower, Calatayud.

ITINERARY V   Church-Fortresses on the Border with Castile

Calatayud

Collegiate Church of Santa María, general view of the tower, Calatayud.

V.5.c Collegiate Church and Tower of Santa María

Plaza de Santa María. Guided tours are organised by the Tourist Office.

This is the main church of the city, and the building, consecrated in 1249, is therefore located on the site of the Aljama or Great Mosque. Of the old Mudéjar church only the apse, the tower and the cloister have survived. The rest was completely rebuilt early in the 17th century at the same time as the Collegiate Church of the Holy Sepulchre in Calatayud. The new cupola was erected over the transept in 1611, and the new altarpiece was put in place behind the high altar in 1614. Predating this complete renovation of the three aisles is the great doorway in the style of a Renaissance retable, a work contracted on 5th February 1525 by the sculptors, Juan de Talavera and Esteban de Obray.

The Mudéjar cloister adjoins the north front of the church, an elongated rectangle with nine spans on the long sides and five on the short. In the south-west corner of the cloister is the old Chapter House, which can be dated, the same as the Mudéjar work of the cloister, to the last decades of the 14th century. The Mudéjar cloister was certainly already in existence in 1412, when Miguel Sanchez de Algaraví founded a Chair of Theology in the precinct. An unfortunate restoration in 1967, with Rafael Mélida Poch as architect and Sabino Llodio Aranzábal as quantity surveyor, completely distorted the original appearance, closing the archways of the patio with false latticework with six-pointed geometric decoration.

In addition to the cloister, the magnificent Mudéjar tower is also noteworthy. Eight-sided and with solid buttresses at the corners, it is without doubt the most interesting tower in Aragon since the New Tower in Saragossa was demolished in 1892. Its plan with a chapel inside the base and two towers – one inside the other above the chapel – was used as a model for the Tower of San Andrés, as has already been mentioned. As was the usual practice, it was built in different stages: the lower part corresponds to the end of the 15th century and the bell tower to the second half of the 16th century.

ITINERARY V Church-Fortresses on the Border with Castile
Torralba de Ribota

Sierra de la Virgen
Some 20 km from Calatayud to the south of Moncayo, at an altitude of 1400 m., the Sierra de la Virgen has a forest of cork oaks unusual at this latitude. This is an indication of the older and wider distribution of the forests of cork oaks in the peninsula. To visit, take the forest track that starts in Sestrica and walk 6 km.

V.6 TORRALBA DE RIBOTA

V.6.a Church of San Félix

10 km on the N 234. A visit can be arranged through the Town Hall. Tel: 976 899302.

The town of Torralba de Ribota had an exclusively Christian population and was an important centre for the production of bricks and roof tiles. According to López Landa, the Bishop of Tarazona, don Pedro Pérez Calvillo, had the Mudéjar church built on a high flat spot overlooking the town in 1367 at a time when the war with Castile was still not completely over. This circumstance undoubtedly caused him to choose the architectonic typology of the fortified church, closely imitating the Church of the Virgin in Tobed. The pace of work was slow since a substantial part of it was still ongoing during the Bishopric of don Juan de Valtierra (1410–1433). It is precisely to this second decade of the 15th century that the upper choir and the west gable-end flanked by two towers corresponds, a work probably directed by the master Mahoma Ramí, once the second stage of San

Church of San Félix, general view, Torralba de Ribota.

ITINERARY V   Church-Fortresses on the Border with Castile
Aniñón

Pedro Mártir in Calatayud had been completed in 1414.

The church has undergone numerous restorations during recent times, notably the one carried out by Fernando Chueca Goitia in the second half of the 20th century. The plan and structure correspond to what has been described already above in the Church of Tobed, although here the nave is shorter as it only has two spans. The interior plan of the two towers on the west front is interesting, as they have a cylindrical central core. This system, atypical in the Mudéjar of Aragon, is found only here and in the tower of the Mudéjar church in Quinto de Ebro. The church has conserved a magnificent series of painted Gothic altarpieces, which again offer evidence of the perfect coexistence of the Oriental and Occidental languages – the Mudéjar spatial one and the Gothic pictorial one.

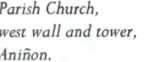
Parish Church, west wall and tower, Aniñón.

V.7 ANIÑÓN

V.7.a West Wall of the Church and Mudéjar Tower

7 km on the N 234. Visits can be arranged through the Town Hall. Tel: 976 899106.

The square Mudéjar tower is earlier than the present building of the Church of Nuestra Señora del Castillo of which it forms a part. Although the extraordinary beauty of the brickwork in relief of the lower of the two sections is noteworthy, the main interest of the tower is the system of vaulting that covers the staircase, which is unique in the genre. The usual system in the Mudéjar style of Aragon is for the vaults formed by converging courses of bricks. Here, however, these are formed with sections of superimposed barrel vaulting. Without any precise documentary

evidence, it has been dated to the first half of the 14th century, nearer 1300. The second interesting element is the great gable or west front of the church which faces the village, the final flourish of the work carried out between 1568 and 1594, the date when the Bishop don Pedro Cerbuna proceeded to bless the completely renovated church. With its ornamental motifs in brickwork and applied glazed ceramics, this magnificent wall reaches its greatest formal beauty for a few brief moments when the setting sun glows on it.

V.8 CERVERA DE LA CAÑADA

V.8.a Church-Fortress of Santa Tecla

9 km on the same road. Visits can be arranged through the Town Hall. Tel: 976 899222.

On top of the hill with the village on its slopes, and with a stone tower that was part of the former castle, the Church of Santa Tecla is an appropriate way to end this excursion, since in it, just as in the last bars of a symphony, we can hear all the themes developed during the time.
Back in 1923, José María López Landa transcribed the Gothic inscription that runs round the railing of the choir loft at the end of the church. It says that the church was finished in the year 1426 when the *jurados*, or elected elders of Cervera de la Cañada, were Pascual Verdejo and Juan Aznar; the *regidores*, or governing councillors, Antón and Miguel Morant, Antón Cuñillo and Mateo Cubero; the procurator was Miguel Fraire

Fortified Church of Santa Tecla, Choir oculo and ceiling, Cervera de la Cañada.

and the master craftsman the famous Mahoma Rami, architect to Pope Benedict XIII.
This church building has caught the attention of the architects, Francisco Íñiguez Almech, who produced a study devoted to it in 1930 and Fernandeo Chueca Goitia, who was in charge of its restoration. The restraints of the previous building have given it a particular personality within the typology of the fortified church, since it only has one chapel in the apse, and this chapel is fitted with an appreciable deviation into the space available between a round and a square tower. On the outside, it has a military air with its great round towers and galleries.
The treatment of the interior space, with the walls painted to look like bricks, the decoration with plasterwork on the windows and railings and the painted decoration of the flat *alfarje*, supporting the upper choir, allows us to relive an ornamental system from the Islamic tradition. It was the perfect solution to the religious needs of the Christian population in the ancient community of Calatayud.

MAHOMA RAMI, MASTER CRAFTSMAN

Gonzalo M. Borrás Gualís

Fortified Church of Santa Tecla, detail of the Choir plasterwork and inscription, Cervera de la Cañada.

The activity of the Muslim master craftsman Mahoma Rami is documented in Aragon during the first quarter of the 15th century, between 1403 and 1426. Because of the transcendence of the works carried out under his direction, this craftsman is considered one of the most important Mudéjar master craftsmen of all time. According to the documentation published by Manuel Serrano Sanz in 1916, on 24th February 1403 a meeting of master craftsmen was held, summoned by Pope Benedict XIII, to determine how the work was to be done on the sanctuary of the Cathedral in Saragossa. Among others, Mahoma Rami attended that meeting and the solution he presented was accepted unanimously. In 1923, José María Landa López revealed a document from the Archive of the Crown of Aragon, provided by don Andrés Giménez Soler. According to this document, in October 1404, King Martín I of Aragon requested some Muslims be despatched from Saragossa to carry out works in his house in Valldaura in Barcelona, while at the same time warning against disturbing Mahoma Rami, since he was working on the Seo in Saragossa by order of the Pope Benedict XIII.

The work to the Cathedral in Saragossa consisted of raising three Romanesque apses to counterbalance the new *cimborrio* that was planned, since the old one, built by the Archbishop don Lope Fernández de Luna, had collapsed.

A new piece of documentary evidence unearthed by Serrano Sanz, mentions that on 26th February 1409 the master Mahoma Rami took on the whole of the decoration of the new *cimborrio* of the Seo himself, once it had been rebuilt.

On the other hand, Ovidio Cuella has considerably widened the documented information available on the master Mahoma Rami, by demonstrating the accounts of the work to extend the Church of San Pedro Martír in Calatayud carried out between 1411 and 1414. Although this church in Calatayud was demolished by a brutal and mistaken decision of the Town Council in 1856, graphic evidence remains to confirm its extraordinary artistic interest.

The last information we have on Master Rami again was brought to light by López Landa, and refers to the inscription in the plasterwork that decorated the upper choir at the foot of the Church of Santa Tecla in Cervera de la Cañada, which says that the work was finished in 1426, with Mahoma Rami as the master. This signature of the work is clear proof of the self-esteem and high social acceptance that the Muslim master craftsmen enjoyed in Aragon.

Various other outstanding works in the context of Mudéjar building in Aragon have been attributed to Mahoma Rami. These are buildings included in our itinerary, such as the final section of the Church of the Virgin in Tobed, the house of the Luna Family in the calle Mayor in Daroca, or the finishing of the Church of San Félix in Torralba de Ribota. Although there is no documentary evidence to prove that they are his work, the attribution to him is based on the formal resemblance they have with other work known to have been done by him.

ITINERARY VI

Castles and Walled Cities

Pedro Lavado Paradinas

VI.1 ARÉVALO
    VI.1.a Castle, Walls and Bridges
    VI.1.b Churches of San Martín, Santa María, San Miguel and el Salvador
    VI.1.c La Lugareja (optional)

VI.2 MADRIGAL DE LAS ALTAS TORRES (optional)
    VI.2.a City Walls and Gates
    VI.2.b Church of San Nicolás

VI.3 COCA
    VI.3.a Castle

VI.4 OLMEDO
    VI.4.a Wall, City Gate and Church of San Miguel
    VI.4.b La Mejorada Monastery (optional)

VI.5 MEDINA DEL CAMPO
    VI.5.a Castle

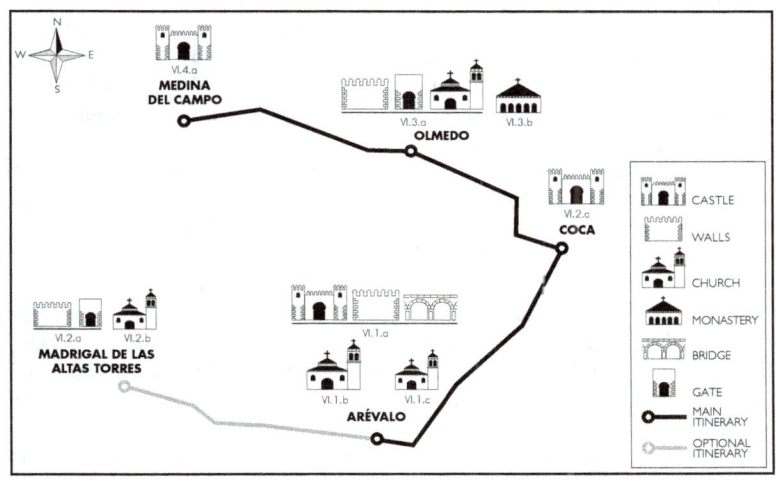

Castle, partial view, Coca.

ITINERARY VI Castles and Walled Cities

City wall, Olmedo.

In the same way as the Mudéjar style played an important part in the religious and civil architecture of the Middle Ages in Castile and León, it was also a very useful style for military architecture, where economy of resources and time were important assets.

The late Middle Ages was not a peaceful period for the inhabitants of the peninsula. Castile had a tense relationship with Aragón, Portugal and the Muslim territories. Now that the fight against Islam had been relegated gradually to the south of the peninsula, the Christian kingdoms attempted to create a militarised frontier with the Muslims – a territory guarded by impregnable castles perched on rocky heights. Yet life carried on between skirmishes, and the knights dreamed of winning honour and spoils in military action.

From the 14th century onwards, the *meseta* of Castile and the valley of the River Ebro suffered an instability that lasted until the union of Castile and Aragón, the result of the marriage of Isabel I of Castile and Fernando II of Aragón in 1479. In these circumstances, the only safe place was a castle, which needed a strong army to defend it. Against the arms available at that time, it was enough to have a stronghold with vertical stone defences, adequate boiling oil to pour over the assaulting troops and offensive weapons with the longest possible range, such as the crossbow and the bow. After the invention of gunpowder in the 13th century, the loopholes had to be enlarged so that the firearms could reach out through them without leaving any blind spots while engaging in crossfire with the enemy, although the shots were still not very accurate.

Of all the defensive requirements, which from the high Middle Ages had meant the building of castles, fortresses, citadels, towers and walled precincts in whatever type of materials were available: dressed stone, masonry, adobe or recycled materials, Mudéjar architecture was an extremely useful form because of its quick, cheap construction techniques. The use of brick, either alone or alongside masonry – in banded courses or with in a mix with rubble – made things easier than building in stone.

In centuries-old walls, like those of Avila, the Roman ashlars coexisted – and still do. There are the Celtiberian stone animals used as building blocks, the stretches of stone masonry and strong, round towers reinforced with brick courses to prevent the walls collapsing. There are sections of wall held together with chains, and brick pillars reinforced after the devastating impact of the catapults, bombardments and other attacks from the siege artillery, which was still rudimentary, designed to breach the walls rather than cause havoc among the troops.

The renewal of some defensive systems were carried out from the 14th century onwards, and the passages between the barbicans and ravelins were widened, the towers were improved with lookout turrets and other elements jutting out from the walls, which were designed to surprise and astonish the enemy rather than to threaten them. In this era, we no longer find enormous fortresses, but rather small castles able to lodge one family and the troops needed to protect them. This was the case in the Castle of Coca, where the workmen achieved an outstanding aesthetic impact with bricks, managing to embellish even the purely defensive elements. Apart from their military function, these castles also tried to offer the best possible living conditions and the atmosphere of a palace in their interior. The great chambers with wooden and plasterwork ceilings, paintings and fireplaces were the interior correlation of an exterior bristling with towers, battlements, moats and loopholes.

Alongside the battering walls and drawbridges typical of the Western world, in Mudéjar military architecture the keep is at one corner of the castle just as in the Hispano-Muslim citadels, the cupolas on *trompa*s, and the multifoil arches and the ceramics from Seville. The military architecture of Toledo reached as far as Burgos, where the master craftsman, Mohammad, built the Gate of San Esteban in the 15th century with a brick horseshoe arch fitted in between two square towers.

Unfortunately, many of these castles and fortresses over time have gradually lost part of their defences and only a few of them allow us to imagine the time when a Moorish guard, seated on carpets and under a shining roof of

City wall, Madrigal de las Altas Torres.

gilded wood, guarded a Christian king in a Muslim fortress. The European travellers of the 19th century fell silent with amazement and envy when they saw them. Primarily because they could not comprehend how, in a country that was theoretically at war with Islam, the Muslim warriors could form part of the Christian stronghold; and secondly because these palace-fortresses were very luxurious compared with the interior of any defensive stronghold in the rest of Europe.

The Muslim craftsmen excelled themselves in the designs of the ceilings and the craftsmanship of the plasterwork during the whole of the first half of the 15th century. Brick castles include La Mota in Medina del Campo, built by the chief craftsman Fernando Carreño in around 1440. The Coca in Segovia, built by Archbishop don Alonso Fonseca before 1473, the Alcázar in Segovia where the Arab master Xalel Alcalde intervened between 1412 and 1456, and the castle in Arévalo, already documented in 1481. These are just some of the most important examples. As well as these, there are many other castles, walls and urban precincts where defensive forms learned from the Almohads were put into practice. The principal characteristics of this building style are the vaulting of towers flanked by gates, the drystone walls and the rubble and puddle walls, all of which are very different from the Toledo style, characterised by the masonry walls, horizontal brick courses and vertical lacing courses, and reinforced pillars. Towns like Madrigal de las Altas Torres and Arévalo in Ávila or Olmedo, Tordesillas, and Medina del Campo in Valladolid are key examples of Mudéjar military architecture in Castile. Many other palaces and fortified houses also survive that at one time accommodated the principal families of the ancient kingdom, to safeguard their lives and property. Some outstanding examples are the Castle of the Velasco Family in Medina del Pomar in Burgos. In Palencia are the Castles of the Tovar Family in Cevico del Torre, of the Delgadillo Family in Castrillo de Don Juan, of the Acuña Family in Dueñas, and of the Almirantes in Palenzuela. There are also the Castles of the Almirante Family in Medina del Rioseco and in Bolaños de Campos, in Valladolid.

Birds of the steppes
Alongside the roads that lead to several different villages, the birds of this area can be seen. The huge fields of cereals on the plains of la Moraña hold a surprisingly rich bird life with species that have adapted to the crops and farming cycles of this area.
One of the most interesting colonies of birds is the great bustard with more than 500 examples recorded. The great bustard is one of the heaviest flying birds, with males weighing anything up to 15 kilos. It is a gregarious bird, which spends the winter in mixed flocks. This is when the fields of alfalfa are of great importance, since they mean that there is a guaranteed food supply.
In the middle of March, the mating displays of the male birds begin attracting the attention of the females with a spectacular display of white plumage, which makes them visible from a good distance away. Other important species are the little bustard, the pin-tailed sandgrouse, the black-bellied sandgrouse, the stone curlew and the calandra lark.

ITINERARY VI *Castles and Walled Cities*
Arévalo

VI.I ARÉVALO

Arévalo, one of the oldest towns in Castile, has seen many of the vicissitudes of the crown of Castile. Isabel la Católica spent her childhood here, as did her grandson, the future emperor of Germany. The Queen's Palace, where Juan II and his wife Isabel also lived, and where María de Aragón died, was converted into the Convent of the Bernardine Cistercian nuns, after it was ceded to them by the Emperor Carlos V in 1542.

The city, which was conquered in 1088 by Alfonso VI, was divided up between five families: the Briceño, Berdugo, Montalvo, Sedeño and Tapia. In the 15th century the Zuñiga, the counts of Plasencia and later the dukes of Arévalo also received portions of the city. The fact that it was a town on the edge of the Tierra de Campos and dependent on Toledo marked its architecture, for we can see the box-shaped sections of masonry edged with horizontal and vertical brick courses, typical of Toledo, while the towers and apses are more like the those found in the Tierra de Campos.

VI.1.a Castle, Walls and Bridges

The Castle and its walls are at the top of the town.

The castle stands imposingly above the town, mentioned in 1481 as a replica of the one in Coca, and much altered in the 16th century to adapt it to the new kind of war that was now gunpowder based. There is a stone tower remaining and a stretch of the wall with a stone base and loopholes. The rest is puddle and brick, with turrets and parapets built out over brick brackets.

The walls, which began at the castle and surrounded the town, are conserved in different parts, especially in

Castle, general view, Arévalo.

141

ITINERARY VI Castles and Walled Cities
Arévalo

Church of Santa María, general view, Arévalo.

the calle Entrecastillos where one of the entrance gates and the prison are to be found. Through this gate, one enters the town itself and three of its squares which were used for markets and fairs surrounded by arcades: the Plaza de la Villa, del Arrabal, and del Real, which all reused columns and arcades from older buildings, although the last two are later.

The two bridges over the Rivers Arevalillo and Adaja are good examples of Mudéjar engineering of the late 14th or early 15th centuries. Constructed in masonry and brick with large pointed arches and *alfices*, both bridges were constructed from similar materials, and indeed the same workmanship, as other Mudéjar monuments. The bridge on the Adaja had a stout crenellated tower with a door, which some scholars classified as Arabic.

VI.I.b Churches of San Martín, Santa María, San Miguel and el Salvador

Guided tours can be arranged through the office in Calle Santa María, 20.
Tel: 619 856821.

There are various Mudéjar churches in Arévalo and they all have very different types of ornamentation, which gives each one of them a different feel. Outstanding in the precinct of Arévalo are the brick towers of the churches, where the ornamentation is simpler than in the Toledo model. Based on double arches of raked bond, they provide a sober challenge to other beautiful examples with multifoil and horseshoe arches.

The Church of San Martín dates from the 13th and 14th centuries. It has one single nave with a transept, three chapels in the apse and, to the south, a portico in Romanesque stonework in the style of Segovia, which was restored in the 16th century. The fact that it has two towers is in itself peculiar and one of them is even more unusual – called *la de los Ajedreces* – because of its decoration of *ajedreces* or chessboard squares. The other tower, called the New Tower, is a copy of the other, which has been restored.

Santa María has a Mudéjar apse in brick with blind arcades on different floors. At the foot, a tower with a great pointed arch gives on to the street. The restored interior con-

serves the remains of *artesonado*, wooden choir stalls, and traces of a 13th-century mural painting in the apse.
San Miguel, built towards the end of the 13th century, was rebuilt in the 15th century. It has a square apse with barrel vaulting. The brickwork alternates with masonry. The north wall lattices in brick are very interesting. It has one single nave with the remains of a coffered ceiling.
El Salvador, built in the 16th century, has three aisles and a brick tower.

VI.1.c La Lugareja (optional)

After 1.5 km take the diversion as signposted and follow the unmade road. Private property.

La Lugareja, also called the Church of Gómez Román, conserves a sanctuary with three apses, the transept and two side-bays. The building is brick with broad joints and squint brick in the windows of the apses; the apses are covered with pointed oven vaulting and are separated by arches on cavettos. Above the transept, there is a lantern with a cupola resting on blind arcades and four squinches. The interior is decorated with multiple stone heads and floral motifs. The exterior has a square tower with arcades.
In 1257, the brothers Gómez Román founded a convent here for nuns and gave their name to the church. The foundations of the nave still exist, but the church must have been unfinished and closed off at the level of the transept. The reason for this was probably that it was considered too far away from the village, so the nuns were transferred to Arévalo and the convent became simply a shrine.

VI.2 MADRIGAL DE LAS ALTAS TORRES (optional)

A walk around the Mudéjar Church of Santa María del Castillo is recommended, it is situated on a hill overlooking the town. Also worth a visit is the enclosed Convent of the Augustinians, the birthplace of Isabel la Católica.

VI.2.a City Walls and Gates

27 km on the C605. Walk along the top of the walls, with access from the Medina Gate.

The town of Madrigal de las Altas Torres, as its name suggests, is surrounded by stout masonry walls and adobe boxed in with brick, square towers and hollow *albarranas*, which reinforce the stretches of wall, and gates that open up between the towers. These consist of a lower part without openings, an upper floor at the level of the battlements that has brick arches for openings, and which pointed arches support in the interior. There are three gates still standing and almost complete: the Cantalapiedra Gate – where the left-hand tower is finished off at an angle on a pentagonal ground plan to strengthen the firing positions – the Medina Gate, similar but simpler, and the Arévalo Gate.
The precinct is circular, and the materials of the borders, gates and towers remind us of their Hispano-Muslim past. Although construction of the walls began at the end of the 13th century, many alterations were made to them up until the end of the 15th century. They are mentioned in 1302 when Fernando IV, recognising the authority of Arévalo under whose jurisdiction Madrigal falls, ordered

ITINERARY VI   *Castles and Walled Cities*
Madrigal de las Altas Torres

the demolition of the walls and towers that had been built without his authorisation. The order, as we can still see, was not carried out. The fortress is built on flat land; this explains the very stout walls and gates, which are intended to protect a small agrarian and commercial town. Isabel La Católica was born in Madrigal de la Altas Torres, in the former Palace of the Kings of Castile, part of which has been attributed to Juan II. The building is a fine example of a noble house, its rooms covered with *alfarjes* around a patio courtyard. Square towers and galleries open onto the exterior, which were covered with latticed screens some time later. Carlos V donated the palace to the order of nuns in 1527. In that same year, the church and the convent buildings were added; the structure of the cells where the nuns lived with their servants and lay sisters can still be seen. The interior accommodates a small museum with exhibits from the time of the Catholic Monarchs.

In the town, two Mudéjar churches are conserved: Santa María del Castillo and San Nicolas de Bari.

Built on a hill, Santa María del Castillo, like so many other churches in this area, acts as reminder of the ancient defensive function of such buildings. Built in the early 13th century, the remains of the earlier Moorish fortress is concealed in its foundations. It has a brick Mudéjar apse with various levels of blind arcades and, at the end, a tower constructed from the same material. The interior has a single nave with a transept, which was covered with a Mudéajr wooden ceiling. The remains of this can be seen still in the small Museum of the Parish of San Nicolás. There are Romanesque mural paintings in a chapel next to the sacristy.

VI.2.b **Church of San Nicolás**

When the church is closed, refer to the priest's house next door.

The Church of San Nicolás de Bari (the present parish church) is the most important church in Arévalo, built in the late 12th or early 13th century. It follows the second type of Sahagún (see Itinerary VIII.1, p. 179 ff.), with three aisles between pillars and pointed arches. Two of the apses are decorated on the outside with blind arcades in brick, with three levels on the main apse. The aisles are covered with a wooden ceiling from the 16th century and there is an eight-sided roof over the transept. There are remains of the polychrome wooden choir stalls, which correspond to the final years of the 15th century or the beginning of the 16th century, and there are the remains of several different ceilings. At the foot of the church, there is one of the most imposing towers in Castile. Almost 50 m. high, it has blank walls in the lower part, while higher up, the walls are perforated by two series of double arches. Its structure is of an *alminar* with a staircase around a central hollow core.

The Bishop Alonso de Madrigal was also born in Madrigal. A prolific writer of the 16th century, and nicknamed "el Tostado" (the Swarthy) because of the colour of his skin, the popular saying – *"to write more than el Tostado"* – refers to him. An inscription on his tomb in Avila Cathedral can be roughly translated as, "... *he was famous for writing / four pages a day. / His teaching thus lighting / even for the blind the way."*

ITINERARY VI   Castles and Walled Cities
Coca

Castle, general view, Coca.

VI.3 COCA

VI.3.a Castle

At 28 km from Arévalo on the SG 351: the Castle belongs to the House of Alba, who ceded it to the Ministry of Agriculture (for all of 100 years but a day, at the peppercorn rent of 1 peseta per year) and at present it is the School of Forestry. The panoramic view from the battlements is not to be missed. Entrance fee. Guided tours are available. Opening times: 10.30–13.00 and 16.30–20.00, Sat, Sun, public holidays: 11.00–13.00 and 18.00–20.00. Closed first Tues of every month.

The Castle of Coca is one of the most significant examples of Mudéjar military architecture in Castile. Its ground plan is rectangular with polygonal towers at the corners, escarpment, moat, outer ward, rampart walk and main building. Its Keep has hexagonal sentry lookouts, or turrets, at the corners, and two semicircular turrets at the centre of each of its sides. In the corner sections with the towers, there are three lookout posts, the central one bigger and longer and the two at the side jutting out. The

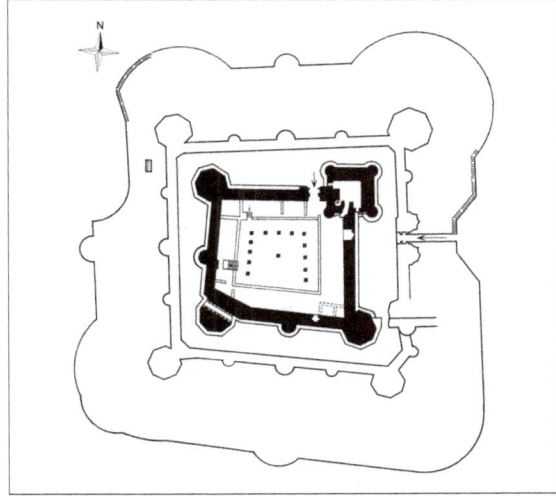

Ground plan of Castle, Coca.

ITINERARY VI *Castles and Walled Cities*
Coca

Church of San Miguel, general view, Olmedo.

walls are finished off with an impost of small arches; above these is another stretch of wall formed by vertical bands, which are semi-cylindrical and pointed. The play between the bare walls and the decorated crown makes this building an excellent example of architecture that was simultaneously courtly and defensive.

The gate once had a pointed arch, covered and painted in red, ochre and black. There were paintings in the interior, some of which are in the Provincial Museum in Segovia. The most interesting of these came from the Tower of Pero Mata.

It is likely that don Alonso de Fonseca the Archbishop of Seville, who died in 1473, commissioned this castle. He left many other buildings in the town and the tombs of some of his family in the Church of Santa María. If indeed the Archbishop did commission the castle, this would explain the contributions to the church of ceramics and paintings from a workshop in Seville, resulting from the connection of Fonseca with the town of Coca. The construction of the castle is probably due to don Alfonso de Fonseca, Archbishop of Seville, who died in 1473, and left many other buildings in the town; and the funerals of some family members took place in the Church of Santa Maria. All this would explain why the ceramics and paintings of the church benefitted from the contribution of a workshop in Seville, which would further consolidate the links of Fonseca with the town of Coca. There are some remains of a masonry and brick wall that at one time surrounded the town and linked it to the castle. The entrance gate is built between two cubes; it has one flattened, and one pointed arch with archivolts and *alfiz*, above which runs a line of blind arcades.

VI.4 OLMEDO

VI.4.a Wall, City Gate and Church of San Miguel

22 km. Guided tours of the entire village are available at weekends. Consult the Tourist Office. Tel: 983 623222. Opening hours: Sat, Sun and public holidays 11.00–14.00 and 17.00–19.00.

The Rivers Adaja and Eresma surround Olmedo — leaving intact, to the northeast — the little that remains of the castle. The cement wall is one of the elements that most attracts the attention of visitors. Long stretches of the wall, square towers and some turrets are still in position and shelter the town, still enclosed partially by these sections of wall. Seven archways gave access to the city, with those named de la Villa, San Miguel, San Martín, la Vega and San Pedro conserved until recently.

The gates in the wall are brick with double semicircular arches and *alfices* and they would have been closed shut with a portcullis. Some, like that of San Martín, form part of one of the brick churches that make up the Mudéjar concentration in Olmedo. In the case of the Church of San Miguel Tower, it represents yet another defensive element for the city.

Outside Olmedo, Juan II and Alvaro de Luna clashed with the Infantes, don Juan and Don Enrique in 1445, which is where the expression comes from *"He who wants to be the Lord of Castilla [Castile] had better have Olmedo on his side"*.

The chronicles relate that the town was conquered by Alfonso VI; in the chronicle of the Archbishop don Rodrigo Ximénez de Rada the town is mentioned as *"Ulmetum"* along with *"Cauria, Cauca, Iscar, Medina, Canales, Ulmus ..."*, which are nearly all castles, some of them Arabic of caliphate origin. It had its own *fuero*, or code of laws similar to that of Roa, which is prototypical, and in 1388, the daughter of Pedro I, Constanza, brought it as a dowry to mark the occasion of her marriage to the Duke of Olmedo.

Ground plan and cross section, the Chapel of la Mejorada, Olmedo.

ITINERARY VI   Castles and Walled Cities
Medina del Campo

Mudéjar Theme Park
In Olmedo, this park brings together a selection of good-quality replicas of the Mudéjar monuments of Castile and Leon. The site also serves as a leisure park with walks, water activities, a train that runs through the park, a children's play area and a well-kept garden with local plants. Opening hours: summer 10.00–14.00 and 16.00–21.00 every day; winter 10.00–14.00 and 16.00–19.00 Closed Mon. For more information telephone: 983 623222.

VI.4.b **Mejorada Monastery**
(optional)

5 km on the outskirts. It is signposted. To visit the Monastery Chapel, ask the guards.

In the 14th century, the Monastery of la Mejorada was a hermitage, then a Franciscan monastery and after that a Hieronymite monastery. The 15th-century church conserves only one memorial chapel with a cupola decorated with plaster strapwork. The chapel houses five stone tombs in the Gothic-Mudéjar style and one in the Plateresque style. In one of these is supposedly buried a stuccoist who was active in Olmedo between the end of the 15th and the beginning of the 16th century, someone whose name can only just be deciphered, "Servendo". On the outside of the chapel an incomplete inscription reads, *"the knight Alonso de Fonseca ... being finished in the year 1514".*
In 1592, Felipe II stayed in this monastery on his way to Tarazona. A member of his retinue, the Dutchman Enrique Cock who called Olmedo the *"well protected"*, did not forget to register the fact: "... *on Wednesday 17th ... His Majesty was lodged in a monastery of St Jerome at a quarter of a league ... which they call la Mejorada".*

VI.5 **MEDINA DEL CAMPO**

VI.5.a **Castle**

30 km on the C 112. Guided tours are organised by the Tourist Office Tel: 983 811357. Opening hours: 11.00–14.00 and 16.00–18.00, Sun and public holidays 11.00–14.00.

During the Middle Ages, this city was very important for its fairs: a contemporary writer relates, *"Every year they hold two fairs of the utmost importance in Spain ... the dealings in Medina reach to all parts of Spain and even outside it ..."*. Sometimes the commercial transactions reached the sum of 53,000 million *maravedis*. In 1496, Muslims were given permission to open shops in the city, providing they were far away from the fair so as not to jeopardise its business, which shows that there was a certain Muslim presence.
Medina had a number of fine palaces and houses. The most important of these was the palace owned by Isabel I of Castile, located in the city square itself, and where she died. This may be what Cock is referring to on the journey of Felipe II when he writes that *"there was a palace and some very noble houses"*, referring perhaps to the Casas Reales in the Plaza of San Antolín, burned down in the War of the Communidades in August 1520. Many buildings were destroyed during this war, when the city, which did not want to give up its artillery to the imperial troops, was set on fire.

ITINERARY VI *Castles and Walled Cities*
Medina del Campo

Castle, general view, Medina del Campo.

The Venetian ambassador Navagero explained it thus, "... *the streets are good since most of them were burned [down] at the time of the Comunidades. The rest of the houses are new* ...". The documents of the time mention many other houses built by merchants and bankers of the town, such as the Dueñas, the Ruiz or the Quintanilla Families.

Many travellers describe the city and its walls; the Flemish Antoine de Lalaing in the retinue of Felipe el Hermoso wrote: *"the city is built on flat ground and is well walled and has two good streets where the merchandise is displayed during the fair* ...". What really surprised the German Baron de Rosmital in the second half of the 15th century was the lack of firewood in the surrounding area, which forced the townspeople to use dried dung and vine clippings.

Built on a rise, the fortress of La Mota dominates the town: arranged on an irregular square ground plan, built of concrete faced with brick, it has a double precinct with a barbican, and a main castle with circular towers. The keep has been erected on top of a ruin of an earlier one. At one time stucco, and plaster strapwork would have decorated the interior. The entrance, with its horseshoe arch, bears the date 1482 and the arms of the Catholic Monarchs. The first architect mentioend is Fernando Carreño, who built the castle on older foundations in 1440 during the reign of Juan II. In 1479, the Catholic Monarchs named *"Alonso Niño as master craftsman"* (also known by some authors as Alonso Nieto). Between 1480 and 1489, two Muslim *alarifes*, called Abdallá and Alí de Lerma, worked there. Throughout its history, the castle has had different owners and suffered various alterations. The most recent restoration eliminated the Mudéjar remains that later were rescued from a nearby rubbish dump.

Tordesillas is recommended for an overnight stop, 25 km away, where the next Itinerary starts.

ITINERARY VII
First day

Daughters of Kings and Nobles: Through the St Clare's Convents

Pedro Lavado Paradinas

VII.1 TORDESILLAS
    VII.1.a Palace of Pedro I,
    present-day Convent of Santa Clara

VII.2 PALENCIA
    VII.2.a Diocesan Museum
    VII.2.b Church of San Francisco

VII.3 ASTUDILLO
    VII.3.a Palace of Pedro I,
    present-day Convent of Santa Clara

VII.4 SANTOYO
    VII.4.a Church of
    San Juan Bautista

VII.5 TÁMARA DE CAMPOS
(optional)
    VII.5.a Church of San Hipólito

VII.6 AMUSCO
    VII.6.a Shrine of Nuestra Señora
    de las Fuentes

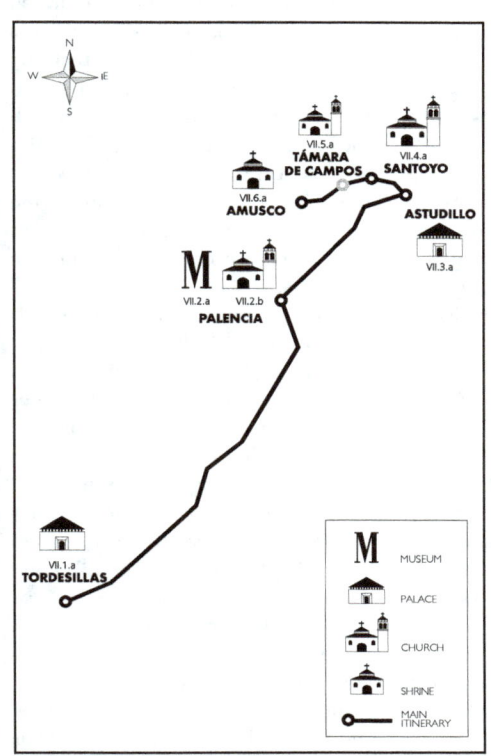

Church of Santa María and Museum; detail of a beam, Becerril de Campos.

ITINERARY VII   Daughters of Kings and Nobles: Through the St Clare's Convents

Palace of Pedro I, façade, Tordesillas.

A number of the daughters of the kings and most important noble families of Castile and León joined the communities of nuns in this region. The Cistercians and the Poor Clares welcomed them gladly and gave them important positions.

The economic contributions of the new arrivals, either in the form of donations of houses or of money, for the improvement of the buildings of their Order, give many of these Cistercian and Order of St Clare convents of this period (between the 14th and 16th centuries) a spaciousness and noble air, which is still their characteristic trait.

María de Padilla (?–1361) and her daughters Beatriz (1353–?) and Constanza (1354–?), the result of her relationship with Pedro I of Castile (1334–1369), utilised the unfinished palaces of Astudillo and Tordesillas. Women from the Manrique, Castañeda or Enriquez families, among others, left their houses and goods to the convents of Calabazanos, Carrión de los Condes and Palencia. It is rare to find a convent in the area without some trace of one of the most important local families.

To find out what life was like in the houses of these religious women a visit one of these convents, where the daughters of noble families lived as nuns, often accompanied by members of their family and servants, is very informative. In Santa Isabel de Valladolid several of the cells and some of the communal areas of the convent can be seen. In Calabazanos, Tordesillas and Carrión the best architectonic structures of this type of convent in the region are conserved, although they are difficult to visit. The aim of this itinerary is to learn about this type of building and about the objects, made specifically for convent life, which are conserved in private museums.

The present-day appearance of the palace buildings of Pedro I (1334–1369), Enrique II (1333/4–1379) and Juan II (1405–1454) are the result of later transformations of these convents, carried out in the effort to adapt them to suit the community's way of life.

The façades and the patios (courtyards) are the most characteristic elements in the cases of Astudillo and Tordesillas, where schemes of Granada or Toledo-influence are repeated: the exteriors of stone doorways in cob walls and brick-edge courses, columns and corners in ashlar stone and multifoil windows; and, in their interiors, richly decorated plaster and polychrome wood with the royal coat of arms. Both buildings are now museums. We can also see the remains, not so well conserved, of the palace of Juan II in Madrigal de Las Altas Torres, but the little that remains of the palace of Enrique II in León is only to be found in the Provincial Museum, and consists of some plasterwork and one or two ceiling fragments.

As well as this convent architecture, there are other representative examples of religious architecture in the main towns of the Tierra de Campos. There, the Mudéjar artists left their mark on ceilings with rich strapwork, on choir lofts, in the figurative themes representing people of the time, in plasterwork in chapels and on pulpits, tombs and tiling. Through the rich typology of buildings used for religious purposes it is revealed how the demands of the time allowed for extremely personal interpretations of Gothic or Renaissance art and created a kind of church which was rural, simple and economically adapted to the local area's existing resources.

This kind of church normally had a single nave with or without two side aisles, and was built in adobe reinforced with brick, or simply faced with plaster on the outside to protect the walls from the damp and then decorated to imitate rough stone. A square tower at the foot and an apse of the same geometry balanced the building. In spite of the simple exterior appearance, the interior is of a sober and astonishing richness. The aisle, with the wooden ceiling enhanced by strapwork- polychrome- and in some cases figurative decorations; the sanctuary, single or triple,

using regular or irregular eight-sided figures in which the *apeinazada* decoration – that is to say structural strapwork which provides volume, and the other decorations – *ataujerada* – with fillets of precious metals, studded and polychrome or gilded, imitated the reality of the heavens. This caused Fray Luis de León (1527–1591) to exclaim in his *Vida Retirada* that "... *the ceiling gilt / can be admired, built / by the knowing Moor in jasper* ...".

Found among the styles of strapwork on these ceilings is a unique variety of images from the Pantocrator with the symbols of the Evangelists (in Santa María in Fuentes de Nava and the Asunción in Villacé) to the humanized representations of the theological and cardinal virtues (in Santos Justo y Pastor in Cuenca de Campos).

In the wooden choir lofts there are representations, painted or carved, of characters from the Bible like kings

Palace of Pedro I, enclosure doorway, Astudillo.

ITINERARY VII *Daughters of Kings and Nobles: Through the St Clare's Convents*
Tordesillas

and prophets (in Bolaños de Campos) or simply characters from everyday life, dressed in contemporary style, and presented in accurate and realistic-type portrayals.

Less frequent are scenes from the Passion of Christ (in the Church of Santiago in Calzada de los Molinos). The figurative themes passed from stone to plaster, and many plasterers copied on tombs, pulpits and chapels the stone representations of the apostles around the Pantocrator in the choir loft in San Hipólito de Tamara. The master Alonso Martínez de Carrión was the most outstanding of all these craftsmen, whose work can be seen in the churches of San Francisco and Santa Clara in the city of Palencia and in those of Santa María in Becerril de Campos and Villalcázar de Sirga, both in the province of Palencia.

VII.1 TORDESILLAS

Church of Santa María, interior, Fuentes de Nava.

Church of San Facundo y San Primitivo, Sanctuary ceiling, Cisneros.

A visit to the convent of Santa Clara in Tordesillas is recommended early in the day to allow time to visit the Diocesan Museum in Palencia.

VII.1.a Palace of Pedro I, present-day Convent of Santa Clara

In the old quarter on the banks of the River Duero. Although this is an enclosed convent, the palace, church and the baths are in the care of the Patrimonio Nacional (National Trust). Entrance charge. Guided tours.

Tordesillas is situated on the banks of the River Duero on a hill that gives it its name "Otero de siellas". The town remains partly enclosed by the cob wall with brick gateways in which the

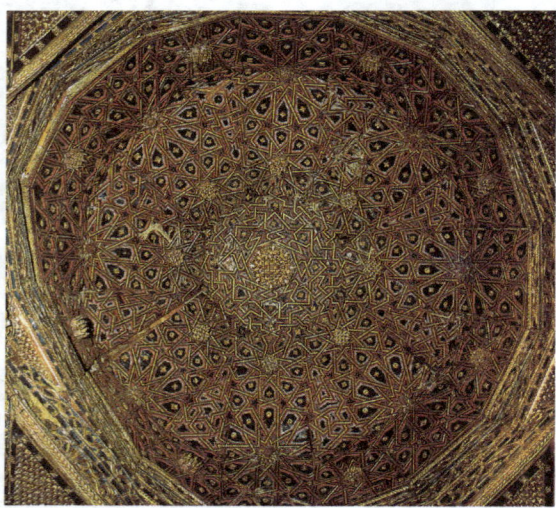

ITINERARY VII   *Daughters of Kings and Nobles: Through the St Clare's Convents*
Tordesillas

Mudéjar workmanship is evident. A palace was built facing the river for the monarchs of Castile. It has been classified by some as an early work of Alfonso XI (1312–1350) on account of the inscribed stones on the façade, although the inscriptions are no longer legible, and on account of the coat of arms of his mistress, Leonor de Guzmán, in the baths. However, the only documented evidence is that Pedro I commissioned the construction and that Beatriz, the elder of the daughters of don Pedro and María de Padilla, later converted it into a convent of the Poor Clares.

The whole palace arrangement has been set according to the water source that comes in through the east wall where the kitchen garden of the monastery is today; from there, the water fills the *aljibes* or water tanks and then flows towards the south and west. To the south is the sanctuary of the present church and the baths. In the west, the water flows into the water deposit of the convent and into a new deposit situated at one end of the present cloister. This gives onto the garden and the patio (courtyard) of another part of the palace, which could date from the second half of the 14th century judging from the numerous remains found during recent excavations. Constructed in the style of the Patio of the Lions in the Alhambra in Granada it had two temples and two fountains one of which still exists, with its tiling and water jet. The restoration work after the excavations has recovered polychrome plasterwork and inscriptions that are in the style of the Patio of the Lions in Granada.

The visit begins in the extreme west of the palace complex, where there is an outstanding trabeated stone façade with indented voussoirs and an upper section with a double window with multifoil arches and a panel with diamond-shaped honeycombing. Inscribed stones placed symmetrically and the decoration of the key and other ceramic elements are reminders of Granada and the workmanship of Muslim Spain. Above this side there is a *qubba* or plaster cupola, which was built between two small patios; one is the present Patio del Yeso, decorated with strapwork and plant motifs and the other, which now no longer exists, was formerly part of the old kitchens. The palace structure opened on the east side onto this second patio through a transverse room that is now the nuns' refectory, and onto another patio, which forms part

Palace of Pedro I, Baths, Tordesillas.

155

ITINERARY VII *Daughters of Kings and Nobles: Through the St Clare's Convents*

Tordesillas

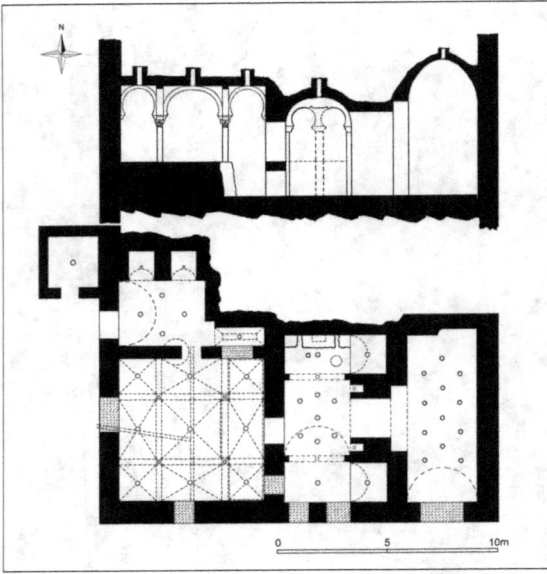

Palace of Pedro I, ground plan and cross section of the baths, Tordesillas.

of the west side of the cloister. In the *qubba*, known as the Capilla Dorada (golden chapel), remnants of Gothic religious paintings remain, which are later than the Mudéjar architectonic work. The vaulting is formed of double ribs that do not cross in the centre and which, starting from alternate crossbeams and eight-pointed stars finish in the keystone of a great 16-pointed star, with a central pendentive.

The palace stretched from east to west (façade and *qubba*) with an intervening patio and two pavilions and pools. On the east side, a new room was opened parallel to the Capilla Dorada. It had two alcoves leading off it through brick archways. The room's floor-standing ceramic-tiled fountain is still conserved with its waterspout.

Towards the south, the palace looked out onto the river through plasterwork arches bearing inscriptions from

Granada, which now having been recovered support the hypothesis that Pedro I ordered a new U-shape room be built that was open to the south on to the river in the same way as the Palace of Galiana in Toledo. The metrology — taking as the unit the Muslim codo or cubit — tells us that the palace was underneath what is today the church and chapel of the Saldaña family, from the name of its founder. However, to discover that this was so, we only have to look at the remains of one of the alcoves in what is the present sacristy, or read the document where the bishop of Palencia don Gutierre allowed the church to be enlarged *"building over the portals of the palace"*.

The adaptation of the palace to a convent in the mid-14th century saw the rooms surrounding the Patio del Vergel, or garden, on the north side, converted into dormitories. In the 17th century these dormitories were again renovated to make two floors of cells, refectory and kitchens (on the east side) and the chapter house, leaving the south side of the cloister as the choir and main church — what is known today as the Long Choir. Later, the Bishop of Palencia gave his permission for the present church to be built, which eliminated communication with the baths; although the baths fell into disuse and were abandoned, still the geometric and heraldic paintings has been conserved in almost all of the rooms. Later, using what had been the façade and porch of the palace, the nuns made a lower choir at the foot of the church and had it decorated with Gothic religious paintings, which alternate with Mudéjar plasterwork and ornamental inscriptions.

ITINERARY VII *Daughters of Kings and Nobles: Through the St Clare's Convents*
Palencia

VII.2 **PALENCIA**

77 km on the N-620 highway. Parking recommended near the Cathedral and then follow the itinerary on foot.

In Palencia, the Mudéjar buildings are restricted to the convents of San Francisco and Santa Clara and the wooden ceilings conserved in the Diocesan Museum.

VII.2.a **Diocesan Museum**

In calle General Mola in the Bishop's Palace. Entrance charge. Guided tours offered by the nuns at 11.30 and 12.30. Closed Sun.

In the Diocesan Museum, currently housed in the Bishop's Palace, three representative wooden ceilings of the area are conserved. The first of these belonged in the church of San Juan in Moral de la Reina. An *alfarje* from the upper choir allows a glimpse of what were possibly scenes from the life of St John in between the remains of the polychrome. This *alfarje* could be related to others of the so-called the Gothic-Mudéjar Burgos School (Silos, Sinovas, Calzada de los Molinos or Amayuelas de Abajo).

The second *alfarje* belongs to the upper choir of the church of San Miguel de Támara; and the third, to the last of the covered towers of the Convent of the Poor Clares of San Bernardino in Cuenca de Campos, founded in 1455 by doña María Fernández de Velasco and her nephew, the Count of Haro. From their privileged vantage point high up in what was known as "the views", the sisters — gathered together to sew or to carry out light domestic tasks —

Diocesan Museum, ceiling, Palencia.

ITINERARY VII *Daughters of Kings and Nobles: Through the St Clare's Convents*
Astudillo

Church of San Francisco, Sepulchre of the Sarmiento Family, Palencia.

could look out on all that was happening in the village below on feast days without being seen.

VII.2.b **Church of San Francisco**

Beside the Plaza Mayor. Ask to visit the Capilla del Sarmiento (Chapel of the Sarmiento Family) and the Sacristy. Mass times: 09.30–10.00, 12.30–13.00 and 18.30–19.00

The convent of San Francisco was founded by Bishop don Tello Téllez de Meneses whose polychrome wooden tomb can be seen under the splendid eight-sided wooden ceiling in the sacristy. Yet these notable achievements, commissioned at the beginning of the 16th century by Bishop don Juan de Castile in the upper choir in the nave, both take second place to the unique funeral chapel built for the Sarmiento family. This chapel, remarkable for its stuccowork, is by a Mudéjar plasterer whose name sometimes appears in the lands of Castile and who here, curiously, has signed his masterpiece *"Alonso Martínes"*.

The chapel holds various statues; in a niche, decorated with Gothic tracery, crests and engravings, the stout person buried there, possibly Juan Sarmiento, kneels in eternal prayer. Under small canopies there are other statues representing apostles and saints.

While in Palencia try a typical dish from the repertoire of local specialities, both **menestra** *(thick vegetable soup) and* **perdiz** *(partridge) are recommended.*

VII.3 ASTUDILLO

VII.3.a **Palace of Pedro I, present-day Convent of Santa Clara**

30 km on the P-431. The church and museum housed in the Palace of Pedro I can be visited, where there is an interesting collection of archaeological finds and works of art. Opening hours: 11.00–13.00 and 16.00–18.30. Closed Mon.

The town of Astudillo has conserved part of its walls, one of the gates, as well as various Gothic churches where Mudéjar works of art can be seen, as for example in the lower choir of San Pedro. Although the town has lost its castle the name – Mota

ITINERARY VII   *Daughters of Kings and Nobles: Through the St Clare's Convents*
Astudillo

– remains, while from the Jewish presence here all that is left is a street-name after the Synagogue.

Pedro I of Castile wanted to build a castle in Astudillo that resembled those the Nasrid monarchs were constructing in Granada at around the same time. It may have been because of his friendship with Muhammad V of Granada, who had been restored to his throne with the help of the king, that craftsmen were sent from Granada who left their best work in Astudillo (1356), Tordesillas (1363), Seville (1364–1366) and Toledo.

The Palace of Astudillo was never finished, and since it did not undergo as many transformations as the palaces of Seville, Toledo or Tordesillas, where the Mudéjar craftsmen sent by Muhammad V from Granada also worked, it allows us to imagine easily the real appearance of the palace dwellings in the middle of the 14th century. Using inexpensive materials like plaster, cob and brick, they built the walls, the window frames and the *arrocabes*, adorned with geometric themes and coats of arms. The wooden polychrome ceilings and the stonework – used only on the façade in a lintel with voussoirs or at the corners in capitals with simple plant motifs – complement a simple but luxurious ornamental system.

What were possibly baths are extant on the western side. These, along with a patio, with pools and galleries of plasterwork traceries in diamond shapes, which filtered the light level on to the chamber, and two private alcoves, reveals a lifestyle and certain courtly luxury that barely fits into the conventional idea of Spain at the time of the reconquest as a society of monks and warriors.

Palace of Pedro I, the nuns' lower choir, plasterwork by Braymi and Alonso Martínez, Astudillo.

ITINERARY VII *Daughters of Kings and Nobles: Through the St Clare's Convents*
Astudillo

Tierra de Campos.

The Pope's threat of excommunication of Pedro I for living "in sin" in the palace with Maria de Padilla, suggested to the latter the idea of converting the palace into a convent. Deciding to assign it to the Order of St Clare, Maria de Padilla was named the founder. After the death of María (1361) and the assassination of the sovereign by the hand of his illegitimate brother Enrique (1369), another of his daughters, Constanza, became the new abbess. She decided to commission a religious building and abandon the palace buildings for good.

During the 15th century, new renovations, including to the plasterwork began on the convent. The Muslim craftsman Braymi was responsible for the renovation carried out in the chapter house. Braymi left his signature on one of the inscriptions of the frieze, along with a pious saying, attributed to St Bernard and written in the corrupt Latin of the time: "*Soli Deo Honor et Gloria*". Braymi also made the pulpit of the refectory, now in the convent museum. At the end of the 15th century, the master Alonso Martínez created plasterwork to embellish the funeral chapel of doña María de Padilla, the foundress of the convent. Here, he repeated the decorative themes of San Francisco and Santa Clara in Palencia.

Dovecotes
On the roads leading to the different villages, you will have the opportunity to see the dovecotes of the Tierra de Campos in their characteristic linear simplicity. Sometimes they are the only buildings that appear in the midst of the unending plains and become the real symbols of the landscape. The material used to build them is fundamentally adobe. For this reason, and because the breeding of pigeons is declining, many have disappeared or are irretrievably damaged. Nevertheless, and thanks to the initiatives undertaken to conserve the rural heritage and architecture of the area, more and more of them are under restoration.

ITINERARY VII Daughters of Kings and Nobles: Through the St Clare's Convents
Santoyo

VII.4 SANTOYO

From Santoyo onwards, gigantic churches begin to appear, almost cathedrals in size and build (Santoyo, Támara or Amusco). These are the products of the enormous wealth created from farming cereals in the area. This district of the Nueve Villas (Nine Towns) became one of the great granaries of Spain in the 16th century.

VII.4.a Church of San Juan Bautista

1 km on the P-431. Opening hours: July–Sept 10.30–13.30 and 17.00–20.00. Rest of the year: Sat and Sun 11.30–12.30 and 16.30–17.30. If the church is closed, ask for Sra. Maruja.

The choir loft of San Juan de Santoyo, dating from the late 15th century, is something more than just a place to pray for an important religious congregation; it is also the scene of a great pictorial representation of a society in the late Middle Ages. Depicted here are not only the clergy, beneficiaries and servants, but also an extensive repertoire of different types of people, dressed in the styles of the time, from the knight to the craftsman, passing by the minstrels and the Jews. We know nothing about the commission or the artist—a master, whose style some experts relate to works of international Gothic painting in Castile, or to the first steps towards this in the Flemish style.

Church of San Juan Bautista, detail of the Upper Choir, Santoyo.

Támara de Campos

VII.5 TÁMARA DE CAMPOS
(optional)

VII.5.a Church of San Hipólito

7 km. If the church is closed, ask for Sra. Concha. Tel: 979 810246.

The Parish Church of Támara de Campos, dedicated to San Hipólito, is one of the most imposing in the district of Tierra de Campos in the area known as the Nine Towns. Some have attributed this building to the Catholic Monarchs whose coat of arms appear on the tower. The Romanesque precedents can be seen in the nearby castle church and other more clearly monastic ones in the Church of San Miguel. This latter church may have formed part of an old Benedictine priory and there are still remains of the ceiling and a beautiful Mudéjar plaster pulpit, from the school of Alonso Martínez.

In San Hipólito – with its upper choir loft worked in stone with a superb group of Apostles surrounding the Pantocrator – the visitor can gain a foretaste of what the master Alonso Martínez de Carrión, or his school, was later to produce in plaster in various convents in the area. A good example of this plasterwork is the pulpit, with Gothic-inspired decorative work.

The Mudéjar workmanship can be traced in different parts of the church and the town, but it is perhaps in the wooden door of the upper choir where the excellent work of a Mudéjar carpenter and cabinetmaker, who could well have come from Granada, can best be seen.

The *taracea* work on the frame and the coat of arms of the Catholic Monarchs, but without the pomegranate, symbolising the definitive conquest of the peninsula by Isabel and Fernando, leads us to date the work before 1492.

Shrine of Nuestra Señora de las Fuentes, Pulpit, Amusco.

VII.6 AMUSCO

VII.6.a Shrine of Nuestra Señora de las Fuentes

14 km. Visits can be arranged with the parish. Tel: 979 802051.

The town of Amusco is mentioned in the medieval chronicles for its important Jewish quarter of which only memories remain. *"From Piña were those who scourged Jesus, in Amusco they dined and in Fromista they had supper and stopped"*, a popular saying of Palencia goes.

On the outskirts of the village, the Shrine of Nuestra Señora de las Fuentes is a Gothic building containing a curious Mudéjar plaster pulpit, one of Castilla-León's most original. The ornamental motifs, which are Gothic and Nasrid, as well as other styles apparently inspired by a printed Renaissance source, show the curious symbiosis of cultures and artistic forms which occurred in Mudéjar Castile. On one side are the Gothic tracery, engravings and festoons; on the other, asymmetrical leaves and *mocárabe*, eight-pointed stars and crossbeams; on yet another the representation of Rhetoric – a very good thing to have mastered to preach from the pulpit – all created in the purest iconographic style of the Italian Quattrocento, and in particular of Andrea Mantegna. This configuration of an artistic hybrid demonstrates very well the uniqueness of the Mudéjar style. It does not seem to have been the work of any plasterer active at the time in the area, but was probably by a craftsman from Granada, or perhaps one of his disciples, who may also have made the pulpit in Santa María del Campo in Burgos.

Shrine of Nuestra Señora de las Fuentes, detail of the Pulpit, Amusco.

An overnight stay in Carrión de los Condes, 30 km away, is recommended. In the renovated Monastery of San Zoilo the remains of the Romanesque façade of the church and the superb Renaissance cloister of Juan de Badajoz can be seen.

ITINERARY VII
Second day

Daughters of Kings and Nobles: Through the St Clare's Convents

Pedro Lavado Paradinas

- **VII.7 CARRIÓN DE LOS CONDES**
  - VII.7.a Convent of Santa Clara

- **VII.8 VILLAMUERA DE LA CUEZA**
  - VII.8.a Nuestra Señora de las Nieves

- **VII.9 BECERRIL DE CAMPOS**
  - VII.9.a Church of Santa María and Museum

- **VII.10 FUENTES DE NAVA**
  - VII.10.a Church of Santa María

- **VII.11 CISNEROS**
  - VII.11.a Church of San Facundo y San Primitivo

Pedro I of Castile

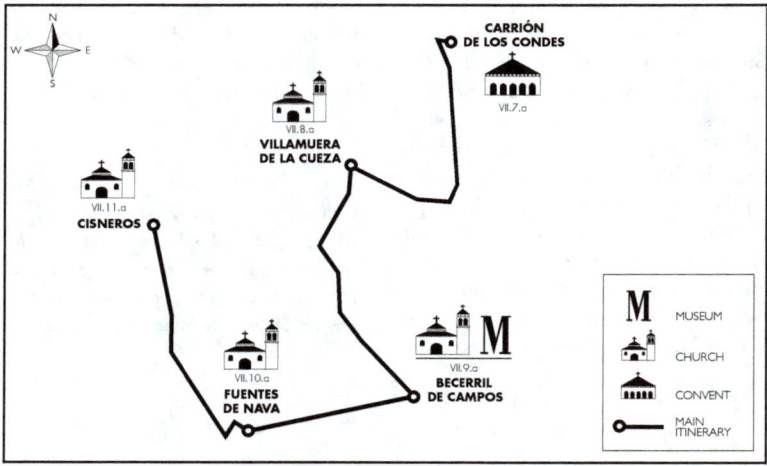

ITINERARY VII Daughters of Kings and Nobles: Through the St Clare's Convents
Carrión de los Condes

Convent of Santa Clara, wooden beams, Carrión de los Condes.

VII.7 CARRIÓN DE LOS CONDES

VII.7.a Convent of Santa Clara

Both the church and the museum are open to the public and have panels and beams from the Mudéjar ceiling as well as everyday objects from the convent and other works of art. The enclosed Convent of Santa Clara still produces exquisite sweetmeats from traditional recipes. Opening hours: summer 11.00–13.00 and 17.00–19.00; winter 11.00–13.00 and 16.30–18.30. Closed Mon.

Recent renovations in the convent museum have made visible the remains of the grille in the parlour of the convent founded by doña Mencía López de Haro, who married the King of Portugal, Sancho II, as her second husband in 1260. Possibly the nuns from Santa María del Páramo lodged first in the Church of the Sancti Spiritus which was founded here before the alternations carried out by the Mother Superior Sor Luisa de la Ascensión in the 17th century. The discovery of a series of wooden beams worked in the style of the Mudéjar carpenters of the 13th century suggests that this was an example of the reuse of beams from a Romanesque church whose wooden ceiling would have been similar to examples in Toledo and Segovia. The alterations made in the 17th century retained the best beams and replaced them haphazardly in the grille of the parlour or *locutory* of the new church. Some fragments were used as wedges for the 15th-century ceiling in the chapter house of the convent.
It is clear that additions to the building were ongoing and that the number of nuns in the order grew. The coat of arms of the families Lara, Castañeda and Zuñiga testify to the patronage of these families in different parts of the convent at the end

165

of the 15th century and early 16th. A number of fragments and boards from different ceilings with the coat of arms of these families are exhibited in the convent museum.

It is not easy to visit the individual cells built by Mother Superior Sor Luisa de la Ascensión, which present obvious similarities with those in the convent in Calabazanos. Built as small cells out of clay (adobe) and accessible through doors decorated with stucco relief depicting religious imagery, each cell consists of a small room equipped with a sleeping alcove including a plaster niche for pictures and images, a shelf and an almery.

Unfortunately, other ceilings and Mudéjar work from Carrión have not survived, some due to ill-advised restorations, as in the case of the important portico with a sculptured frieze that at one time sheltered the Romanesque door of Santa María.

The documents, however, speak not only of Muslims but also of Jews: *"... populatores in barrio Sancti Soyli, tam christianos, quam iudeos sive sarracenos ..."* (1220) (the populace in the quarter of San Zoilo, both Christians and Jews or Saracens).

The community is still mentioned in 1465: *"... those who live within the walls and will live here from now on ..."*, which is quite likely to be an accurate report since the Census of the Inquisition in 1594 and of the Expulsion in 1609, again, mentions a certain number of *moriscos*.

One of the town's most famous personages was Rabbi don Sem Tob, also known as don Santos de Carrión, whose poems, collected in the book *Proverbios Morales*, dedicated to King don Pedro, are a good example of the hybrid nature of Hispanic medieval culture in which there is a place for the Bible, the Qur'an and the Talmud: *"En el mundo tan cabdal / non hay commo el saber: / más que heredad val, / nin thesoro, nin aver / ... nin mejor compañía / que el libro, nin tal; / tomar grande pofía / con Él, más que paz val"*
(In this world there is nothing as perfect as knowledge; it is worth more than a heritage, or any treasure or possession. ... There is no better company than the book, none ... to wrestle with it is worth more than peace ...).

VII.8 VILLAMUERA DE LA CUEZA

VII.8.a **Nuestra Señora de las Nieves**

20 km on the C-615 and at Villafolfo take the P-963. If the church is closed, ask for Sra Jacoba. Tel: 979 883162.

The three-aisle church of Nuestra Señora de las Nieves in Villamuera de la Cueza is built of adobe faced and plastered to imitate the joints of cut ashlar stone, but today disguised and covered up with modern and tasteless brick.

Inside, it is a typical church with columns of the Tierra de Campos. It has lost – or perhaps still has hidden under the false ceiling – the great wooden boards of the nave, although, fortunately, it has preserved the eight-sided wooden ceiling in the sanctuary, a Mudéjar masterpiece from Castile. Its author signed it on the *arrocabe* in among a tangle of vegetation, which makes it quite difficult to find: *"Esta obra yço Juan Carpeil"* (Juan Carpeil did this work). The eight-sided ceiling,

ITINERARY VII   *Daughters of Kings and Nobles: Through the St Clare's Convents*
Villamuera de la Cueza

Nuestra Señora de las Nieves, detail of the Sanctuary ceiling, Villamuera de la Cueza.

which begins from the square ground plan of the sacristy, is divided into eight by *trompas of* gilded *mocárabes*. It then subdivides into other smaller *trompas* until it reaches 16 sides, and then returns to the eight-sided form by alternating triangular and trapezoidal pieces, which culminate in an octagonal *almizate* with a central pendentive of *muqarnas*, which is also gilded.

This ingenious solution, which approaches a cupola of the Seville type, can be found in plaster in Tordesillas, La Mejorada de Olmedo and in Seville in the chapels of la Quinta Angustia and Omnium Sanctorum. And it is also found in wood, in the Patio of the Lions in the Alhambra in Granada, in the Salon of the Ambassadors in the Alcázar in Seville, in the ceiling of the Palace of the Cárdenas family in Torrijos (now in the National Archaeological Museum in Madrid), in the ceiling of the staircase of the Casa de Pilatos in Seville and in a number of other variants.

It is possible that the same artist or workshop made this type of ceiling popular, and examples can be seen in other buildings. The same Juan Carpeil made the ceiling in the chapel of the Virgen del Castillo, in San Facundo de Cisneros, and possibly made the ceiling in the sanctuary of the nearby shrine of Villafilar as well. We do not know, however, anything about who commissioned the work: perhaps it was the result of one of the generous legacies donated by don Luis Hurtado de Mendoza, Abbot of Covarrubias (Burgos) and of the Sanctuary of Atocha, in the city of Madrid. In his will of 1507, Mendoza donated many artworks, furniture and ornaments to different monasteries in the area, but there is no mention of this chapel. The suspicion that Mendoza may have commissioned the work is down to the fact that, only

Becerril de Campos

Church of Santa María and Museum, Pulpit, Becerril de Campos.

Of the seven churches in Becerril at one time, only two remain standing: one still used for services (Santa Eugenia) and the other used as a parish museum (Santa María). The original wooden ceilings of San Martín, San Pedro and Santa María have been irretrievably lost. The conversion of the Church of Santa María into a museum saved it from abandonment and consequent ruin, but at the expense of the museum installations, which denies visitors the chance of seeing one of Tierra de Campos' most unusual churches.

This is a church with a single, very high and wide nave, surmounted by a wooden ceiling, and another smaller aisle on the Gospel side, which until a few years ago still had the remains of murals by an artist called Pedro Alfonso; unfortunately, these have now disappeared. Signed by him in 1432, they decorated a sarcophagus. Besides this one, later on, at the beginning of the 16th century, another mural was painted.

two days after making his will, he died in Nuestra Señora de las Nieves, where he is buried in a chapel at the foot of the church. If Mendoza did not in fact leave anything towards the building of the church, it may have been the monks of San Zoilo de Carrión.

VII.9 BECERRIL DE CAMPOS

VII.9.a Church of Santa María and Museum

23 km on the P-693 towards Paredes de Nava and then on the C-613. Opening hours: 11.30–13.30 and 17.00–20.00. Sat, Sun and public holidays 10.30–13.30 and 17.00–20.00. Closed Mon.

The wooden roof of the church, especially the almizate, suffered severe damage in the Baroque reform that covered up the ceiling with vaulting and did away with the roof trusses and strapwork. A *par y nudillo* design with the boards intricately decorated and a polychrome or gilded background, the roofing system of Santa María is very similar to that of the Franciscan churches – and in some cases to the Franciscan churches in Levante and Galicia – from the early 15th century. The only other example nearby is the superb ceiling of the Abbey church in Husillos.

At the foot of the nave is a choir loft in wood, one of the most unusual and humorous in the whole of Castile.

VII.10 FUENTES DE NAVA

VII.10.a Church of Santa María

13 km on P-953. Visits can be arranged with the Parish Priest D. Joaquín: Tel: 979 842027, in the late afternoon or early morning.

In the interior of the church of Santa María the best example of Mudéjar work in the Tierra de Campos has been preserved. The church belongs to a common type of *iglesia columnaria* (column church), of three aisles with a transept and a single square sanctuary, a cupola, added in 1562, and a tower at the foot, which today is in ruins and disused. In this case, the columns that separate the aisles are octagonal pillars that, while extremely slender, are able to bear the weight

On the heads of the beams is a procession of carved and painted characters, some male, wearing a beard, moustache or goatee beard, and others female, wearing a necklace and low-cut gown; in addition there are other male and female portraits painted in the style of the late 15th or early 16th century.

In all likelihood, the work to the ceiling was completed during this time, although the choir was being refurbished in 1545 according to a note in the baptismal register. It is also possible that the open portico and the ceilings of the south or Epistle side, were constructed at the same time. However, the mural paintings by Pedro Alonso on the Gospel side make it prudent to date the first construction of the ceiling to the first quarter of the 15th century.

Another important piece of data is the plasterwork by Alonso Martinez, who signed his work on the pulpit: *"Alonso Martines de Carrión me f ..."*. This is a polygonal five-sided pulpit with panels which alternate in flamboyant Gothic and openwork decoration, and which has certain similarities to other examples in the area. It is possible that this craftsman is also responsible for the plasterwork of the windows of the apse and the now non-existent pulpit in plaster of San Pelayo in Becerril de Campos.

A cattle-rearing market town, the only remnants of this extant today are the wooden galleries in one of the squares and the arcaded streets. Inexpensive materials such as adobe, brick and wood were used, practically the same as the materials for the vernacular architecture of the area. Although much of this has survived to the present, it is now fast disappearing due to ignorance and neglect.

Church of Santa María, interior, Fuentes de Nava.

ITINERARY VII Daughters of Kings and Nobles: Through the St Clare's Convents
Cisneros

Church of Santa María, detail of the ceiling, Fuentes de Nava.

of the magnificent eight-sided ceiling with wheel-shaped blue and red strapwork and 16-strand knots.

In the transept, the church has an eight-sided ceiling on *trompas*, with twelve-, 16- and 24-strand knots. Curiously, in the centre, instead of a cone-shaped pendentive, there is a hanging polychrome figure of the Saviour in the centre of four stars and surrounded by the animals usually seen accompanying the four evangelists, who are holding phylacteries. This is a unique example of an ostentatious display of the mixing of elements from the Christian and Muslim traditions. The Master of Fuentes de la Nava – a name given in the hope that it would appear in some document at some point in association with his craft – had a considerable influence in the area (in Boada de Campos, Añoza and Villalcón). Evidence that Fuentes de la Nava's activity reached as far as the area surrounding León can be seen in the ceiling of the Asunción in Villacé,

which is certainly also his work. In the centre of the strapwork ceiling, note the figure which could represent Christ or the Eternal Father.

Perhaps it would be possible to confirm the activity of a workshop of carpenters of some sophistication in Fuentes de Nava – a workshop that continued to be active until the mid-16th century – if we were able to see the roof of the Church of San Pedro in this same town. Unfortunately, that ceiling although preserved almost intact, is trapped between the vault and the roof; this is why, even though we know of its existence, we don't know anything about it. The same until recently could be said of other ceilings and carpentry works still in existence and examined in the city some years ago, as in, for example, the house of calle Rodriguez Lagunilla. Today, the only evidence that can be seen in Fuentes de la Nava are some awnings and houses bearing a coat of arm from the 16th century.

VII.11 **CISNEROS**

Cisneros is the name of this town in Palencia, named after one of the town's most important families from the late 15th and early 16th centuries. The presence of a powerful family in Cisneros can probably explain the artworks in its churches. However, there is evidence of only three knights of the name Cisneros buried in this town: don Álvaro and don Toribio Ximénez de Cisneros are buried in San Pedro, and don Antonio Ximénez de Cisneros in San Facundo. The tombs of the first two are from the mid-15th century (the second of them is dated 1455); the third, who was the cousin and secretary of the great cardinal Fray Francisco Ximenez de Cisneros (1436–1517), was buried in the sanctuary of the church of San Facundo, following his death in Cisneros, in 1517. Cardinal Cisneros himself perhaps paid for some of the works, but there is no documented evidence to support this.

VII.11.a Church of San Facundo y San Primitivo

25 km on the P-944. If the church is closed ask for Sra Maruja (next door). Tel: 979 848485. There is an interesting Parish and Provincial Museum in the Church of San Pedro.

The church of San Facundo y San Primitivo shows a new kind of roof with a complete ornamental system in wood for the choir, the chapels and the tribune. The Gothic header, a polygonal, eight-sided structure covered with a half-ceiling with polychrome strapwork, has its twin in Santo Tomás de Revellinos and at least partly seems to repeat the same solution as the ceiling of the Convent of Santa Clara in Tordesillas. The whole church also has a very special type of roof on a structure of columns typical of this district of Campos. The ceiling, of unpainted pinewood, eight-sided and studded, is formed of chamfers that make diminishing rhomboid- and octagonal-shaped squinches. Decorated entirely with strips worked in wood and with floral motifs of a Renaissance provenance, the system of transition between the central nave and the side aisles is reminiscent of Mazuecos de Valdeginate; and the workmanship and resulting shapes are not dissimilar from those of Santos Justo y Pastor in Cuenca de Campos.

In the first span of the nave on the Epistle side is the Chapel of the Virgen del Castillo, probably by Juan Carpeil, since the same structural and decorative solutions appear similar to those already mentioned in Villamuera de la Cueza. An upper choir, displaced to the side of the church, with heads of animals and heraldic risers referring to Castile, establishes another relationship with the work in Santa María in Becerril de Campos.

An overnight stay is recommended in Sahagun as it is the starting point of the next Itinerary.

Church of San Facundo y San Primitivo, detail of the ceiling, Cisneros.

PEDRO I OF CASTILE

Pedro Lavado Paradinas

Pedro I, sculpture, National Archaeological Museum, Madrid.

Pedro I of Castile (Peter of Castile) has become something of a legendary king. The nicknames "el Cruel" (the Cruel) or "el Justo" (the Just), given him respectively by his enemies and his partisans, could only be worn by a personality that was contradictory in itself, as well as historically controversial.

Born in Burgos in 1334, the son of Alfonso XI of Castile and María de Portugal, it was Pedro's lot to live in a confused world that was in a state of permanent civil war. Pedro came to the throne of Castile when he was still at the very young age of 15 (1350), while the favourites and their families – the Alburquerque and the Coronel – governed the country. The following year, his mother ordered the assassination of Leonor de Guzman, his father's mistress, which gave the new king even more new and closer enemies, such as his illegitimate half-brother, Enrique de Trastamara (Henry II of Castile), the son of Leonor. He made himself new enemies outside Spain of his own accord as well, because of his erratic policy with France and England.

All of his politics, both internal and external was tremendously personal and his actions were extremely contradictory. While on the one hand he was living with María de Padilla in 1352, on the other, he celebrated his marriage to Blanca de Borbón in Valladolid the following year, but then abandoned her two days later, returned to his mistress, and had his wife incarcerated in Toledo. The result of this action was the rupture of the alliance with France, and this led to the rebellion of Toledo. In the same year he married another noble woman from Castile, Juana de Castro, but he abandoned her almost immediately as well. Until 1356, he lived in a state of permanent crisis, which he would try to escape, invariably aggressively, starting a war against Pedro IV of Aragón. His life, as recounted in the chronicles, in the literature and in popular ballads is an important source of the Romantic legend, which also includes his contemporaries Pedro IV of Aragón (1317/19–1387) and Pedro I of Portugal (1320–1367), this latter also known as "the Cruel".

Different impressions of the monarch of Castile come to us through the chronicle of his contemporary, the Chancellor Pero López de Ayala (*Crónica de don Pedro de Castilla*), through Félix Lope de Vega in seven of his comedies and through Prosper Mérimée (*Histoire de Pedro I, roi de Castille*, 1848), to mention only the best-known examples.

His relationship with the Jews and the Muslims also caused difficult diplomatic and political situations and was much criticised, because no sooner had he left the royal finances in the hands of Jehuda Haleví, he was confiscating his goods, and condemning him. As far as the Muslims of Granada were concerned, he took the part of Muhammad V against Muhammad VI, *el Rey Bermejo*, assassinating the latter and gaining the friendship and favour of the former.

His amorous intrigues led him into very complicated situations that never have been clarified fully. The Pope had threatened King Pedro with excommunication on various occasions for living "in sin" with María de Padilla. Yet, in 1361 – the year in which both Blanca his legitimate wife died and also María, supposedly his mistress – the king declared that only the latter had been his legitimate spouse and that the children he had fathered with her – Alfonso, Beatriz, Constanza and Isabel – were his legal heirs. His contemporary Pedro de Portugal took the same position with the children he had fathered with Inés de Castro, with the difference that Pedro of Castile, at least, prevented the partisan of his wife from murdering his lover.

In 1369, after the murder of Pedro I in Montiel – by his half-brother Enrique de Trastamara, supposedly assisted by the mercenary Beltrán Duguesclin – the daughters of the monarch of Castile inherited and then governed the houses and palaces that don Pedro and doña María de Padilla had built between 1354 and 1361 in Astudillo and Tordesillas. These were now converted into the convents of the Order of St Clare, with the daughters of King don Pedro their first abbesses or priors.

These buildings, which in general would have been unfinished at the time of their founder María de Apdilla's death, constitute one of the clearest examples of Mudéjar civil architecture in Castile and its later conversion into convent precincts. The walls and structures are mainly of adobe and brick, with a simple façade of cut stone, and spans with archways in brick or plaster. The interiors are decorated with polychrome wood and have plasterwork ornamentation on the ceilings and arches. The patios or courtyards furnished with pools and temples, the fountains, the baths and the heating by underfloor *glorias* were the main refinements in the buildings which were simple and sober, but certainly not uncomfortable. Possibly Mudéjar craftsmen from Granada designed and decorated the buildings, although some scholars believe they may have been from Toledo while still others argue that they were from Burgos.

Whatever the truth may be, these early examples of Mudéjar civil architecture in Castile happened at a moment in the mid-14th century when this region, and a large part of what was later to become Spain, was suffering the scourge of the Black Death and experiencing political and economic turmoil. This atmosphere of crises often escalated into civil wars and other conflicts between the various Christian kingdoms of the Peninsula.

ITINERARY VIII

Consequences of the Birth of Gothic Cathedrals: Working with Brick

Pedro Lavado Paradinas

VIII.1 SAHAGÚN
  VIII.1.a Church of San Tirso
  VIII.1.b Sanctuary of La Peregrina

VIII.2 SAN PEDRO DE LAS DUEÑAS
  VIII.2.a Monastery of San Pedro de las Dueñas

VIII.3 SANTERVÁS DE CAMPOS
  VIII.3.a Parish Church

VIII.4 VILLALÓN DE CAMPOS
  VIII.4.a Church of San Miguel

VIII.5 MAYORGA DE CAMPOS (optional)
  VIII.5.a Church of Santa María de Arbás

VIII.6 VILLALPANDO
  VIII.6.a Church of San Nicolás (optional)
  VIII.6.b Church of Santa María la Antigua

VIII.7 TORO
  VIII.7.a Church of San Lorenzo
  VIII.7.b Church of Santa María de la Vega
  VIII.7.c Convent of Santa Sofía

Fairs and Markets

Monastery of San Pedro de las Dueñas, general view.

175

ITINERARY VIII Consequences of the Birth of Gothic Cathedrals: Working with Brick

Parish Church, apses, Santervás de Campos.

Contrary to what school textbooks would have us believe, the history of art is not a linear process where each new style only appears when the preceding one has already disappeared. The beginning of the great Gothic cathedrals in Castilla-León – Burgos (1222), León (1255) or Palencia (1321) – and of the great monastic foundations – Las Huelgas in Burgos (around 1180), coincides historically with the conversion of unfinished Romanesque buildings into brick architecture.

The enormous sums in tithes and taxes that was necessary for the construction of such colossal works, and the vested interests of all the guilds of master craftsmen involved in their construction – stonemasons, carpenters, plasterers, stucco artists or painters – in ensuring that the work lasted as long as possible, undoubtedly explains why so much rural religious architecture remains unfinished and was left very badly off in so far as materials, transport and workmen were concerned.

A scarcity of resources in the rural parishes as well as a lack of the social organisation or a religious order able to finance the cost of the work (which frequently took more than a century to complete) meant that Gothic buildings – frequently built on top of Romanesque ones – would be left unfinished in the hope of better times to come.

Away from the Camino de Santiago (The Way of St James) and a distance from the great monastic centres, it is difficult to find completed Romanesque buildings and even more unusual to find Gothic buildings begun in stone, which made use of a specialist workforce. Only in the province of Burgos at the centre of the important wool trade, and along the route from Burgos to the ports on the north coast in Cantabria, could a development of significant Gothic architecture take place. Inspired in part by the plans of Burgos Cathedral, sometimes even the same master masons who undertook worked there were recruited. Such is the case in the Church of San Gil and San Esteban in the city of Burgos or of the Asunción, in Laredo (Santander).

The decided royal preference for Burgos and León is patent in the Gothic cathedrals constructed in both places, and makes them authentic islets in a vast area that is also lacking in churches for the rural population and the secular clergy. The few Gothic works that exist in the province of Burgos are the result of the develop-

ITINERARY VIII Consequences of the Birth of Gothic Cathedrals: Working with Brick

ment of the capital itself – for example Sasamón – a copy of Burgos Cathedral, and Villamorón and Grijalba. In the rest of the region, Gothic churches were built only in places that depended on the Military Orders, such as the Templars in Villalcázar de Sirga or the Knights of St James in Villamuriel de Cerrato, both in Palencia.

Generally, Romanesque buildings in this region conserve their sanctuaries and the front parts of their original bays, vaulted in the early years of the 13th century and left waiting in an unfinished state for a chance to complete them. In this way, brick architecture was popularised in Castile, which helped to satisfy the demand for workers for these rural buildings in a simple and economical way.

Very possibly the first centre of Mudéjar architecture in Castile was in Sahagún, a conclusion that may be drawn from looking at buildings which have been conserved, to illustrate that they are even earlier than the Mudéjar buildings in Toledo. In both cases, the procedure was the same. The Cathedral in Toledo, begun in 1226, absorbed all the available workforce and resources for its construction, leaving the use of brick, wood and other more economical materials for secular architecture.

But the problem was not only one of economic resources. It was also a question of adapting to the environment, insofar as the quarries were exhausted and the transport routes inadequate, with the main routes taking the direction of the building sites of the great cathedrals. The great masters from abroad and their workshops tried out new forms in stone, while the craftsmen, very possibly of Muslim origin, turned to brick and other decorative and constructive elements which in the case of secular architecture reproduced Romanesque stone forms in brick.

The Mudéjar art of Castile initially was evident in the churches of Sahagún (San Tirso), Santervás de Campos (Santos Gervasio y Protasio), San Pedro de Dueñas (the Monastery Church), Fresno Viejo (San Juan Bautista) and Alba de Tormes (San Juan).

Nevertheless, the dates suggested for these buildings are clearly earlier than the beginnings of the Gothic cathedrals in Burgos, León or Palencia, so that we have to think of other reasons to explain the rise of a rural Mudéjar architecture and consider why it is that so many Gothic buildings were never finished. One of these could be the enormous prestige and power of the Monastery of Sahagún, where these other churches grew up in its shadow and dependent on it. Another reason could, of course, be the wars – such as those that broke out after the death of Alfonso VI and during the reign of doña Urraca and don Alfonso el Batallador, which left unfinished works not only in Castile but also in Aragón.

Church of La Peregrina, general view, Sahagún.

Church of San Miguel, painted brick, Villalón de Campos.

The second Mudéjar period in Castilla-León is characterised by brick architecture: cruciform brick pillars, which support pointed arches on which the wooden ceiling rests.

The apses in this style are made completely of brick and although on the outside these are covered with blind arches, they are two or three storeys high and squared off and framed at the top in *alfices*. In this case, the similarities with the Mudéjar style seen in Toledo is self-evident. The most important examples are in the Church of San Lorenzo and Santiago in Sahagún, the Church of San Feliz in Sahelices del Río, San Lorenzo de Villapeceñil and the Parish Churches of Arenillas de Valderaduey and Gordaliza del Pino, all in León. Other concentrations of Mudéjar craftsmanship appear in different towns in Castilla-León, creating specific local variations with repercussions in their various geographical areas. This is the case of Toro and its churches, which have high blind arcades in brick on the exterior, or the variants in Olmedo (Valladolid), Arévalo (Ávila) and Cuéllar (Segovia.) In this way, in the border area of the three provinces, there is a multiplicity of churches with more ornamental variants than structural ones.

The same applies to the churches in Daroca (Saragossa), which also began as Romanesque buildings and finished as Mudéjar, in brick, with similar motifs.

In Castilla-León, other variants of early Mudéjar exist inspired by the Romanesque architecture in the area, and producing a very special type of building. An example of this are the churches with flat apses in the area of Villalpando (Zamora) that are reminiscent of the Romanesque architecture of Zamora, especially in the valley of the River Tera. In Mayorga de Campos in Valladolid and its surroundings, there is a type of semicircular apse in adobe, which reflects a Romanesque concept of space and the use of local materials.

However, in the same way that Sahagún and its area of influence interprets the Romanesque – creating a first architectonic typology of Mudéjar, the so-called pre-classical Mudéjar or Romanesque-Mudéjar, and other local variants of the Romanesque (that is, the classical Mudéjar with evident parallels with the Toledo style already mentioned in Villalpando, Mayorga, Toro, Olmedo, Arévalo and Cuéllar) – in the second half of the 13th century, a new version of Gothic-Mudéjar architecture appears with its polygonal apses and *estribos* appearing on the outside, something that is also earlier than the Toledo model, and which can be seen at its exemplary best in the Church of the Franciscans (Sanctuary of La Peregrina) and in the Shrine of the Virgin del Puente.

Curiously enough, two religious orders had no relationship with the Benedictines of Sahagún and had to build their own churches, Gothic in structure, outside the city walls: the Franciscans and the Canons of St Augustine.

Other later variants of Gothic architecture in Castilla-León, which we owe to Mudéjar *alarifes*, are outstanding examples of Gothic-Mudéjar. The first group of variants was formed by the buildings that had royal patronage after the period of Pedro I and Enrique II of Castile (mid-14th century), with recollections in some churches of the Convents of the Order of St Clare. A second group would be the buildings due to the patronage of the Enríquez family, such as in the cases of San Andrés in Aguilar de Campos (Valladolid). Then there are the churches whose patrons were the Pimentel family in San Miguel and San Pedro de Villalón de Campos (Valladolid). A fourth and final group can be recognised in the adaptations of a Gothic style with roots in the Levante, such as in the cases of the Abbey of Husillos and in Santa María in Becerril de Campos (in Palencia), some of the churches in the capital, and other places in the province of Zamora, such as Ayo de Vidriales.

What is certain is that the Romanesque typologies survived for a long time, adapting buildings that were impossible to construct out of stone, because the means to do so was unavailable, to brick. In this way not only was the transformation of the epidermis of those rural churches achieved, but also the basis for great architectural developments was established. Thanks to the simple and economical materials used, the Muslim craftsmen created new structural concepts such as lighter wooden ceilings, *cimborrio* towers and ornamental themes worked or painted directly on to the brick itself. Their work showed sophisticated details that turned chessboard patterns into raked courses, the corbelled eaves into coving and components of the arches into trimmed and moulded brick. Their work introduced *alfices*, barge courses and horizontal and vertical brick courses, which reinforced the box-shaped sections of masonry and adobe, and introduced an extensive range of spans or arches: multifoil, pointed, interlaced, horseshoe, double or single, and also exquisite variants of brick, which was trimmed or cut after it had been fired.

VIII.I SAHAGÚN

VIII.1.a **Church of San Tirso**

The Church is no longer in use for services, but there is a guide. Opening hours: 1 May–1 Nov 10.00–14.00 and 16.30–20.00. The rest of the year 10.00–14.00 and 16.00–18.00. Closed Mon.

The Church of San Tirso is mentioned in documents of 1123, making it contemporary with the Romanesque buildings of the monastery (1100–1110), a project that would appear to have been interrupted by

ITINERARY VIII   *Consequences of the Birth of Gothic Cathedrals: Working with Brick*

Sahagún

Church of San Tirso, apse and tower, Sahagún.

the death of the Abbot don Diego in 1111. This church building shows its Romanesque foundations in stone and the continuation in brick, a change that would have involved considerable effort in order to adapt the forms of the stone to the brick: blind arcades with brick mouldings and a new proportion of materials. San Tirso is a building on a pseudo-basilica ground plan with three aisles separated by semicircular brick arches, making use of the remains of the Romanesque foundations. Over the first bay of the central aisle, a tower, remodelled extensively in brick, has reused Romanesque elements. The only document that makes mention of the church is a donation by doña Sancha, the sister of Alfonso VIII, to the Monastery of San Pedro de Dueñas: "*Facta ... huius ... per manun adefonsi ecclesie sancte tirsi in ...*", dated 7th September 1126.

VIII.1.b Sanctuary of La Peregrina

Opening hours: 1 Jul–1 Oct 10.00–14.00 and 16.00–20.00. In the winter, visits can be arranged with the guide at San Tirso. Tel: 626 077663.

This Franciscan Convent known as the Sanctuary of La Peregrina (the Pilgrim), named after a statue of the Virgin Mary that is in safekeeping there, was founded in 1257, roughly at the same time as the church. The latter has a single nave with a polygonal chancel, while on its walls there are a wide variety of blind arcades of different types including multifoil and lancet arches. Although some of the motifs used here more usually appear in the Mudéjar architecture in Toledo, this church is earlier than Santa Fe in Toledo, which means that it might be considered the first example of the Gothic type. On the other hand, the ornamental motifs of the arches are found a century later in San Pablo de Peñafiel in Valladolid.

Perhaps the most unusual aspect of the Sanctuary is the burial chapel of don Diego Gómez de Sandoval located on the Epistle side of the church. This square chapel's interior is decorated with polychrome plasterwork that surrounds a substantial tomb and covers the walls completely with friezes of geometric latticework. Below, on the lower parts, strapwork and Gothic plant motifs alternate on a background of small-scale *ataurique*. An inscription in semi-uncial Latin letters runs around the wall: *Domine: Jhs: Xpe: Fili de(i) ... (p)ecatori: Q(ui):*

ITINERARY VIII   Consequences of the Birth of Gothic Cathedrals: Working with Brick
San Pedro de las Dueñas

Moribu. The Sandoval family coat of arms – with one diagonal band – is arranged in different parts of the plasterwork, supporting documentation tells us that the first Conde de Castro, don Diego Gómez Sandoval, who died in 1455, is buried here. The will of his second son, whose name was the same, reads: *"Furthermore I leave to the monastery of San Francisco de Sahagún, where my Ancestors are buried, because they are charged with praying to God for their souls and my own, and for certain things which have to be done in the tombs of my parents and my brothers ... 3200 maravedíes ..."*.

The plasterwork itself is evidence of a Mudéjar School of plasterers working in this area between 1430 and 1450 and who must have specialised in decorating memorial chapels. They have left important work in Sahagún and in Mayorga de Campos in Valladolid.

Church of La Peregrina, detail of plasterwork, Sahagún.

VIII.2 SAN PEDRO DE LAS DUEÑAS

VIII.2.a Monastery of San Pedro de las Dueñas

6 km on the LE 941. An enclosed Convent of Benedictine Nuns. If the church is closed, ask for Sra Maruja in the bar in the square. Tel: 987 780850.

Although there is nothing left of the original monastery, the church is another example of the primitive or pre-classical Mudéjar in Sahagún. The church, with a Romanesque ground plan and elevation, has three apses on the exterior; the two lateral ones covered with barrel vaulting, while the central one has tiercerons on facings of masonry.

The stone corbels and eaves that remain on the outside are devoid of carving at the top of the apses. The system of blind arcades on columns, which are attached to brackets on the central apse and finished in brick without any decoration on the sides, continues throughout the building. While the main apse has parallels with the Church of San Tirso in Sahagún, in San Pedro de Dueñas the main apse was continued at the top with a frieze of nine double-brick blind arches, semicircular in shape, even if somewhat flattened. The brick tower is situated over the straight stretch of the apse following the model of the towers, which imitate *cimborrios*.

Santervás de Campos

Monastery of San Pedro de las Dueñas, interior.

Another parallel with Sahagún is that the same stonemasons and Mudéjar *alarifes* were re-employed. In San Pedro de Dueñas the aisle on the Gospel side was used for the public while the other two were reserved for the nuns.

The place is mentioned between the years 973 and 976; in 1076, the abbess was doña Urraca, and a donation was made to her in 1086 in the name of the king; but it only came to be called de las Dueñas after 1107. The epitaph of the Abbot don Diego de Sahagún reads: "*Monasterium Sancti Petri de Dominabus construxit et moniales ibidem instituit ...*". In another document of 1126 we find the following: "*Basilica fundata extat super crepidinem aluei que dicitur ceia secus stratam in quo loco permanet ecclesia miro honore fabricata in qua presidet domna tarasia abbatisa cum magno agmine monachorum*".

The church, which belongs to a type known as "*de peregrinación*" (pilgrimage church), can be related to the Monastery in Sahagún. Similar to the Church of San Tirso in the same place or in Santervás nearby, it clearly shows how, after the Romanesque style remained unattainable – first because of economic and social reasons, and later due to the lack of the workforce and craftsmen required for the construction of the great monasteries and cathedrals of the region – we witness the emergence and rapid development of an efficient and financially convenient local workforce made up solely of the Mudéjars. They worked all over the region and other workshops took over at a later stage: not only brick and plaster craftsmen in the 15th century, but also carpenters in the 16th century. We can see evidence of this in the vaulting of the Church of San Pedro de Dueñas, where plasterers, who combine Gothic motifs with Mudéjar themes, worked the geometric strapwork.

VIII.3 SANTERVÁS DE CAMPOS

VIII.3.a Parish Church

15 km on the LE 942 turning off in Melgar de Arriba. If the Church is closed, ask for Sra Jani or Sr. Hipólito. Tel: 987 785097.

This Parish Church is dedicated to the saints Gervasio and Protasio and sits on top of a hill within the area of influence of the Monastery of Sahagún. Of the three apses, the

ITINERARY VIII Consequences of the Birth of Gothic Cathedrals: Working with Brick
Villalón de Campos

central one is built in Romanesque masonry, with attached columns and figurative corbels under the eaves. The two side apses and the interior of the central one are in brickwork, again suggestive of the building crisis in the early 12th century, coinciding approximately with the death of Alfonso VI in 1109, and with the beginning of the instability that led to the wars between Castile and Aragón. The decoration of the brick is very unusual. The lower frieze of the apse on the Epistle side – just as the interior of the main apse – utilises niches and responds in brick, something which also appears in French Romanesque and in some examples of the Romanesque art of upper Aragón, combined with raked courses and semicircular blind arches. Meanwhile, the apse on the Gospel side has two bands of semicircular blind arches and eaves with double coving, and the straight section has a frieze of interlaced arches.

In 1130, the church and the village were donated to the Monastery of Sahagún. The stonemasons who worked on this church are the same as those who worked in Sahagún, as can be seen from the workmanship on some of the capitals in both places.

VIII.4 **VILLALÓN DE CAMPOS**

Villalón was resettled by a Mozarab called Alón according to some chroniclers, or by others, by a Christian called Alfón or Alonsi. Fernando III and Fernando IV granted commercial privileges to the town and Juan II gave it to don Rodrigo Alonso Pimentel, the Count of Benavente, in 1434. The successors of don Rodrigo were the patrons responsible for the town's most important buildings.

The commercial development here resulted in the design of squares and porticos, both of which were very useful for agricultural transactions. The wealth and patronage of the Benavente family is evident in the churches built here and their contents.

VIII.4.a **Church of San Miguel**

17 km through Villacarralón or on the VA 930. Visits can be arranged through the Parish. Tel: 983 740041. Open from 1 April–1 October, visits can also be arranged through the Tourist Office. Tel: 983 740011.

Parish Church, central apse, Santervás de Campos.

ITINERARY VIII *Consequences of the Birth of Gothic Cathedrals: Working with Brick*

Villalón de Campos

Church of San Miguel, interior, Villalón de Campos.

The Church of San Miguel is an important Gothic building either dating from the end of the 13th century or beginning of the 14th. Gothic remains can still be seen in the lower part of the tower and in the chapel, which may be dated any time after 1258. The building works continued between the end of the 14th century and beginning of the 15th, resulting in a brick building of three aisles on eight-sided pillars, which form four pointed arches with covered *extrados*. The aisles on the Epistle and Gospel sides finish in a polygonal brick apse with *estribos* on the exterior: the central aisle must have been similar, although later alterations eliminated all evidence of it.

The most important thing about the church is that the brick walls have retained their original painting, which imitated perfectly brick facings on white plasterwork, while false spans and windows repeated the forms of a clerestory. The polychromed *par y nudillo* ceiling is decorated with tracery, small crosses and heraldic elements. These latter, which celebrate the patronage of don Rodrigo Alonso Pimentel, Count of Benavente, and of his wife, Leonor Enríquez, the granddaughter of Enrique II with the quartered shield, was later commonly used by the royal family, and *el ala* (the wing), the symbol and nickname of the family and subsequently of the town.

When the first count of Benavente renounced his allegiance to his lord the King of Portugal, for injuries that the king had done to him, the king said: "*A bird in the hand is worth more than vultures on the wing*", to which don Juan Pimentel replied: "*On the wing is worth more*". This is where the nickname "the wing" comes from.

Inside the church there is also evidence of the patronage of the Bishop of León, don Juan Rodríguez, who in a letter dated 12th July 1422 wrote that "*he used cut stone to build the tower* that today has and his [coat of] arms to be seen which are a fleur-de-lis, the retable and the choir". These fleurs-de-lis are repeated on the ceiling.

At the end of the 15th century, a new aisle was opened up in the church, breaking through the wall on the Epistle side and at that point made of brick, with ribbed vaulting. The work may have been commissioned or paid for by the fifth count, don Alonso de Pimentel and his wife, Ana de Velasco Herrera, who held the title of count between 1499 and 1527. It is probable that this work was undertaken at the same time as the church was converted into a collegiate church in 1513, when the count and his wife were also responsible for the *alfarje* under the choir loft.

Also of great interest are the remains of the 16th-century coffered ceiling in the Chapel of the Rosary, which was later reused. Due to the quality of the caissons and the gilding work, it may very well have been the ceiling of the sanctuary or of the memorial chapel of Bishop Barco, whose marble tomb is on the Gospel side of the church.

This church is possibly one of the most representative of the Gothic influence on the Mudéjar art and architecture in Castilla-León, where the colour of the walls, certain ornamental brickwork, ceilings from different periods and the original paintwork have all been well preserved.

The link is evident between the Mudéjar artists who worked here and those who had built the Church of San Andrés in Aguilar de Campos in Valladolid some years earlier, under the patronage of the Almirantes of Castile.

VIII.5 MAYORGA DE CAMPOS (optional)

There are two historical facts, which in artistic terms have influenced Mayorga de Campos. The first is its dependence on the Monastery of Sahagún, against which the villagers rebelled in 1270, destroying the houses and palaces of the abbot. The second is their dependence on the Counts of Benavente after 1430.

Most of the walls and the fortress built by Fernando II have disappeared, except the Puerta del Sol, or Sun Gate; little remains of its parish churches. Some are closed for religious services and others have been put to various and inappropriate uses. The basic trait of the churches in Mayorga is their semicircular apse, in the Romanesque manner, built with cob walls and plastered over. This is a characteristic repeated in the other churches of the area, such as the one in Castrobol (Valladolid).

VIII.5.a Church of Santa María de Arbás

23 km on the N 610. The Church is under repair at present

The Church of Santa María de Arbás is a National Monument not only because of the carpentry work, but also for the plasterwork. Mentioned as San Nicolás de Arbás, in 1537, this church, along with the primitive Church of San Andrés documented since 1191, formed part of the Parish of Santa María. It has two aisles, the principal one with the characteristic semicircular apse with cob walls, while on the Epistle side are the

ITINERARY VIII *Consequences of the Birth of Gothic Cathedrals: Working with Brick*
Villalpando

Church of Santa María la Antigua, general view, Villalpando.

Chapel of San Andrés and the portico.

The church is covered with a wooden armadura of the *par y nudillo* type, and in the *arrocabes* there are Renaissance devices such as triglyphs, arches and rosettes. The Gospel side aisle has a roof of single *limas* with cross braces, which ends in the sanctuary in a three-part coffer-shaped wooden ceiling inlaid with metals and unpainted. At the entrance to the nave there is a coat of arms depicting an eagle with outspread wings and a heraldic device of two chequered vessels with the heads of serpents. These may relate to a daughter of the fifth Count of Benavente, who was married to Juan Fernández Manrique, third Marquis of Aguilar. What is strange, though, is that while the coats of arms of the Aguilar appear those of the Pimentel do not.

Perhaps the most representative work of the church is the Chapel of San Andrés on the Epistle side, with an inlaid coffered ceiling of double *limas* with strapwork and cone shaped pendentives. The frieze or *arrocabe* that runs around beneath it is a good example of 15th-century plasterwork in the area. The arms and inscription refer to don Pero García Dévila Gómez and his wife, who ordered this chapel to be built in 1422.

The use of geometric motifs with multifoil arches, diamond-shaped networks and plant motifs of Hispano-Muslim and Christian origin seems to have originated in Seville in the early 15th century. From here it reached Castile, either through the influence of the Velasco family in their palace in Medina de Pomar and the Tower of Lomana (both in the province of Burgos) or perhaps through the examples in Mayorga (1422), Valladolid (1429) and Sahagún (1455), in this latter case in the valley of the River Cea in León.

VIII.6 **VILLALPANDO**

Very near the road to Villalpando is the village of Castroverde de Campo. A lunch break here is recommended.

Unfortunately, all the churches of Villalpando have suffered various mutilations over the course of time. What remains there of the Mudéjar period can be seen principally on the exterior of the sanctuary at the head of the church, since the rest of the walls and ceilings have disappeared. These exteriors are interesting because they are flat and made of brick, a unique shape in the Mudéjar of Castilla-León. They came about when the Mudéjar *alarifes* who were working here decided to copy the Romanesque variants of the flat end wall in the city of Zamora (in San Cipriano) and in the valley of the River Tera.

VIII.6.a **Church of San Nicolás** (optional)

40 km, take the N 610 to Villanueva del Campo and then the ZA 511. Arrange a visit through the Parish of the Inmaculada. Tel: 980 660272.

Although the present parish church of San Nicolás has undergone excessive renovations over time, it nonetheless retains its frontage wall with blind arcades on two levels. Initially it was a classic Sahagún-type of brick church with three naves. It is said that the church was built in 1164 by order of the brothers Lorenzo and Domingo Pedro, canons of San Isidoro of León.

VIII.6.b **Church of Santa María la Antigua**

A National Monument since 1935, the church is in a very poor state of conservation. Visits can be arranged through the Parish of la Inmaculada.

The Church of Santa María la Antigua is 12th-century Mudéjar with three naves in brick of the second style of Sahagún. It has three apses with two levels of blind arcades in brick, those on the higher level larger in proportion. It is finished off with a frieze of raked courses and a *scotia* under the eaves. The interior decoration has two similar levels, which converge in an apse vault. The aisles and part of the apses were renovated some time later, but now neither the roof nor the vaulting is preserved. The plasterwork realised by the Corral de Villalpando family has also disappeared. The tower and part of the original walls can still be seen at the base, since this church, along with others in the town had a dual religious and defensive function. This wall is from the end of the 12th century and possibly dates from the resettlement of the town in 1170.

The Lagoons of Villafáfila
18 km from Villalpando is the National Hunting Reserve of the Lagunas de Villafáfila, which has been declared an Area of Special Interest for Birds; remarkable for the presence of black winged stilts, great bustards, little bustards, black bellied sandgrouse, lesser kestrel, common crane and avocet. The colony of bustards (otis tarda) may reach 1,500 or 1,800 birds and is undoubtedly the main attraction of the area.

Urueña
211 km on the N VI there is the turn-off to the unusual and enchanting village of Urueña. The village, strategically situated on top of a hill, has conserved its medieval appearance inside the walls. Different crops are cultivated at the foot of the hill and there is a magnificent panoramic view over the countryside, which changes completely according to the season. Of the four museums in the village, the Museo de Campanas (Museum of the Bells) is the most interesting.

ITINERARY VIII   *Consequences of the Birth of Gothic Cathedrals: Working with Brick*

Toro

Church of San Lorenzo, apse, Toro.

VIII.7 TORO

Resettled from the 10th century, in the 16th century, Toro was a city which was *"prosperous, fertile and with good wine"* according to the historian Marineo Sículo. There are remains of the concrete walls, trimmed with calyons, which Gómez Moreno describes as *Moriscos* (Moorish), and which protected three communities: a Christian one, a Jewish one and a Mudéjar one. It is thought that Samuel Haleví, the famous treasurer of Pedro I, was born into the Jewish community here. As far as the existence of Muslims is concerned, paying attention to the buildings they left rather than to their names or social positions is more fruitful, although in the census of the Inquisition in 1581 and 1589, *Moriscos* from Granada are mentioned.

What is decisive in Toro is the brick architecture, which makes this town one of the most important centres of Mudéjar art and architecture in Castilla-León. In contrast to the Romanesque Collegiate Church in stone, the apses of the churches of Toro have blind arcades in brick.

The stone foundations of the churches do not recall the first style of Sahagún, rather, the aim of this simple system of laying foundations was to insulate the building against the damp ground. In general, the walls of these churches correspond to the 12th and 13th centuries, while their roofs, where they have been preserved, belong to the 15th and 16th centuries. There is a certain influence of the Church of San Lorenzo, in the same town, with its double arcade on the exterior of the apse and long continuous friezes in the nave, as is usual in the sanctuaries and naves of other churches in Toro.

VIII.7.a Church of San Lorenzo

50 km on the N VI until the C 519. The Church is under restoration presently, but visits can be arranged through the Tourist Office. Tel: 980 691862.

The Church of San Lorenzo has one nave with single and double blind arcades on the exterior, tiny windows and squared frames in raked brick. On the Gospel side of the sanctuary are the tombs of Beatriz de Fonseca (died c.1487) and of her husband Pedro de Castile (died c.1492), the grandson of Pedro I of Castile. The wooden *par y nudillo* ceiling with anchor ties and the balcony of the choir loft are works dating from the end of the 15th century.

VIII.7.b Church of Santa María de la Vega

Also called Cristo de las Batallas or the Church of Christ of the Battles. 1.5 km on the road to the station. The Church is not in use for services. Open Sat 16.00–18.00. Visits can be arranged through the Tourist Office.

The Church of Santa María de la Vega, also known as Christ of the Battles, is on the outskirts of Toro, beside the River Duero. There is evidence that it was handed over to the Order of the Knights Hospitallers by the Bishop of Zamora in 1208. It has one nave with high double arcades, except for the gable end, which is plain. The doors in the sides have pointed arches and cove mouldings. It has pointed barrel vaults and the interior is decorated with two levels of blind arcades. The scenes of the Coronation of the Virgin were painted in distemper at the time of the

Church of Santa María de la Vega, general view, Toro.

ITINERARY VIII *Consequences of the Birth of Gothic Cathedrals: Working with Brick*

Toro

Convent of Santa Sofía, Sanctuary ceiling, Toro.

Catholic Monarchs, and an inscription on the cornice alludes to an altarpiece that was ordered by don Rodrigo de Ulloa and doña Aldonza de Castile in 1481.

VIII.7.c **Convent of Santa Sofía**

Enclosed Convent of the Order of Santa Sofía Premostratense. Opening hours: 10.00–13.00 and 16.00–20.00. To visit the tower and patio, ask at the torno or revolving window.

The Convent of Santa Sofía dates from the early 14th century and is built on the site of the houses of doña María de Molina. In 1316 it received the goods of the Abbot of San Andrés, don Nuño Pérez, and of his brother, don Alfón, Bishop of Coria, on condition that the benefactors would be buried there. Both the original houses and the 13th-century door were preserved until they were destroyed in a fire at the beginning of the 20th century. Nevertheless, the ceilings of the church are still in perfect condition: an eight-sided *armadura* in the sanctuary and another eight-sided *armadura* over the nave. These are works from the 16th century and nothing is known about either the craftsmen or the patrons.

FAIRS AND MARKETS

Pedro Lavado Paradinas

The inadequate transport systems and even worse roads in medieval Spain made it essential to build up stocks of merchandise in specific places on the peninsula from where the goods were transported two or three times a year. The organisation of Trade Fairs meant exemption from the payment of taxes, which obviously stimulated the activity of both merchants and their customers. From the time of Alfonso VII, abundant royal privileges were conceded authorising fairs in different places in Castile. Alfonso VIII granted Sahagún a fair that was to be celebrated on the Feast of the Nativity of Our Lady on 8th September. For the celebration of these events, normally a date between the Feast of St Michael on 29th September and that of St Martin on 11th November was chosen, since that way the products of the harvest and the vintage would be available for sale.

A decree of the *Partidas* of Alfonso X el Sabio reminds us that the authority to establish new fairs and markets corresponds to the King's wishes:
"*Fairs or markets which the people use to sell or buy or exchange should not be held in any other places, except where they have always been held. Nevertheless, if the King should by his privilege authorise that new places might be opened to fairs, the fairs can take place there*".

The exemption from taxes is mentioned in the *Tratos y contratos de mercaderes y tratantes* of Fray Tomás del Mercado: "*A fair signifies something free, isolated and economic, because anything sold in those places at those times does not pay a tribute.*"

Arcaded street, Villalón de Campos.

The fairground was protected by a special judicial regime that guaranteed law and order for the duration of the fair. Anyone who breached the peace was ordered to pay a fine and suffer other punishments. The city that enjoyed this privilege was guaranteed rapid commercial and industrial development, since it could count on an outlet for the products of its *alfoz*, or district, and with the basic products that reached it from all around it could manufacture equipment and consumer goods. The fairs offered outlets for both local agricultural produce and products produced by transhumant herdsmen, such as wool, butter and cheese.

From the 15th century onwards, the fairs in Castile became very important and experienced considerable growth. Segovia, Valladolid, Alcalá, Salamanca, Seville, Villalón, Medina de Rioseco and Medina del Campo were where the most important fairs were held.

Medina del Campo was without doubt the most important of all. Its precise origin is not easy to define. It is thought that it may have been don Fernando de Antequera who created it when he governed Castile in the name of don Juan II. The chronicler don Alvaro de Luna comments on this fair: *"And at that time there was held the fair in Medina del Campo, where there come and meet together great numbers of peoples of different nations, from Castilla and from other kingdoms …"*.

It was the biggest trading centre in Spain, which to some extent determined the way the city developed. The opening up of squares with arcades for the market and churches, meant that ceremonies could be followed from a distance by merchants and buyers without any need to abandon their stalls in the public square.

Added to this were a flourishing number of private houses, the property of some of the most important merchants, such as the Dueñas or Quintanilla families.

At these fairs, bills of exchange were a common currency, an ancient practice where the presence, patent or not, of the community was always supposed. Another method of ensuring the mutual confidence between buyers and sellers was the existence of money changers and bankers whose job it was to make all the coins in use in commercial transactions available. The pragmatic decrees of 1551 and 1552, which intended to regulate the issue of bills of exchange by forbidding them to be carried over from one fair to another, was one of the reasons for the decline of the fair in Medina. Later on, at the time of Felipe II, taxes were increased so that the fiscal advantages and exemptions of the medieval period disappeared; and since they could not use credit, the merchants of Medina abandoned the fair. The creation of a bank specifically for the fair was an attempt to revive the commercial life of Medina, but it did not have the required effect. Finally, its transfer to Burgos put an end to the most famous fair of medieval and Renaissance Spain.

The by-laws of Medina del Campo in 1421 established 100 tax-free days for the purposes of the fair. Later, the months of May and October were fixed because of the advantages for the agriculture and livestock industries, and in addition, so as not to interfere with the dates when fairs were held in other towns that enjoyed the same privileges.

In Medina de Rioseco it was the Enriquez family, and in Villalón de Campos and Benavente, the Counts of Benavente who obtained the royal privileges to hold fairs. Don Alonso Pimentel, Count of Benavente, obtained permission for two fairs in Villalón from King Felipe el Hermoso. One was at Lent and the other after the Mysteries or Easter. These fairs each lasted 20 days and exempted the merchants from taxes. On the death of Felipe el Hermoso, the Count of Benavente tried to find favour with the regent Fernando el Católico, who granted him 200,000 *maravedies* and confirmed the fair in Villalón. In 1519, because it had taken sides with the cause of the *Comuneros*, Villalón lost the privileges of its fair; these privileges then passed to Medina de Rioseco, where they remained until the 17th century. In 1644 Felipe IV tried to get the fair back for Villalón through a decree issued in Saragossa; this gave the town the privilege *de jure* of not paying taxes on either fountains or rebuilding, since the town was so densely populated that the houses were deteriorating over the cellars and silos, but his attempt failed.

In Medina de Rioseco fairs were held in April and August and there was a free market granted by the Catholic Monarchs in 1477. This, in addition to the cloth industries and other commercial activities, meant that the town flourished until the 18th century. The calles de la Rúa and Pañeros are reminders of this activity, where the fairs and markets were held under the wooden-pillared arcades. Today it is still easy to imagine the stalls and *zaquizamíes*, where the merchants *"with sackcloths, matting and boards put up on top of the stalls tried to make it darker within so that the buyer could not properly see the goods"*. Confronted with a complaint, the Council of Medina de Rioseco would take action, without any right to appeal, and remove the offending elements from the stalls.

Another commercial phenomenon that has left its mark on many cities in Castile are its markets. In Castile, there were monthly and weekly markets, both for agricultural supplies and for other more restricted merchandise. Apart from the mandatory keeping of the peace for these markets, the exemptions from tithes and tolls were fundamental for their development. In Castilla-León, the everyday markets were given the Arabic name *azog* or *azogue* as is still reflected in some of the place names in the urban geography of the region: el Azoguejo in Segovia and the variants Azogue or Azoague in the Zamora area (Santa María de Azogue in Benavente and Villanueva de Azoague nearby). In fact in Benavente the two terms coexist: Santa María de Azogue and San Juan del Mercado, as if to distinguish between two types of market: one with Islamic and the other with Christian roots.

The market cross which presided over these markets was a symbol of royal power *de jure* a reminder of the ever-present justice and authority and the transformation of the cross, which had originally been put in place there as an instrument of public and exemplary punishment. A representative example of these is still evident in Villalón de Campos. The *zabazoques*, or justices of the peace, were the eyes and ears of the judges and inspectors of the markets, and they had officials or bailiffs at their disposal who were responsible for the control of weights and measures and for the upkeep of law and order.

ITINERARY IX

Traces of the Past: Churches, Synagogues and Palaces

María Teresa Pérez Higuera

IX.1 TOLEDO
    IX.1.a Puerta del Sol
    IX.1.b Mosque of Cristo de la Luz
    IX.1.c Church of San Román
    IX.1.d Synagogue of Santa María la Blanca
    IX.1.e Synagogue of el Tránsito
    IX.1.f Palace of the Taller del Moro
    IX.1.g Palaces of the Toledo and Ayala Families
    IX.1.h Church of San Andrés
    IX.1.i Church of Santiago del Arrabal

Mudéjar plasterwork in Toledo

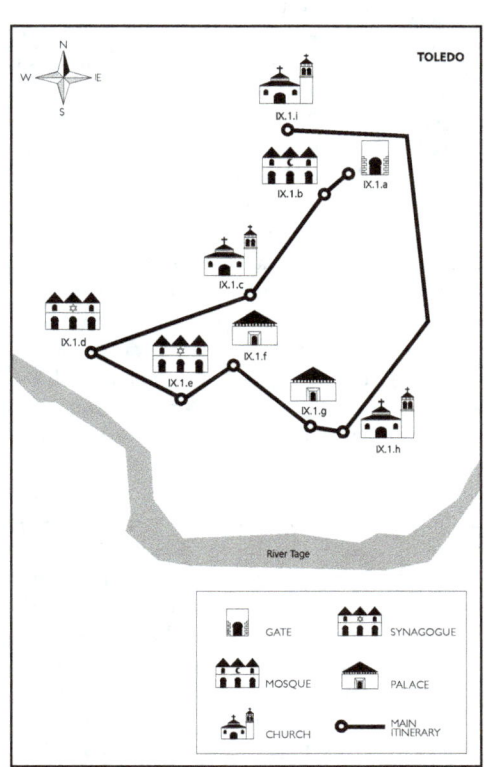

Synagogue of Santa María la Blanca, Toledo.

ITINERARY IX   Traces of the Past: Churches, Synagogues and Palaces

Church of Santiago del Arrabal, apses and tower, Toledo.

Among the many Mudéjar buildings conserved in Toledo, those chosen for this itinerary are the most representative to illustrate both the various functions of churches, palaces, synagogues or gates in the city walls as well as to explore the stylistic evolution of these models. In accordance with this concept, this itinerary includes a church that represents the Mudéjar of Toledo – Santiago del Arrabal – as well as other buildings documenting the various construction processes. For example, the adaptation of a mosque as a Christian church – Cristo de la Luz, a church that corresponds to the early Mudéjar phase – San Román – and another – San Andrés, which today is the result of many later reforms, although, largely, it still keeps its Mudéjar appearance. In the case of the two synagogues – Santa María la Blanca and el Tránsito – the only two conserved in Toledo, their interest lies in their marked difference from each other, both in the architectonic models they represent and in their decorations.

To become more familiar with Mudéjar palaces, one of them – the Taller del Moro – hosting also the Museum of Toledo, has a Mudéjar interior; with regard to examples of palace exteriors, the doorways of the palaces of the Ayala family have been selected, situated in the Plaza del Rey don Pedro. Finally, the Puerta del Sol is an example of the Mudéjar-period rebuilding of part of the fortified precinct of the city.

As these buildings are in different parts of the city, this itinerary leads visitors through the streets to see the Islamic traces in the urban plan and encourages them to appreciate the various functions of the different sectors – commercial, residential, the Jewish Quarter – which defined Toledo as a Mudéjar city, heir of the earlier Hispano-Muslim Toledo.

The ancient capital of the kingdom of the Visigoths, Toledo was conquered by the Muslims in the year 711 and remained under Islamic domination until 1085, when Toledo first submitted to the central power installed in Córdoba, and which, then, from 1031, became the capital of a *taifa* governed by the Banu Din-l-Nun. Incorporated into the crown of Castile in 1085, the conditions of the capitulation guaranteed the Muslims who remained in the city the right to retain their goods and religion as well as their own language and judgement according to their own laws. These guarantees explain the large number of Mudéjars, who, along with the Jews and the older nuclei of *Mozárabes*, formed the basis of the population, which grew as new resettlers from Castile, León, Galicia or France arrived.

In this way, Toledo became the prototype of what Torres Balbás called the "Mudéjar cities", the result of the transformation of Muslim cities once occupied by Christians. Gradually, the city adapted itself to the way of life of its new inhabitants who built churches, streets and arcaded squares. However, Toledo always kept hold of the traces of its Islamic past, which still exist today in its narrow twisting streets, cul-de-sacs and in the famous *cobertizos*, which like covered alleyways join the upper floors of the houses on both sides of the street. The unique attraction of Toledo, however, is undoubtedly that it has been able to perpetuate the memory of the different sectors that make up the Muslim city. These are defined by their specific functions: *alcazaba* (citadel), *zocos* (markets) and dwelling houses in the *medina*, the *arrabales* (outskirts) outside the walls, the cemeteries and the *almunias* or vegetable gardens. Even today, the commercial area of the city is easily distinguishable from the residential areas and the *arrabales* or outskirts. The former *zocos* were transformed into the markets around the cathedral, which occupied the site of the main mosque. The northern *arrabal* and the Jewish Quarter remain in the same place they occupied in the 10th century. In addition, in the *cigarrales* or country houses that surround the city, we can still see the survival of the *almunias* of the Muslims.

The identification of the city with its Muslim past justifies the term "Toledo Mudéjar" which is applied to its architecture. This is the sense in which we

Mosque of Cristo de la Luz, apse, Toledo.

ITINERARY IX   *Traces of the Past: Churches, Synagogues and Palaces*
Toledo

Cobertizo *or covered passageway, Barrio de San Blas, Toledo.*

should interpret the contraposition of the Gothic art of the Cathedral, imposed by the Episcopal power, and related to the European Christian West, and the preference for the Mudéjar style in the palaces, houses and religious buildings used by the people, such as in the parish churches and synagogues.

In the process of its formation, an initial stage of the Mudéjar style of Toledo can be distinguished that corresponds to the 12th century, when the insecurity of Castile, threatened with assaults from the Almoravids and Almohads, limited architectonic works to the reconstruction of the ancient Mozarab parish churches and the adaptation of some mosques for Christian worship. These works make up what is called the "first phase" of Mudéjar in Toledo, which is characterised by a certain archaism in some of the elements used, such as the semicircular horseshoe arch to divide the nave from the aisles and the reuse of Visigothic columns as supports. Later, after victory at Navas de Tolosa in 1212, the definitive consolidation of the conquest justified the construction of new buildings that clearly show the Castilian influence. The Mudéjar architectonic model is derived from the Romanesque, although it is always modified by the use of a local formula like the enclosed masonry bond, the brick decoration based on the combination of horseshoe and multifoil arches or interlaced arcades, the plasterwork facings of the interiors and the use of carved beams in ceilings and eaves. From the 14th century on the same traits as seen in the Nasrid architecture of Granada appears, visible above all in the extraordinary richness of the plasterwork that decorates both the palaces and synagogues of this period such as el Tránsito. This capacity to assimilate new forms explains precisely how Mudéjar art in Toledo managed to survive in the 15th and 16th centuries, and then coexisted closely with the end of the Gothic period and the introduction of the Italian Renaissance.

IX.1 TOLEDO

IX.1.a **Puerta del Sol**

In the calle Real del Arrabal. It is better to use the car park opposite the Puerta del Sol and then continue on foot.

Although the Puerta del Sol (Sun Gate) was completely rebuilt at the time of the Archbishop don Pedro Tenorio (1357–1399), it forms part of the fortified precinct that surrounded the Islamic *medina* and was the principal access gate from the northern suburbs from the 10th century. It is even possible that the horseshoe archway, which the Mudéjar construction made use of, dates from this period.

The gate is composed of a central section between two towers, one square, where it links to the wall, while the other tower is semicircular to defend it better from outside attacks. This military function, as well as providing permanent control over the entrance to the city, explains its internal structure: an upper floor used as a watchtower, with windows and three machicolations on the rounded tower and a flat roof above, level with the battlements. The gateway itself is of a fortified type, with a guardroom positioned in the separation between the lower horseshoe arch and the higher pointed one, and with a portcullis in the interior passageway, which is no longer there, but the slit into which it once fitted still visible. This defensive function is disguised partly by the brick façade that is embellished by friezes of interlaced arches, which repeat the ornamental scheme of the Mudéjar style in Toledo found in the churches and palaces. In this way, the military function is married to the concept of the monumental entrance inspired by the triumphal arch. In 1575, during the time of the Corregidor Tello, a medallion was added depicting the Virgin presenting St Ildefonso with a chasuble, as a symbolic element of Visigothic Toledo.

IX.1.b Mosque of Cristo de la Luz

In calle Cristo de la Luz. Go up the stairs on the right. Visits by arrangement with Sr. Manzanares. Tel: 925 223081.

This mosque, in fact, is two buildings adjoined to become one. One of the buildings is the former Mosque of Bab al-Mardum, which from its inscription dates it to 999 (390 of the Hegira). The building, which is on a square ground plan with a roof composed of nine small domes, has Islamic precedents in North Africa, and the characteristic features of its architecture link it directly with the work of the Caliphate era in the Córdoba Mosque.

Puerta del Sol, general view, Toledo.

ITINERARY IX   Traces of the Past: Churches, Synagogues and Palaces

Toledo

After the Conquest of Toledo by Alfonso VI in 1085, the mosque was consecrated as a Christian church; and in 1182, it was donated to the Order of the Knights of the Hospital of St John of Jerusalem and dedicated to the Holy Cross. The building of the apse adjoining the east end of the old mosque must date from this time. The decision to reuse older buildings including mosques, as churches, was usual in Toledo during the 12th century,

Mosque of Cristo de la Luz, painting of the interior, Toledo.

Church of San Román, detail of an arch, Toledo.

because of the instability caused by the constant threat of the Almoravids and Almohads, who were determined to reconquer the city. In the case of Cristo de la Luz, the joining together of the two buildings is resolved with absolute uniformity through the use of the same materials – brick and banded masonry – and by combining the same formal elements – horseshoe and multifoil arches – both of which prove that the 10th-century mosque was used as the model for the Mudéjar church. At the same time, the apse establishes a Toledo prototype, with a foundation of masonry and the upper part in brick. The decoration of the upper brick section comprises superimposed blind arcades of pointed horseshoe arches under other multifoil arches, separated by raked brick courses and with eaves resting on brick corbelling.

Conserved in the interior are the remains of murals representing the Pantocrator, and the Tetramorph, in the Romanesque tradition, and dated to the first half of the 13th century.

IX.1.c **Church of San Román**

Calle San Román. Follow the Cuesta de las Carmelitas and continue up to the Church of San Román, which is now the Museo de los Concilios y Cultura Visigoda (Museum of the Councils of Toledo and Visigothic Culture), and used for temporary exhibitions. Opening hours: 10.00–14.00 and 16.00–18.15, Sun and public holidays 10.00–14.00. Closed Mon.

It seems probable that the church already existed in Visigothic times, which would explain the reuse of various capitals belonging to this period in the Mudéjar building. In

ITINERARY IX *Traces of the Past: Churches, Synagogues and Palaces*
Toledo

the years immediately after the conquest of the city in 1085, the church was cited among the so-called "Latin parishes of the Christian cult". The family of the Illán belonged to it, a lineage connected to the kings of Castile, an ancestor of which had been the *caudillo* or military leader of Alfonso VI. This evidence proves the existence of a church before the year 1221, the date when it was consecrated by don Rodrigo Ximénez de Rada, Archbishop of Toledo, as is recorded in the *Anales Toledanos* (Annals of Toledo).

Keeping this information in mind, when examining the present building it is easy to distinguish two different architectural projects. One, which coincides with the main part of the nave, must belong to the church when it was in use in the 12th century. The type of horseshoe arch resting on brick pillars with attached columns corresponds to this period – the Visigothic columns and capitals mentioned above – along with the organisation of the upper part of the spans, which are not for the purposes of illumination, but simply lighten the load of the wall. These characteristics coincide with those of the other churches in Toledo from the so-called "first phase" of Toledo Mudéjar, like San Lucas, Santa Eulalia, or San Sebastián. The sanctuary belongs to a later phase of work, which may have coincided with the date of the consecration of the church in 1221. Here, in spite of the remodelling of the interior carried out in 1553 by Alonso de Covarrubias, there are still the remains of the exterior decoration of the primitive apse, with blind arcades following the Castilian model, which became the dominant style

from the 13th century, within the "second phase" of Toledo Mudéjar. Also dating from the 13th century are the murals, discovered in 1940, which in all likelihood were painted to unify the old aisles with the new sanctuary.

Although they are within the Romanesque tradition, certain details hint at the influence of the Islamic tradition, such as the use of imitation voussoirs in white and red on the arches of the nave, the multifoil arches of the windows and the plant motifs of the *ataurique* in the spandrels of the arches.

The tower, which must have been built at the end of the 13th century or in the early 14th century, is notable for its use of multifoil arches, which

Church of San Román, tower, Toledo.

ITINERARY IX   *Traces of the Past: Churches, Synagogues and Palaces*

Toledo

rest on small columns of vitrified ceramics, a solution, which although quite rare in Toledo is seen in some other buildings, for instance in the Tower of Santo Tomé.

Since 1971, the interior of the church has housed the Museum of the Councils of Toledo and Visigothic Culture.

IX.1.d Synagogue of Santa María la Blanca

Reyer Católicos 4. Taking the calle de San Clemente, walk down through the streets to the synagogue. Entrance fee. Open 10.00–14.00 and 15.30–18.00 (summer until 19.00).

The synagogue is situated in the old Jewish Quarter, which even in the Muslim period was an independent district surrounded by its own wall, the *madinat al-yahud* or City of Jews. During the late Middle Ages it was called the *Judería Mayor*, or the main Jewish Quarter. It was one of the most famous in Castile and existed until the expulsion of the Jews in 1492. There are documentary references to various synagogues in Toledo and this must have been one of them. From 1401 onwards when it was consecrated as a Christian church, it was dedicated to and called Santa María, but among the names cited in texts before this date the name for this building has not been definitely identified. Probably it was the *Sinagoga Mayor* or Main Synagogue, or perhaps the *Sinagoga Nueva* or New Synagogue. Whichever is the case, an examination of its artistic features dates it to the first half of the 13th century.

Santa María la Blanca is a unique building that attracts much discussion

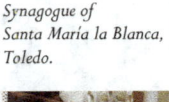
Synagogue of Santa María la Blanca, Toledo.

ITINERARY IX   Traces of the Past: Churches, Synagogues and Palaces
Toledo

as to whether to consider it Almohad or Mudéjar. The opinion that it is Almohad is based upon the evident parallelisms it has with other works from the Almohad period. The opinion that it is Mudéjar, which has become the generally accepted one in recent years, points out that not only is it from Toledo, which was already under Christian domination, but also that it is related to other Mudéjar buildings of Castile in the Monastery of Las Huelgas in Burgos.

Enclosed within plain exterior walls, the interior, on an irregular rectangular ground plan, divides into five aisles separated by horseshoe arches, drawn on a circumference very similar to those of San Román. However, the visual impression here is completely different because of the presence on the low pillars of large stuccowork capitals decorated with enormous pinecones, which Gómez-Moreno called *"a sovereign invention"* of the master carver who worked them. Both above and around the arches is delicate ornamentation mixing plant and geometric motifs, outstanding among which are the medallions with different strapwork designs. At the end of the aisles a sanctuary was introduced formed from three chapels, its interior decorated in the Renaissance style, and probably made between 1550 and 1556 and attributed to Alonso de Covarrubias.

IX.1.e Synagogue of el Tránsito

Calle Manuel Leví. Take calle Reyes Católicos. At present, it houses the Museo Sefardí (Sephardic Museum). Entrance fee. Open 10.00–13.45 and 16.00–17.45, Sun and public holidays 10.00–13.45. Closed Mon.

Synagogue of el Tránsito, detail of the plasterwork, Toledo.

The other synagogue conserved in Toledo is known as el Tránsito (the Assumption of the Virgin), a name that is also the consequence of its dedication to the Christian cult after the expulsion of the Jews in 1492. It was built around 1357 under the patronage of Samuel ha-Leví, the treasurer and councillor of King Pedro I of Castile, and a member of the ha-Leví Abulafía family, which had been established for generations in Toledo.

This building along with some adjoining rooms was used as the *yesibah* or school of religious teaching, it has a large rectangular room devoted to prayer, which in its eastern wall holds the *heckal* or tabernacle where the sacred scrolls of the Torah were kept.

ITINERARY IX   Traces of the Past: Churches, Synagogues and Palaces
Toledo

Palace of the Taller del Moro, interior, Toledo.

foil arches, some blind and others latticework, to let in the light; these act as supports for a splendid ceiling of the *par y nudillo* type.
On the south wall, the women's balconies have similarly conserved plasterwork to that of the main room.
In 1971, the Sephardic Museum was inaugurated in the building.

IX.1.f **Palace of the Taller del Moro**

Calle Taller del Moro. Follow the paseo del Tránsito to the calle Taller del Moro. Entrance fee. Opening hours: 10.00–14.00 and 16.00–18.30, Sun 10.00–14.00. Closed Mon.

This central rectangular room with a square alcove at each end is all that is left of what was once a Mudéjar palace. The patio garden, which was also rectangular, has also been destroyed. On the shorter sides of this garden were the principal rooms accessible via porticoes or galleries, one of which is this rectangular room. Certain elements show solutions typical in Nasrid domestic architecture, such as the use of the *arco angrelado*, or the placing of small latticework windows over the door for ventilation, as much as to filter the light entering the room. Additionally, the walls would have been decorated completely following the model of Hispano-Muslim living areas: a dado of tiles in the lower part and cloth or leather covering the upper walls; the square surrounds of the archways would have stood out in polychrome plasterwork, similar to the broad frieze that runs around the top of the room and the alcoves as a support for the ceiling. At present, with

To highlight this function the wall is covered with rich decorative plasterwork divided into three sections, of these the central one includes a niche with three small multifoil arches. The whole complex reveals evident parallels with Nasrid art in Granada, above all in the network of diamond-shaped patterns or *sebka*, the background of which is filled with tiny plant motifs, or *ataurique*, and in the cornice, *muqarnas* to finish it off.
On the other walls a broad frieze runs round the upper part, where plant motifs of Muslim inspiration are joined by naturalistic motifs such as vine or oak leaves, clearly inspired by the repertory of Gothic art in Toledo. Above this and around the whole room runs a gallery of multi-

the ornamentation of the dados and walls now lost, only the plasterwork remains that shows several different decorative systems. On the arches there is a simple network of diamond shapes filled with plant motifs, while on the upper frieze there is a strapwork pattern in which, as a substitute for some of the stars or wheels, there appear the arms of the Palomeque and Meneses families. All these clues have prompted scholars to identify the palace as one that belonged to Lope González Palomeque Lord of Villaverde, who was married to María Tellez de Meneses. In turn, this dates the work to between 1325 and 1350. Finally, the *alfices* that frame the arches have inscriptions on them, which complete the three basic elements of Islamic decoration – geometric, plant motifs and epigraphic – and in this case, present a clear expression of Mudéjarism; mixing Arabic characters which repeat praises and desires for prosperity, with Gothic lettering which copies in Latin the beginning of the Gospel of St John.

The first part of the name used today – *Taller* or Workshop – was given in the 16th century when the original owners no longer used it and rented it to the cathedral, which used the plot immediately next to it for cutting stone and the large room as a store. However, the origin for the other part of the name – *del Moro*, or the Moor's – is not known, although the street and nearby square are known by the same name. The Museum of Mudéjar was inaugurated here in 1963. Among the exhibits of Mudéjar craftsmanship from Toledo are outstanding examples of tiles, jars and well-heads in clay, some of them vitrified. In the right-hand alcove are some examples of carved wood, which came from different buildings in Toledo.

IX.1.g Palaces of the Toledo and Ayala Families

Plaza de Santa Isabel. Take calle Santa Úrsula and at the end turn left into San Marcos; then turn right into travesía de San Marcos, turn left along travesía de Santa Isabel and then right into the square. The Convent Church of Santa Isabel is open all day.

Palace of Pedro I, façade, Toledo.

ITINERARY IX   *Traces of the Past: Churches, Synagogues and Palaces*
Toledo

Convent of Santa Isabel de los Reyes, Apse of San Antolín, Toledo.

Although the interiors of the palaces are within the enclosed area of the Convent of Santa Isabel de los Reyes, which occupies one side, the small square really deserves a visit as it is one of the most typical and representative corners of Toledo's town plan, and an example of the continuous transformation of the medieval city. In the Islamic period the site lay in the district of the Dyers, which was still there in the 12th century, and from the 13th century was called the Old Dyers, as the workshops had been moved to the south of the city by then. Construction of the Parish Church of San Antolin probably took place around this same time. During a reconstruction at the beginning of the 16th century as the Conventual Church of the Monastery of Santa Isabel, a small Mudéjar apse was retained from the primitive church where the usual Toledo Mudéjar type is repeated, very similar to that of Cristo de la Luz.

In the Middle Ages, the palaces of the Toledo and Ayala families – two of the most important lineages of Castile from the mid-15th century – stood beside the church. All the members of these families, in turn, built their own houses on this land, of which four still survive today. These were donated in 1488 to found the convent. Still visible in the high walls is a small doorway, dating from the end of the 14th century, which belonged to the Palace of don Pedro Suárez de Toledo y Ayala. The door's decoration, made up of the owner's coat of arms, emphasises the combination of arch and lintel as the Mudéjar version of the Hispano-Muslim scheme that can be traced back to the façades of the Mezquita in Córdoba. Originally, on either side, small pilasters ending in brackets with figures of lions – very mutilated now – supported wooden eaves. This formula is considered a characteristic of Toledo; a variant of the same scheme, including the window on the upper floor, is repeated in the building commonly called the Palace of Pedro I on the other side of the street, which still conserves its original wooden eaves. Although named after King Pedro I of Castile, in fact, the palace once belonged to doña Teresa de Ayala, wife of Fernán Álvarez de Toledo, Lord of Higares, as is shown by the arms over the doorway. In the nearby travesía de Santa Isabel, another palace – that of doña Inés de Ayala – was linked to the palaces already mentioned by a *cobertizo*, a gallery passageway that can still be seen at street level. Here, the patio and part of one room are preserved. Finally, next to the present entrance to the church, are the remains of the doorway of yet another of the palaces, that of doña Juana Enríquez, granddaughter of the above-mentioned Inés de Ayala, who donated the entire complex of houses to found the convent.

IX.1.h Church of San Andrés

Calle Ave María. Go around to the end of the palace. Opening hours: 18.30–20.00, Sun and public holidays 09.00–13.30.

The present condition of the church is the result of successive artistic periods, all of which have left their mark, in a process that ran in parallel to the historical development of the city of Toledo itself. Probably there was already a church here in Visigothic times, to which a relief that now forms part of the façade and two pilasters in the interior must have once belonged. It was probably a Muslim mosque at the beginning of the 11th century, an era from which a memorial funerary stone dated 1001 has survived and, very possibly, the lower part of the mosque's tower. After the Conquest of Alfonso VI in 1085 and the building's consecration as a Christian church, the building caught fire in 1150, as is recorded in the Annals of Toledo. It must undergone repair straightaway, since in 1156, Mozarabic documents cite it.

Two parts of the church can be dated to the end of the 12th century and both are interesting because of the Almohad influence they show. This includes the doorway, which is unique in Toledo because of the type of small blind arcades in the frieze on the upper part, and two vaults of *muqarnas* in the transept, which can be related to others that exist in Las Huelgas in Burgos. Also corresponding to the Mudéjar period are three aisles with horseshoe arches in brick and a cloister that was destroyed several years ago.

A tomb from the last third of the 14th century in the Gospel side aisle is decorated with plasterwork depicting two enthroned figures against a background of plant motifs. This theme – one that can be interpreted as an allusion to the Blessed in Paradise – is repeated in other examples in Toledo,

Church of San Andrés, doorway, Toledo.

ITINERARY IX   *Traces of the Past: Churches, Synagogues and Palaces*
Toledo

Church of Santiago del Arrabal, aisle arches, Toledo.

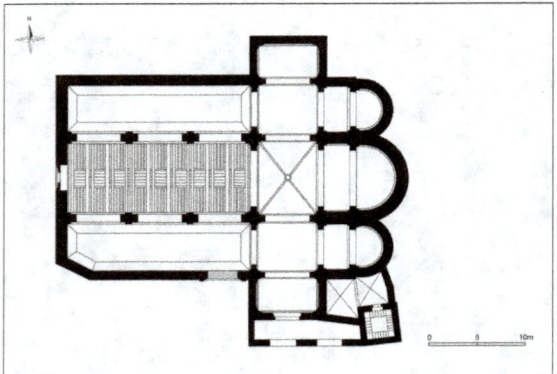

Ground plan of the Church of Santiago del Arrabal, Toledo.

which are also Mudéjar, and date from the same time.

A Gothic sanctuary with splendid ribbed vaulting was added to the church in the nave area; it was built from 1507 onwards by don Francisco de Rojas, ambassador of the Catholic Monarchs, as a burial chapel for his lineage.

Finally, between 1630 and 1637, the aisles underwent a reconstruction carried out by Francisco Espinosa, with the supports replaced by Classical-style Doric columns of the period, designed by Bernardo de Portillo. The appearance of the church today is the result of the restoration of 1975 that eliminated the portico adjoining the north side, which consequently hid the Mudéjar doorway.

IX.1.i Church of Santiago del Arrabal

Calle Real del Arrabal. Mass times: 08.00 and 19.30 (20.00 in summer), Sun 08.30, 12.30, 13.15 and 19.30.

The church is so-named because it is situated in the *arrabal*, or outskirts to the north, which were already in existence in the Muslim period. It is the only parish church in Toledo to have completely preserved the primitive structure, recovered after the restorations in 1958 and 1973. Also on this site were earlier buildings, as can be seen from the fragments of the Visigothic-period friezes built into the apse. It is possible that the *alminar* from another mosque was reused as the tower; this is suggested by the fact that it is an isolated construction in terms of the type of masonry used for the walls and the double horseshoe arch of the window. The top

208

ITINERARY IX   *Traces of the Past: Churches, Synagogues and Palaces*
Toledo

part of the bell tower must have been a mid-13th-century addition at the same time as the present church was under construction; this would help bear out popular belief that the work began in the year 1245 under the jurisdiction of King Sancho II of Portugal.

The model of the church is representative of what is called the "second phase" of the Mudéjar era in Toledo, characterised by the influence of the Romanesque of Castile on the type of ground plan with three semicircular apses and the incorporation of the transept into the nave. The same origin explains the decorative organisation in the sanctuary, which has a superimposed series of blind arches. These characteristics, clearly archaic at the time of building, are mixed with references to Gothic art, such as the slender proportions or the use of ribbed vaulting in the central section of the transept. The aisles are covered with wooden Mudéjar ceilings and the central aisle preserves an old *armadura* of *par y nudillo*. As far as the Islamic heritage is concerned, it is visible in the schemes used on the façades that are derived from the architecture of the caliphate of Córdoba. These include the horseshoe arch inside another multifoil one and a frieze of intercrossing arches above, with the outstandingly novel feature of two pilasters that frame the doorway, a solution frequently seen in later buildings in Toledo.

As you leave the city, we recommend driving up to the viewpoint near the Parador Nacional, from where there is a spectacular panoramic view of the city and the curves of the river. The best time to do this is at sunset.

Church of Santiago del Arrabal, cross section, Toledo.

Church of Santiago del Arrabal, aisle arches, Toledo.

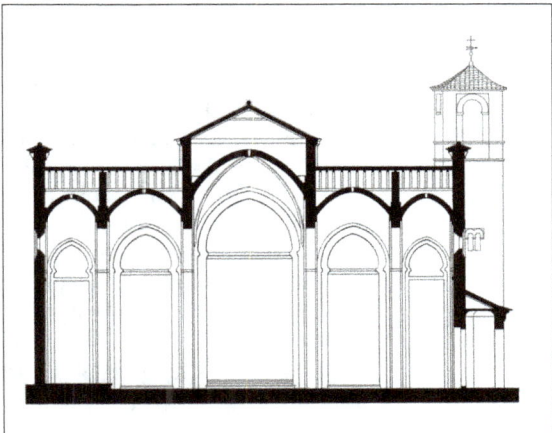

MUDÉJAR PLASTERWORK IN TOLEDO

María Teresa Pérez Higuera

Franciscan Convent of la Concepción, Chapel of San Jerónimo plasterwork arch, originally from the Palace of Pedro I. Detail of peacock, Toledo.

The use of plasterwork to cover the interior walls of buildings was a common decorative system in Hispano-Muslim art, and, as such, plaster was much utilised in Mudéjar architecture. The examples that have survived have lost their polychrome features, but originally the plasterwork was coloured with an abundance of red and blue. This allowed the plasterwork to imitate the tapestries and silk hangings that adorned the walls in the rooms of palaces, with the advantage that plaster was much cheaper and more resistant than cloth.

Interest in Toledo plasterwork is due above all to the fact that a whole repertory of unique motifs was created for it, which then spread out beyond the immediate geographical area, up to the point where much of the work found in the north of Castile and Andalucía can be classified as the work of master craftsmen from Toledo. In addition, the dating — exact in some cases and approximate in others — allows us to understand the evolution of the themes used, from the remains of the oldest, which correspond to the 11th century, to the typical ones of the Renaissance period, with some from the mid-15th century in between.

Generally, the study of plasterwork in Toledo allows us to establish two main stages. In the first, the elements of Islamic origin predominate. This can be appreciated above all in the decoration with small plant motifs reminiscent of the Almoravid repertory, such as those found in Santa María la Blanca or that preserved in one of the palaces of the Convent of Santa Clara. At times, these motifs are mixed with tracery panels that derive from the Almohad tradition as can be seen in several tombs in the cloister of the Franciscan Convent of the Concepción. These characteristics survived until the first half of the 14th century, in the so-called Salón de don Diego located in the Plaza de la Magdalena and in the Taller del Moro, although they also include motifs similar to those used in Nasrid art. From the mid-14th century and after the decoration in the Synagogue of

Church of San Andrés, detail of Sepulchre plasterwork, Toledo.

el Tránsito (in around 1357) other forms directly inspired by naturalistic Gothic floral motifs, such as the vine or oak leaf, joined the Islamic repertoire. This combination defines the Toledo repertory in works such as the Salón de Mesa and several rooms in the palaces of the Ayala family in Santa Isabel de los Reyes. A characteristic and original note from the final stages of the 14th century is the presence of figures in flat silhouette. Figures, ranging from peacocks to people, include examples of the former seen in the arch of the Chapel of San Jerónimo in the Convent of la Concepción and others outside Toledo: in Tordesillas and in the Alcázar in Seville. The silhouettes of people, on the other hand, appear in what is called the Arco del Obispo in the Cuesta de San Justo; on a tomb in the Church of San Andrés and in a frieze preserved in the interior of the Seminario Menor in the Plaza de San Andrés. This last is an exceptional example since it still has remains of the polychrome decoration. Examples from the mid-15th century include motifs from the Flamboyant Gothic period, such as those in the Palace of Fuensalida Those from the Renaissance belong to the so-called Cisneros style, and one of the most representative examples of this can be seen in the Chapter House in the Cathedral in Toledo.

ITINERARY X
First day

Noble and Monastic Patronage

María Pilar Mogollón Cano-Cortés

This itinerary is part of the programme "**Gateway to the Mediterranean**", co-funded by the European Union within the framework of the Pilot Project Spain-Portugal-Morocco, Art. 10 FEDER.

X.1 GUADALUPE
- X.1.a Royal Monastery of Our Lady of Guadalupe
- X.1.b College of Humanities or Grammar and Choir School (optional)
- X.1.c Grange at Mirabel

X.2 LLERENA
- X.2.a Tower of the Parish Church of Nuestra Señora de la Granada
- X.2.b House of Zapata – Residence of the Court of the Inquisition
- X.2.c House of the Prior
- X.2.d Houses in the Old Quarter

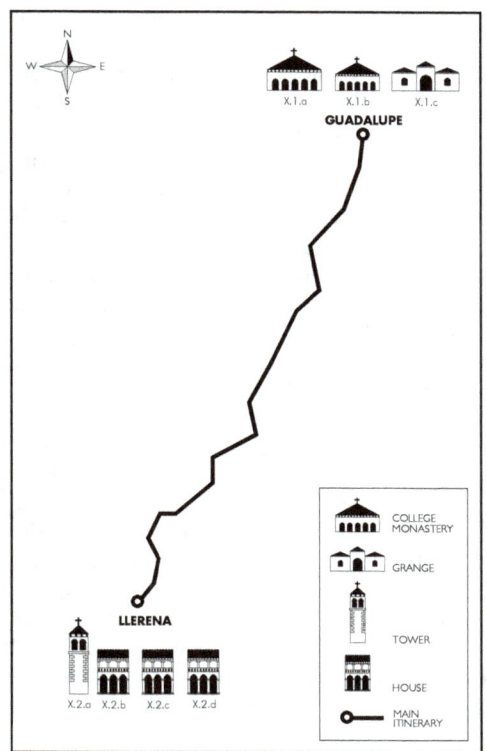

Royal Monastery of Nuestra Señora de Guadalupe, central temple of the Mudéjar Cloister or Cloister of the Miracles.

ITINERARY X   *Noble and Monastic Patronage*

Monastery of Santa María de Tentudía, general view, Calera de León.

During the period of Almohad domination in al-Andalús, what is now Extremadura was the military frontier between the Christians to the north of the Tajo and the Muslims to the south of the Sierra Morena. The conglomeration in Extremadura, therefore, played an essentially military function, as can be seen from the important Almohad defence systems that survive at strategic points, such as Cáceres or Badajoz, or on a smaller scale in Montemolín and Reina.

The definitive possession of this extensive border area was of great importance, not least for the definition of the political and ecclesiastical boundaries of the crowns of Castilla-León. In the mid-13th century, Transierra having been definitively reconquered and, with the aim of consolidating the advance of the Christians in Andalucía, a large part of what is nowadays the region of Extremadura, at that time practically uninhabited, was given over to the control and power of different Lords. Large areas also remained under the power of the Military Orders of the Temple, Alcantara, and Santiago (St James). The first of these orders disappeared at the beginning of the 14th century and its possessions passed into the hands of the other two, increasing their power, as well as that of some of the land-owning lords who enlarged their territories in the 15th century.

Among the landowners, the Military Orders accepted the greatest number of Mudéjars: at the end of the 15th century, more than 80 per cent of the Mudéjars in Extremadura were in their territory, occupying the fertile lands of Baja Extremadura. The most powerful and extensive estates of the region, which belonged to the Feria family, included 13 villages and, in comparison with the other large estates, it accommodated the greatest number of Mudéjars.

It is to these political and religious organisations, which were the Military Orders, that we owe the majority of the Mudéjar artworks in Extremadura. To these material remains of the time should be added the works carried out in the Conventual Priory of Guadalupe, a Marian centre of special devotion and extraordinary historical importance in the Middle Ages as in the modern era.

ITINERARY X Noble and Monastic Patronage
Guadalupe

X.1 GUADALUPE

In the extreme south-east of the province of Cáceres and straddling the provinces of Toledo and Badajoz, extends the region of the Villuercas, a mountainous land, where the Mountains of Toledo penetrate into the province of Caceres. With several rivers running through it, the slopes of the mountains and the valleys beneath them form a wild landscape, untouched, and full of game.

Guadalupe stands out from all the rest of the villages in the area. The medieval origin and later development of Guadalupe links to the veneration of the Virgin of Guadalupe, who gave her name to this place, and on whom the village has depended throughout its existence.

As you get closer to Guadalupe, a leafy valley, surrounded by mountains, comes into view. There, on a hilltop, is an enormous stone fortress surrounded by a village of whitewashed walls. This is the Puebla de Guadalupe, in the centre of which stands the Real Monasterio de Nuestra Señora de Guadalupe (Royal Monastery of Our Lady of Guadalupe), which was declared a UNESCO World Heritage Site on 8th December 1988.

X.1.a Royal Monastery of Our Lady of Guadalupe

Entrance fee. Guided tours to the Museum and Church. Opening hours: 09.30–13.00 and 15.30–18.30.

The monastery is a complex of buildings, from different periods, dominated by contrasts. Its defensive exterior appearance hides its palatial function, with great chambers and patios, and an abundance of water and plants. In spite of the austerity its walls of stone suggest, however, the interior glitters with shining polychrome tiling, paintings and gilt work. In contrast to the military rigour of its profile, the rich artistic treasures kept safely within its walls dazzle any travellers that cross the threshold of this monastery. The origin of this famous shrine goes back to the Middle Ages – to the moment when, according to legend, the statue of the Virgin Mary was discovered. Some chroniclers say that St Luke the Evangelist carved this statue and that, with time, it came into the hands of the Archbishop of Seville, San Leandro. Then it was buried in this out-of-the-way region of the Villuercas to

Royal Monastery of Nuestra Señora de Guadalupe, bell tower and apse of the primitive Mudéjar church.

ITINERARY X   Noble and Monastic Patronage
Guadalupe

Royal Monastery of Nuestra Señora de Guadalupe, ground plan.
1. Basilica of Santa María de Guadalupe
2. Chapel of Santa Paula
3. Sacristy
4. Bell tower
5. Mudéjar Cloister or Cloister of the Miracles
6. Pavilion of the Majordomo and gatehouse
7. Pavilion of the Pharmacy and Infirmary.

protect it from Arab invasions. It stayed hidden for centuries until, in the third quarter of the 13th century, the Virgin revealed the whereabouts of the hidden statue to a local cowherd, Gil Cordero, who was watching over his herd in the area. A small shrine was built that was visited by pilgrims from very early on.

Guadalupe, as well as being an important centre of devotion and pilgrimage, played an important historical role during the Middle Ages and in the modern era, as the place for fruitful diplomatic meetings, as a Royal Pantheon and as a place of recreation for some of the kings of the period.

Buried in the church are Enrique IV and his mother, Queen María of Aragón, both of whom were devoted to the Virgin of Guadalupe. The Catholic Monarchs visited the Monastery on repeated occasions. For them, in the last quarter of 15th century, a Hospedería Real or Royal Guest House was built, but this was destroyed in the middle of the 19th century. Nearby, in Madrigalejo, King Fernando el Católico died on route to Guadalupe. Another visitor here was Christopher Columbus, who gave the name of Santa Maria de Guadalupe to one of the Antilles. Felipe II, and his successor Felipe III, visited Guadalupe on many occasions, and this tradition of royal visits has continued right up to the present day.

The economic power of the monastery became huge, due to the numerous alms, donations and royal privileges, which allowed the monks to acquire lands and cattle and to construct important buildings.

The different phases, which gradually made up the monastery during the first three centuries of its existence (14th–16th century) are all Mudéjar, which makes the monastery the most representative complex of Mudéjar art in Extremadura.

Nevertheless, the monastery complex continued to expand in later years. Thus, there are interesting Renaissance and Baroque elements concentrated in the eastern part, including those of the last years of the 16th century, when the Chapel of San José, or reliquary, was introduced. The Sacristy was an addition of the mid-18th century, and at the end of the same century the *camarín* or Chamber of the Virgin was added, together with the new church (today used as the auditorium), the latter built by Manuel de Larra Churriguera.

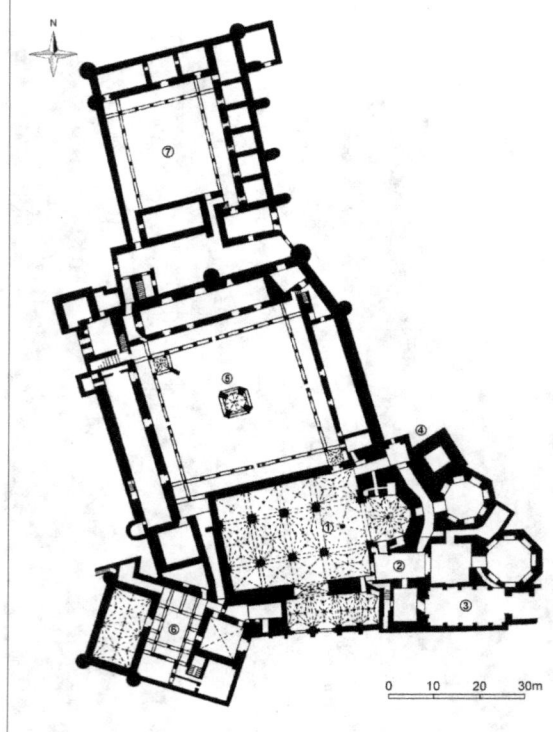

ITINERARY X   *Noble and Monastic Patronage*
Guadalupe

Royal Monastery of Nuestra Señora de Guadalupe, general view.

Given the complexity of the monastery, we have chosen an itinerary through the Mudéjar of Guadalupe in chronological order.

The first area proposed for the visit is the church where the statue of Our Lady of Guadalupe was discovered, and this was the origin of the monastic foundation.

We then move north of the church, where the magnificent Mudéjar cloister is located, built after the arrival of the Hieronymite Order in Guadalupe between 1389 and 1405. In the 15th century, in the south-east corner of the complex, a building intended for the chapter house and library in the inner part, and the porter's lodge and *majordomo*'s offices, were added to the area adjoining the atrium of the church. The last important Mudéjar work in the first third of the 16th century was a new infirmary and pharmacy to replace the existing one that dated from the 14th century.

On arrival, visitors tend to head straight to the Church of Our Lady of Guadalupe, which was built over the place where the statue of the Virgin was found. The statue is a Protogothic sculpture from either the end of the 12th century or the beginning of the 13th century. Made in cedar, she appears as she has done for centuries wearing her veil.

In the Archivo Histórico Nacional (National Historical Archives), a conserved document, dated 1340, explains how King Alfonso XI, after the Victory of Salado, conceded a series of privileges and donations to the Sanctuary. The document, furthermore, says that the king ordered the building of a new church in Guadalupe because the existing one was too small and in ruins. It is possible that the document refers to the remains of a Mudéjar apse, which still exists in the eastern part of the present church, beside the *camarin* and the bell tower.

ITINERARY X   *Noble and Monastic Patronage*

Guadalupe

Royal Monastery of Nuestra Señora de Guadalupe, rose window with traceries in the gable wall of the church.

The part of the semi-cylindrical towers that still survives is made of brick and has lobed modillions that support the eaves of the roof. Blind arcades framed in rectangles form the front of the apse, and in succession from bottom to top, with alternating axes, there are *tumidos* or pointed horseshoe arches, semicircular, pointed and, again, horseshoe-type arches. The arch-type employed, with its semicircular form and the alternating arches in the axes, produces artworks combining typical elements of the Mudéjar style from Toledo with Mudéjar from Castilla-León. This suggests that one should consider this model as independent from realisations in other Mudéjar regions, although this does not imply a lack of knowledge about styles in use elsewhere, but quite the opposite, as Professor Borrás has already demonstrated.

This church was replaced by another which, as the 16th-century chronicles inform us, was built at the beginning of the 15th century, after the arrival of the Hieronymite monks in Guadalupe. In the opinion of some scholars, the work carried out then by Father Yañez was limited to certain modifications to an already existing church, from the time of the secular priory in the third quarter of the 14th century. It is highly probable that the work of adapting and extending the church, which was carried out in the first years of the 15th century, is by the master craftsman Rodrigo Alfonso. He began the construction of the cloister of the Cathedral in Toledo in 1389, and possibly it is to him the funeral epitaph refers seen

ITINERARY X Noble and Monastic Patronage
Guadalupe

on an 18th-century *azulejo* tile at the entrance to the church.

The present church is a Gothic construction of three aisles, with a transept unmarked on the ground plan. The aisles are separated by pointed arches framed in *alfiz*, which rest on clustered Gothic columns of great sobriety. The upper part of the church, enlivened by the presence of numerous pointed windows with rich Gothic traceries and by the rose windows with Mudéjar strapwork in the arms of the transept, is made with gauged brick- and plasterwork, the dominant construction technique in these high areas and in the main façade of the church. Different types of vaulting – ribbed, simple, tierceron and star-shaped – form the roof of the various parts of the church.

With the arrival of the first Hieronymite monks the magnificent raised choir was constructed, which was a necessary addition for the large religious community that spent many hours each day in the Divine Offices. The chapel of Santa Paula adjoins the Epistle, or east side of the church, and preserves murals based on Mudéjar strapwork and an illegible inscription in Gothic lettering. The chapel connected with the old sacristy, but now forms the entrance to the present one, and was finished, according to an inscription, in 1647. Here, there are eight outstanding canvases by the artist Francisco de Zurbarán, who was from Extremadura.

The bell tower of the church is situated *extra muros* – that is, outside the walls of the precinct – but links with the wall that protects the monastery through two bridge-arches, as a defensive, or *albarrana* tower. The bell tower has a solid lower part onto which various chambers are superimposed. According to an inscription that remained covered when the *camarin* was built, the original tower was built in 1363, at the time of the Prior Toribio Fernández.

When the Hieronymites reached Guadalupe, they had to adapt the existing buildings to the needs of a regular Order. This is why it is reasonable to suppose that around the year 1389, the date when the monks arrived there, work began on the Mudéjar cloister, which adjoins the north wall of the church.

The same north wall of the church formed part of the defensive walls built in the third quarter of the 14th century, during the Secular Priorate. Square towers adjoin sober stretches of wall and semi-cylindrical towers crowned with merlons.

Built on a rectangular ground plan, the fortress has communicating walkways at the top as part of its defences, a common feature of castles at the time. The cloister, which was built within the walled precinct, has various chambers, kitchens, a refectory, vestiary, chapter house, cells and chapels. The work, by Fray Juan de Seville, must have been finished in around the year 1405, when the small central temple was built. The whole complex evokes Paradise, with the same elements as the patio of a Muslim palace: cruciform walkways, a small central temple reminiscent of an Islamic *qubba*, rich vegetation and splashing fountains. The famous Mudéjar cloister, also called the Cloister of the Miracles because of the canvases that hang there, can be considered a unique example of the purest and finest Mudéjar art. A 15th-century document states that the monks took part

Guadalupe

in its construction alongside the master craftsmen.

The cloister is rectangular, with two rows of arcades on each side, and twice as many arches on the upper level as on the lower. The galleries are formed by squat arches known as *arcos tumidos*, the springers of which are organised following the Almohad tradition, although on the east side there are some simple horseshoe arches, probably because it was here that the cloister was started. The arches, framed in *alfices*, rest on square pillars with chamfered borders, and their original polychrome is still visible. The roof of the galleries is formed of Mudéjar *alfarjes*, decorated with painted plant motifs and royal emblems.

In 1405, Fray Juan de Seville built a small temple to house a fountain in the centre of the cloister; this disappeared in the 18th century. This small temple is the richest example of Mudéjar in Extremadura and is reminiscent of some of the Mudéjar work in Aragón. The felicitous combination of gauged brick, plaster and tiles, as well as its obviously original design, produced an exceptional piece of work in honour of the Virgin.

The different wings on the ground floor of the cloister are now galleries exhibiting the rich arts of the monastery: embroidery, sculpture, painting and illuminated books. The upper level comprises the dormitories.

The entrance to the monastery from the atrium is through the *pabellón*, or building with the library and *majordomo*'s offices, which date from two periods close to each other in the second half of the 15th century. The library is from the first stage, built with the money donated expressly to that effect by Father Illescas, who had been the Prior of Guadalupe, and at that time was the Bishop of Córdoba. Some years later, the buildings showed signs of structural weakness and were restructured; the cylindrical towers were then added at each of the corners. The community took the opportunity to build what became the monastery offices and a gatehouse – with an office for the prior as well as other offices, and the strongroom, where the money was kept. Displayed at the gatehouse entrance, according to Father Talavera, there were statues of Our Lady, St Jerome and St Augustine, but these have now disappeared.

At the same time, a small cloister linking both buildings was constructed. Called the Patio de la Mayordomía or *Majordomo*'s Patio this has undergone various renovations, but still conserves its Mudéjar character on one side. The arches are semicircular although somewhat stilted, framed in a very pronounced *alfiz* that extends to the base of the octagonal pillars. The roof of the original bays was of wood, but the current vaulting replaced this in the 18th century.

The final important Mudéjar intervention was during the first third of the 16th century, in the shape of a new area for the infirmary, pharmacy and medical school. Called the *Pabellón de la Bótica y la Enfermería* (Pavilion of the Pharmacy and Infirmary) it replaced a hospital from the mid-14th century, and is now the monastery guest house. The final result, very different from the original plan, is a complex on a rectangular ground plan with masonry walls and semi-cylindrical turrets that polychrome capitals crown at three corners. A spacious patio with a triple

ITINERARY X   *Noble and Monastic Patronage*
Guadalupe

Grange at Mirabel, general view, Guadalupe.

arcade on three sides brings the different chambers into line. Although the patio is known these days as the "Gothic" patio, it should be considered Mudéjar for a number of reasons relating to elements of its style. These elements, which have been present in the monastery since the building of the first cloister, are the use of gauged brick, chamfered pillars – Almohad in origin – and plasterwork. Because of the late date of this patio, it has structural and decorative elements that are not Mudéjar.

X.1.b College of Humanities or Grammar and Choir School (optional)

The college is opposite the monastery. Now the Parador de Turismo. The patio and public areas are open to visitors.

In the second quarter of the 16th century, the Hieronymites constructed a new building to house a school for the large group of children who made up the choir, teaching them choral singing and grammar. Separating the school from the main complex of the monastery was a street, and nearby was the Plaza Mayor. Since 1990, the former school has been a Parador Nacional de Turismo, one of the state-run hotels, and as such has undergone much alteration.

The main patio has many reminiscences of the Mudéjar cloister and of the *Majordomo*'s Pavilion in the neighbouring monastery. From the old Mudéjar cloister come the *arcos túmidos*, which form the upper storey, and from the *Majordomo*'s Patio come the semicircular arches of the lower arcades framed in *alfiz*. The *arcos tumidos* of the upper storey double the number of semicircular lower ones, but unlike them, they are not framed in *alfiz*. The patio of the School also copies the Mudéjar cloister in its use of chamfered pillar supports, on both levels.

ITINERARY X   *Noble and Monastic Patronage*
Guadalupe

Highly recommended is a stroll through the "Barrio Viejo", or Old Village, with its medieval town plan and many typical arcaded houses.

X.1.c Grange at Mirabel

6 km. Take the Old Road and, after a very sharp bend, follow the unmade road through spectacular countryside. Opening hours: Thurs 09.00–12.30 and 17.00–20.00.

The Grange at Mirabel was used as a house of rest and retirement for the Hieronymite monks and some other important personages. Presently it is in private hands although it is a National Monument.

The building does not present very many artistic elements from the outside, but inside, the pools, rhythmic galleries, ample patios, comfortable rooms and the intimate chapel, as well as its excellent situation, made it an idyllic place wherein the monks chose to rest.

The main nucleus of the grange, constructed in the last 20 years of the 15th century, consists of a patio that, following the building formulae of the nearby monastery, provides access to different rooms. It is a square space, bordered by galleries, with two floors of arches, semicircular on the lower and basket-handled on the upper, framed in *alfices* and resting on chamfered pillars. Three of the galleries lead into rooms, but the fourth gives on to the waters of a pond in the middle of a garden. The chapel, dedicated to la Magadelena (St Mary Magdalene), is interesting, and reachable through one of the galleries of the cloister. Here there are a wooden door decorated with Mudéjar strapwork and an *armadura de limas* ceiling in the sanctuary. Recent restoration work has uncovered Gothic paintings.

Villuercas-Ibores
To the north of Guadalupe is the Sierra de las Villuercas and the region of Los Ibores. Mixed woods of holm oak, oak, cork oak and chestnut cover large areas, along with moorland, rockrose and heather. The jagged crests of the quartzite mountain ranges running north-west—south-east give the area its wild character, and big game hunting abounds.
The climate of these regions is the mildest of Extremadura and so a well-ordered agricultural landscape stretches out planted with crops typical of the climate, in olive groves, cherry orchards, chestnut and pinewoods.
The traditional buildings use materials that have been available locally for centuries, including slate and fruitwood, which has left a very interesting architectural heritage.

Grange at Mirabel,
Chapel of
La Magdalena,
Guadalupe.

ITINERARY X *Noble and Monastic Patronage*
Llerena

Parish Church of Nuestra Señora de la Granada, tower and façade, Llerena.

X.2 LLERENA

Llerena is in the south of the province of Badajoz in the district of the same name. In the varied countryside of this area, the plains stretch out in the north and a more abrupt relief in the south begins the foothills of the Sierra Morena. The town is on a plain where wide extensions of cereals are grown.

The origin of the City of Llerena (given by Charter of Felipe IV in 1641) dates back to the Middle Ages, and from that time on, its history is linked to the Military Order of Santiago, or St James. Once conquered in the mid-13th century, Fernando III handed Llerena over to this Order for defence and resettlement. In 1297, its *"fuero"* or set of Municipal code of Laws was granted. From the 14th century onwards, because some of the Grand Masters of the Order of Santiago came to live here, its prestige increased, since it was the meeting place for some of the important occasions in the life of the Order. In the 15th century, it became the capital of the diocese of the priory of San Marcos de León, belonging to the Order of Santiago, which had some 50 villages depending on it. In 1478, the Catholic Monarchs established the Court of the Inquisition in Llerena,

ITINERARY X   Noble and Monastic Patronage
Llerena

Tower of the Parish Church of Granada, detail of the tower, Llerena.

which held wide powers. All of this meant that, by the 16th century, Llerena was an active and prosperous town with a growing economy and flourishing population. The fact that it was one of the most important centres in the region generated a highly diversified architecture and, consequently, great dynamism in construction and building works.

X.2.a Tower of the Parish Church of Nuestra Señora de la Granada

In the Plaza Mayor. The interior of the tower is open to the public. Opening hours: Mon—Fri 10.00—12.00 and 19.00—21.00, Sat 19.00—21.00, Sun 12.00—14.00.

The Parish Church occupies the centre of the walled town dominating the Plaza Mayor. It appears in documents dedicated to Nuestra Señora (Our Lady) until the 16th century, and then to Nuestra Señora de la Granada (Our Lady of the Pomegranate) from that time on.

According to some documents, the church was founded in the last third of the 14th century by don García Fernández Mexía y Guzmán, who was the Master of the Order of Santiago at the time. Thanks to the data available in the registers of visits to the Order of Santiago, we know that at the end of the 15th century the church had three aisles, separated by arches and wooden ceilings, the central one with strapwork. It is very probable that it was a Mudéjar building, of which the only part to have survived is the lower part of the church tower.

This is the oldest tower façade to have survived in Extremadura. Built of stone masonry, the two lower sections are still standing. The bell tower repeats the typology of the Almohad *alminares*, with access ramps around a core, holding various superimposed chambers, just as in the *alminar* of the Giralda in Seville. However, the decoration and the composition of the bays, two doors and a mullion window, tell us that this is a Christian work. The western front of the tower forms the façade of the end of the church. In the lower part is the entrance door with a splayed Gothic arch decorated on the archivolt with plant and heraldic motifs and diamond-shaped points. The separation between the two sections is composed of a line of corbelling in the Islamic tradition, over which there must have been eaves with a diamond-toothed pattern. Of interest in the second section is a mullion window with multifoil arches over a marble monial,

ITINERARY X   Noble and Monastic Patronage
Llerena

enclosed in a Gothic arch with an engrailed edge or *angrelado*, which lets light into the interior of the tower. The upper storeys must have been added in the second half of the 16th century.

X.2.b House of Zapata – Residence of the Court of the Inquisition

Go down calle Corredera. The building is used as the Palacio de Justicia (Court House). Opening hours: 09.00–14.00. Closed Sun.

What is now the Court House, in its day was the residence of the Llerena-born lawyer Luis Zapata, who was Counsellor to the Catholic Monarchs. Zapata was an active figure who played an important part in the politics of the kingdom. The palace was built during the first 30 years of the 16th century; it was then rented by the seat of the Holy Office or Inquisition in 1570, which later bought it and carried out a series of alterations. There is little left of the original 16th-century building that, at the time, was as notable as *"the best of the knights' houses ... and better than many noble ones"*. It had two entrance doors: one on the east side, which today is walled up, and about which there is only some data about its Hispano-Flamboyant Gothic style; and the north door, which gives on to the calle de la Corredera, and is the one used today. This north façade has two rows of semicircular arches on columns with twisted shafts and a cornice with pommels.

We know from the register of visits of the Order that the palace had

House of Zapata, main façade arcades, Llerena.

House of Zapata, patio, Llerena.

225

ITINERARY X *Noble and Monastic Patronage*

Llerena

three patios in the 16th century, two of them with corridors, a yard, and two towers that had 34 rooms. The principal chamber of the palace of Luis Zapata, which the documents refer to as *Sala Dorada* or the Golden Chamber, was on the second floor. It had an oratory and very probably a Mudéjar ceiling.

To have survived out of all of this is a square cloister with two floors of arcades in brick. The galleries of the lower floor have three stilted arches framed in *alfiz* on octagonal pillars, while the upper floor has four semicircular segmental arches also framed with *alfiz*.

X.2.c House of the Prior

In Plaza de España; access via the calle Zapatería. Opening hours: Mon–Fri 10.00–14.00 and 17.00–20.00.

House of the Prior, the patio, Llerena.

Construction of this house was in two different stages: the main work was carried out at the end of the 15th century, when García Ramírez was the prior, since the house was in a bad state of repair and inappropriate to its function. Dating from this time is the façade that is somewhat set back from the street; it has a doorway with a flat arch, over which is the arms of the Priory of San Marcos de León.

Entering through this door, a passageway communicates with the main part of the palace, organised around a patio that initially had only one gallery of arches on its eastern side. This gallery is a Mudéjar construction that has two storeys of arcades, in a combination that the extension carried out in the mid-16th century also adopted.

At the beginning of the 16th century, the prior's house became the primary headquarters of the Inquisition in Llerena and remained so until the middle of the century, at which time it reverted to the Prior's residence. It was at that time that a series of works gave the building its definitive shape.

The most noteworthy of these works was the completion of the principal patio, adding galleries on two of its sides, with the final configuration being that of a square with two floors of arches on three of its sides. The arches on the lower level are stilted and semicircular, while those on the upper floor are basket-handled. In both cases, the *alfiz*-framed arches rest on octagonal pillars with a base and a capital. The patio was whitewashed, and the galleries covered by a wooden roof. Around the patio are 30 rooms, while behind it is a vegetable garden with a waterwheel.

ITINERARY X *Noble and Monastic Patronage*
Llerena

X.2.d Houses in the Old Quarter

Stroll around the Old Quarter (calles Bodegones, Cristóbal Colón, Cristo de Palma, Sánchez Prieto, Plazuela de la Fuente). The Town Council is at present restoring the Mudéjar façades.

Llerena's interesting remains of what were Mudéjar dwellings makes it one of the best complexes in Extremadura for this genre, in spite of the many alterations the houses have undergone over the centuries. Strolling in the streets around the medieval area one enjoys a balance of white two-storied façades with mullioned windows on the upper floor; the windows are formed by horseshoe, multifoil or pointed horseshoe arches, framed in *alfiz*. Lines of imposts define the rectangular façades, whereas, at the top, Islamic modillions, lobed or coved in shape, support the eaves. At one time, the houses had lively decorations of scratch work (*sgraffito*) and mural paintings of which hardly any examples still exist.

Some of these details can be seen while strolling through calles Cristóbal Colón, Rodrigo de Osuna, San José, Cristo de Palma, Sánchez Prieto, Bodegones or the Plazuela de la Fuente. Also recommended is the Plaza Mayor, with its rhythmic arcades formed by Mudéjar galleries, the likes of which are documented throughout the 16th century.

The Dehesa in Extremadura
The dehesa is an agricultural method used on large estates that ensures biodiversity and protects the environment. The soil of the area, which is of a quality too poor for agriculture, is used for growing pasture for extensive cattle farming. The holm and cork oaks, which are sufficiently spaced to allow their full development, offers the shade that protects the pasture in the heat of the summer, as well as providing the acorns that feed the cattle. The maintenance of balance in this way respects the environment as much as giving rise to the typical and emblematic landscape of Extremadura.

Houses in the Old Quarter; mullioned window in calle Corredera no. 10, Llerena.

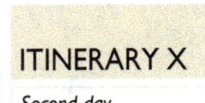

ITINERARY X
Second day

Noble and Monastic Patronage

María Pilar Mogollón Cano-Cortés

X.3 ZAFRA
    X.3.a Alcázar
    X.3.b Convent of Santa Clara
    X.3.c Convent of Santa Catalina
    X.3.d Plaza Chica
    X.3.e Hospital of San Miguel (optional)

X.4 CALERA DE LEÓN
    X.4.a Monastery of Santa María de Tentudía

The Military Orders

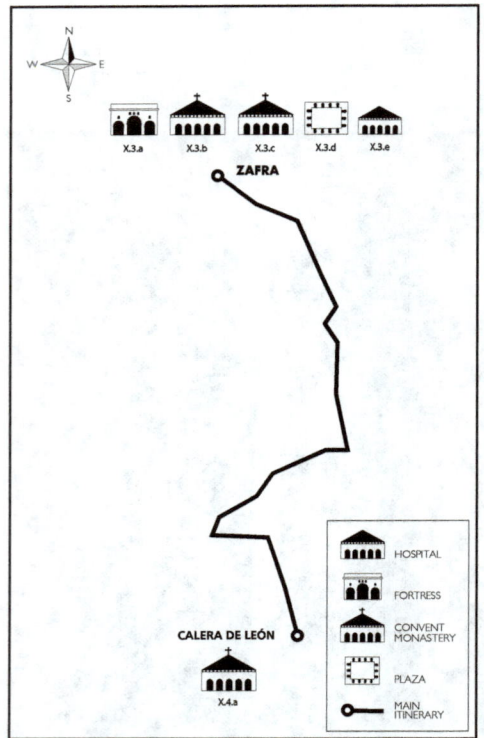

ITINERARY X   Noble and Monastic Patronage
Zafra

X.3 ZAFRA

Situated in a broad valley in the south of the province of Badajoz, Zafra is a town that conserves interesting traces of the patronage of the House of Feria, which is why it was declared a Complex of Historical-Artistic Interest in 1965.
It seems that Zafra was originally an Islamic foundation, which enjoyed a strategic situation on three ancient roadways, and that Fernando III definitively reconquered it in 1241; and from that date on it flourished in commerce and crafts. It was the property of various nobles until 1394, at which time don Lorenzo Suárez de Figueroa handed it over along with other villages that belonged to the province of Badajoz, although some years later Figueroa set up his household there. The Suárez de Figueroa family controlled the town's destiny, first on the part of the properties there and later as part of the estates of the County and Duchy of Feria. When it became the centre of a great estate, Zafra benefited from the construction of important buildings such as the Alcázar, the walls, different convents, hospitals and other public spaces, a great number of which were the work of a Mudéjar workforce. In the 17th century, the Duchy of Feria was joined in marriage to the Marquisate of Priego; then, in the 18th century, to the Duchy of Medinaceli.

X.3.a Alcázar

Parador Nacional. Visits can be arranged through the Tourist Office: Tel: 924 551036. Access to the chapel, which is now the conference room, and to the Sala Dorada, which is a hotel bedroom, depend on whether they are vacant. The recently restored tower may be visited; and the Parador bar has an interesting coffered ceiling.

Alcázar, murals in the Keep, Zafra.

Within the city walls, in the extreme south-east of the old city, is the Alcázar, which was the Palace of the Dukes of Feria.
Two inscriptions tell us that the Alcázar, corresponding to the plan for a military building, was built by don Lorenzo Suárez de Figueroa, Counsellor to the King and Head of the Queen's Household. The inscription above the entrance to the Alcázar has the date when works started, 1437, and the date on the keep gives the date of completion as 1443. Significant alterations were made to the building in the 16th century, among which is the outstanding construction of a Classical-style patio in white marble, while some earlier parts that were retained include, for example,

ITINERARY X   Noble and Monastic Patronage
Zafra

Convent of Nuestra Señora del Valle, gallery and ajimez *in the gatehouse patio, Zafra.*

Convent of Nuestra Señora del Valle, detail of the gallery and ajimez *in the gatehouse patio, Zafra.*

the sanctuary of the church on the upper floor and the mural paintings that decorate the cylindrical keep.

In the interior of this tower there has also survived a polychrome dado painted with frescoes on figurative, plant, heraldic and geometric themes, with varied strapwork that remind us of Mudéjar tiling.

The chapel, now used as a conference room, has an interesting ceiling in which the dominant decoration is Flamboyant Gothic, while the structure is from the Islamic tradition. It is a wooden cupola on an octagonal base made of eight double-pitched sides, crowned by a pendentive of *muqarnas*. The whole composition is covered with a delicate design of gilded plant motifs that contrasts with the blue of the background, imitating a dazzling celestial firmament.

The Sala Dorada also owns a conserved Mudéjar wooden ceiling. This is an *artesonado*, where the dominant feature is a geometric composition based on eight-pointed stars in between which are caissons with splendid gilded fleurons. It has rich polychrome with plant motifs and heraldic devices referring to the House of Feria.

X.3.b Convent of Santa Clara

From the Plaza de Corazon de María, take calle Seville. Enclosed Convent of the Order of St Clare and former Monastery of Santa María del Valle. The church can be visited. Mass times: 17.00–19.00, summer 18.00–20.00.

The Church of the Convent of Santa Clara was designed as the burial pantheon for the House of Feria. Until

ITINERARY X   Noble and Monastic Patronage
Zafra

the 18th century the marble urns of the first lords of Feria, don Gómez Suárez de Figueroa and doña Elvira Laso de Mendoza, were kept in the sanctuary, but they are now located in a side aisle. In the nuns' choir other members of the family rest, such as don García Laso, who died in the War of Baza in the mid-15th century. According to an inscription over the door of the enclosure, building began in 1428 and the Bishop of Badajoz took possession of the monastery, still not complete, two years later.

Many alterations have modified the original building, with those of the 17th century having the most effect. Nevertheless, the original sanctuary in the church can still be a seen today: a Mudéjar construction that repeats the models of the Islamic *qubbas* that were so widespread in the Mudéjar memorial chapels. The sanctuary is a cube, with a ceiling that has a cupola of 16 sides mounted on two lines of *trompas*, the lower with arrises, the upper with small triangular *trompas*.

Other areas in the convent preserve Mudéjar work too, such as the first patio in the enclosure behind the gatehouse where on one of the sides there is still an elegant gallery of five stilted semicircular arches framed in *alfiz*. These, mounted on Classical marble columns of quite late date, are from the last years of the 16th century. This gallery has Extremadura's only surviving *ajimez*.

X.3.c Convent of Santa Catalina

In the calle Seville turn left into calle Fuente Grande, which leads out into calle Santa Catalina. This Dominican convent is

not currently in use. Visits can be arranged through the Tourist Office.

It seems that this modest building owes its foundation to doña Inés de Santa Paula in the year 1500.

The beauty of its sober façade, finished by a 17th-century bell gable, prepares us for the severity of the interior of the convent church, which has a single nave enclosed in plain walls, and a wooden ceiling, of the *par y nudillo* type, with pairs of anchor ties joined by strapwork. The ceiling of the sanctuary is richer; eight-sided and with pitched beams joined with *limas moamares*, which two bands of edging, forming eight-pointed stars and X-shaped crosses, surround. The *almizate* has a relatively complicated knot system with a double quadrangular network overlaid with an eight-sided knot, and the wood retains its natural colour.

Convent of Santa Catalina, detail of the eight-sided ceiling in the Sanctuary Chapel, Zafra.

ITINERARY X *Noble and Monastic Patronage*
Zafra

Plaza Chica, arcades, Zafra.

X.3.d Plaza Chica

Continue up calle Santa Catalina to the Plaza Grande and then turn left.

The city has carried on a busy commercial life since Arab times, an activity that took place, above all, around the Plaza Chica or Small Square. Evidence of this is the measuring rod or yardstick engraved centuries ago on the Arquillo del Pan.

This square was in the centre of the town and the Town Hall was established there in 1430. The square is surrounded by arcades formed of semicircular segmental arches in brick, which rest on pillars or granite columns with varied capitals. In some sections of the galleries, the spans are framed in different systems of surrounds, *alfices* or sunken rectangles, which keeps the Muslim aesthetic alive. In the opinion of José Ramón Mélida, the façades of either one or two floors above the galleries would have been decorated with tiling similar to that which decorates a window in the nearby calle de Pedro de Valencia. Today, however, only a few façades still hold traces of this Islamic tradition.

The main streets that lead from the eight gates in the city walls all con-

ITINERARY X   Noble and Monastic Patronage
Calera de León

verge on this square and, through the Arquillo del Pan and de la Esperanza, lead into the open space that was at one time in front of the Parish Church of la Candelaria. This church was demolished in the 16th century because it was in a ruinous state, and the *Plaza Grande* or Great Square was created in its place. Although of a later date, this square still keeps alive some of the Mudéjar elements of the composition of the Plaza Chica.

X.3.e **Hospital of San Miguel**
(optional)

Behind the Town Hall, on the corner of calle San José and Ronda de la Maestranza, is the Hospital of San Miguel. Although now abandoned, the hospital can still be visited thanks to the initiative of the Town Council and the Plan de Dinamización de Zafra (Zafra Rehabilitation Plan). Visits can be arranged through the Tourist Office.

The hospital was founded by doña Constancia Osorio; a fact that is verified by her will dated 1480. Although the building has been deteriorating since the beginning of the 20th century, it is still clear how the Chapel of la Magadelena follows the typology of the Islamic *qubbas* described in the Convent of Santa María del Valle, and how the brick arcades of both the chapel and infirmary are in the Mudéjar taste.

*From Extremadura the link can be made with the MWNF Portuguese exhibition, "***In the Lands of the Enchanted Moorish Maiden: Islamic Art in Portugal***", alternatively, the journey can be continued southwards over the Sierra Morena to link with the two itineraries in Seville.*

X.4 CALERA DE LEÓN

In the south of the province of Badajoz, on the border with the province of Huelva, this district is in a mountainous area of great natural beauty where the predominant vegetation is the Mediterranean forest with holm and oaks. A few kilometres away, in the Sierra Morena of Extremadura and on the highest point of the province of Badajoz, on top of Mount Tentudía (1.104 m. above sea level), the patron of the area is venerated at the Monastery of Santa Maria.

X.4.a **Monastery of Santa María de Tentudía**

On the N630 towards Seville, we recommend turning off after 716 km, to join an unmade road that goes through beautiful

Monastery of Santa María de Tentudía, cloister, Calera de León.

ITINERARY X   Noble and Monastic Patronage
Calera de León

dehesa countryside. There is a spectacular view, 9 km from the village at the top of the highest peak. Opening hours: 10.15–17.15 and every second Sunday. If the Monastery is closed, contact the Town Hall. Tel: 924 584101.

According to the chronicles, the origin of the name and the foundation of this monastery go back to a miracle that took place in the mid-13th century, when this area was the scene of fighting between Muslims and Christians. According to tradition, the Master of the Order of Santiago, Pelay Pérez Correa, won an important victory over the Islamic troops thanks to the intervention of the Virgin, who, when the Christians were on the point of winning the battle held back the sunset, thus prolonging the fight, and preventing the Muslims from seeking salvation under the cover of darkness. To commemorate the event the master had a shrine built dedicated to the Virgin.

The monastery of Tentudía or Tudía, now a National Monument, was in the vicariate of the Military Order of Santiago and belonged to the province of the Vicar General of Llerena.

The outside appearance of the building is one of great sobriety, with a few simple windows and masonry walls, with horizontal courses of brickwork at some points, and irregularly cut granite blocks at the corners. From the east side, the building looks like a fortress because of the battlements that top it; these must have been added at the same time as the side chapels were built. These fortified churches are relatively common in the province of Badajoz, and even more common in the land that belonged to the Order of Santiago.

The whole complex is a Mudéjar construction including a church, which has two memorial chapels flanking the sanctuary, a cloister with a well on the south side of the church, and some rooms on the east side, which have an independent corridor and entrance.

The church is the oldest part, although modified in the 17th century; the walls belong to an earlier building from the 14th century, which was replaced at the beginning of the 16th century. The nave was remodelled in the 17th century; the original church had three aisles separated by brick arches and a wooden ceiling, but the Baroque reform converted the three aisles into a single nave.

The sanctuary is eight-sided on the inside, with a star-shaped roof formed of ribbed-vaulting. In it, there is a simple sepulchre holding the remains of the master Pelay Pérez Correa, one of the most outstanding personalities of the Order – and of the reconquest – in the area. The sepulchre is a simple urn, raised up and joined onto the wall, and covered with tiling from Seville. The most interesting artwork in the church is the ceramic altarpiece, commissioned from Francisco Niculoso Pisano in 1518.

The high altar, which two memorial chapels on a square ground plan flank, has a roof furnished with interesting cupolas of clear Islamic influence. These 16-sided vaults, which rise above two lines of small *trompas* with arises, date from the end of the 14th, or beginning of the 15th century. In the side chapels, the altarpieces, altar steps and the altars themselves are covered with painted tiles from the second half of the 16th century. Hernández Díaz attributes the deco-

ITINERARY X Noble and Monastic Patronage
Calera de León

Monastery of Santa María de Tentudía, Chapel of the Masters, Calera de León.

rative titling to the master craftsman Alonso García.
In the Chapel of the Masters are the sepulchres of two 14th-century Masters of the Order, Gonzalo Mexías and Fernando Ozores and, under an arch set into the wall, the tomb of García Hernández, the chamberlain of Enrique II. A large "Cross of the Order" in the centre of the vault is all that remains of the frescoes that once covered the chapel.

The Chapel of Juan Zapata, the Knight Commander of Medina de la Torre, has a Mudéjar strapwork composition that resembles the wooden ceilings.
On the south side of the church is a Mudéjar cloister dating from the first decade of the 16th century. It is of great simplicity, with a square plan and modest size. The cloister, formed of two sets of galleries on each of its four sides, is covered with a simple

235

Calera de León

wooden *alfarjes*. The arches on the lower level are stilted and semi-circular on octagonal pillars; those on the upper level are segmental arches on the same kind of pillars and, in all cases, framed in *alfiz*.

This model is common to other patios in Bajo Extremadura from the late 15th and 16th centuries, showing the Andalucían influences. Different rooms, such as the kitchens, dormitories and the refectory, unfold throughout.

In 1511, a guest house was added to the eastern side of the cloister, it had rooms for the Knights of the Order who came to pray before the Virgin, and a gallery, similar to those in the cloister, was added at the same time.

The Sierra de Aracena and Picos de Aroche Natural Park
On the N630 towards Seville, the Sierra de Aracena and Picos de Arroche Natural Park, covering 184,000 hectares, belongs to the western part of the Sierra Morena.
The orographic effect produced by the shape of the relief favours rainfall, which has given rise to climatic conditions ideal for dense leafy woods with more than 4,000 hectares of chestnut trees. The vegetation is mainly of holm oak, cork and gall oak. In the wetter parts are willow, elder and ash trees.
In spite of the human interference in the sierra, the biodiversity of the Park is astonishing. It is still possible to see the Iberian lynx, as well as boar, genet, marten and deer. Among the birds are black storks, golden eagles and black vultures.
The economy of the area relies on agriculture and cattle rearing. The most important activities are the extraction of cork from the cork oaks and the curing of top-quality hams.

THE MILITARY ORDERS

María Pilar Mogollón Cano-Cortés

The Military Orders appeared in medieval Europe during the Crusades to the Holy Land. Their mission was to protect the holy sites and ensure the safety of pilgrims. It was with this aim, at the beginning of the 12th century, that the Orders of the Knights Templars and of the Knights Hospitallers or the Knights of St John of Jerusalem were founded. In 1123, the Council of Lateran declared the peninsula to be under the protection of the Crusaders, and because of this decree new Military Orders were founded, which collaborated with the Christian Monarchs in the reconquest, defence and resettlement of the territories that had recently been taken back from the Muslims. Among the different Orders created in the peninsula, the most important were those of Calatrava, Santiago or St James, and Alcántara. The last two of these were founded in Extremadura in the 12th century.

The Military Orders were religious Orders whose members took vows of poverty, chastity and obedience, and were subject to monastic rule. A Grand Master, who was a figure of considerable social and economic importance governed them, elected in the General Chapter of the Order. Their territories were divided into Commanderies, each with its corresponding forts, villages and towns. At the head were the Commanders, who were obliged to pass a certain amount of time in their possessions, and from which they received substantial benefits.

Painting by J. Sigüenza and Chavarrieta: "Meeting of the Military Orders". *(From the Historical – artistic heritage collection of the Senate).*

On the ecclesiastical plane, at the pinnacle in the hierarchy was the Prior of the Order, who had the rank of Abbot of the Mother House – a Priory – and of Prelate of a titular diocese. In 1873, Pope Pius IX suppressed the ecclesiastical jurisdiction of the Military Orders, which came to depend on their respective dioceses.

Their main mission was to fight to ensure the stability of the Christian territories; the monarchs, in the form of extensive territories, castles, towns and villages, rewarded this military activity. Thanks to this immense patrimony, the Orders did not take long to turn themselves into an economic power of the highest order. After the Conquest of Granada, the Catholic Monarchs gradually incorporated the territories of the various Grand Masters into crown Lands.

ITINERARY XI

Temples and Palaces of Seville

Alfredo J. Morales, Alfonso Pleguezuelo Hernández

This itinerary is part of the programme "**Gateway to the Mediterranean**", co-funded by the European Union within the framework of the Pilot Project Spain-Portugal-Morocco, Art. 10 FEDER.

XI.1 SEVILLE
- XI.1.a Church of Santa Marina
- XI.1.b Church of Omnium Sanctorum
- XI.1.c Church of San Marcos
- XI.1.d Church of Santa Catalina
- XI.1.e House of Pilate
- XI.1.f Palace of the Counts of Altamira
- XI.1.g Real Alcázar (Royal Palace)

Nature and Architecture

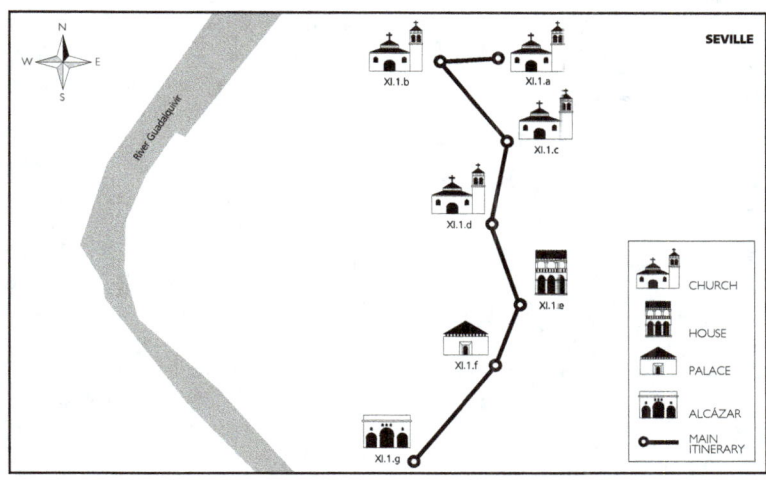

Royal Alcázar, general view of the Patio de las Doncellas *arcades, Seville.*

ITINERARY XI   *Temples and Palaces of Seville*
Seville

Church of Omnium Sanctorum, façade and tower, Seville.

House of Pilate, view of the patio, Seville.

Immediately after the capture of Seville in 1248, works began to convert the mosques to Christian churches. Many of the Muslim buildings, repaired and updated, aesthetically speaking, in different periods, survived until very late dates. The reuse of the Muslim buildings went practically in parallel with the construction of new churches in which a clear relationship with the courtly Gothic style is evident, although concealing the survival of construction techniques and compositional schemes of clear Islamic origin has not been achieved. Starting from these precedents and under the ever-increasing influence of Hispanic-Muslim art, the prototype of the Seville-type Mudéjar church appeared during the 14th century. In the Sevillian parish-type, the Almohad Muslim heritage and the Gothic postulates combine harmoniously and mutually compensate for each other. This well-balanced synthesis was very successful and lasted for a long time. The model not only extended throughout the whole of the Diocese of Seville and in general throughout Baja Andalucía, but also served as inspiration for the Mudéjar parish churches of Malaga and then, somewhat more developed, passed to the Canary Islands and to the New World.

Muslim palaces also underwent conversion, becoming the houses of noblemen and monasteries. This discreet appropriation was made easier by the small number of new inhabitants and by the need to concentrate all efforts into more urgent tasks than the unnecessary remodelling of houses, which probably were, anyway, well above the average standard of living the warrior classes from Castile were

ITINERARY XI   *Temples and Palaces of Seville*
Seville

used to. This meant that there was strong familiarity with Muslim architecture, which led to the adoption of much of the lifestyle and culture of the people who had been defeated politically.

XI.1 **SEVILLE**

XI.1.a **Church of Santa Marina**

Santa Marina 3. It is best to follow the itinerary on foot, entering through the archway of la Macarena within the Muslim walls and then taking the calle San Luis. Opening hours: 11.00–13.00 and 18.00–20.00. Sat 11.00–13.00.

The Parish Church of Santa Marina is a rectangular structure. It has three aisles separated by eight pillars that support pointed arches, and a polygonal apse divided into three unequal spans with buttresses on the exterior. The roof of the aisles is formed from modern timber structures and the apse has ribbed vaulting. Three gothic mullioned windows light up the interior. Outside, the apse has brick buttressing and a cornice resting on rolled modillions.
The brick-built tower on a square ground plan has reinforced stone corners at the base. The stairway rises up around a central square pillar, with vaulting of various kinds. A crenellated parapet, added in the restoration of 1885, tops the belfry.
In the gable wall of the church, three *oculos* in stone allow light into the interior. Nevertheless, the most outstanding feature of the west wall is the stone-built doorway, its jambs finished in figurative capitals with plant, animal and human motifs. At the

Church of Santa Marina, façade and tower, Seville.

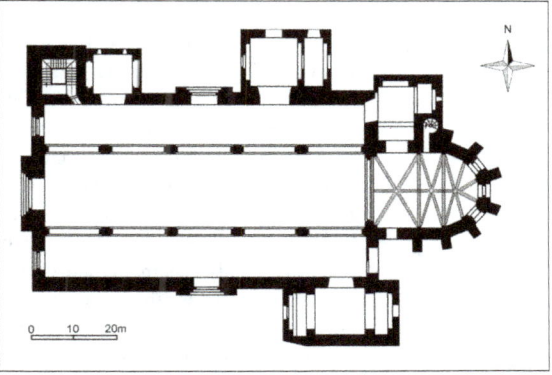

Church of Santa Marina, ground plan, Seville.

241

ITINERARY XI Temples and Palaces of Seville

Seville

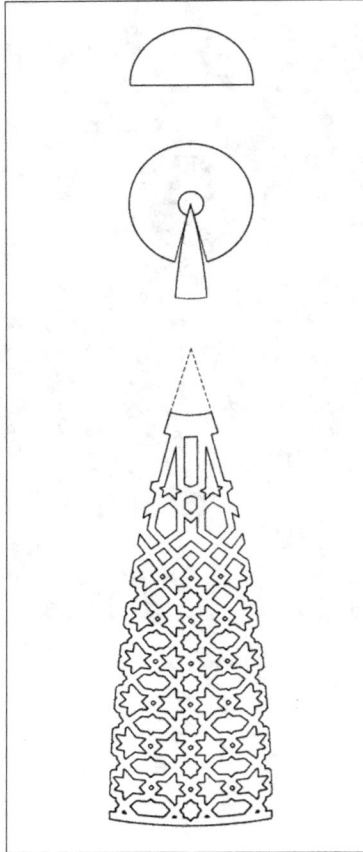

Church of Santa Marina, Chapel of la Piedad cupola, drawing of the strapwork, Seville.

level of the capitals there is a frieze with geometrical and plant themes in relief, as well as two figurative scenes which have been interpreted as scenes from the lives of Santa Marina, Santa Margarita, Santa Catalina and Santa Bárbara, whose statues appear under canopied niches around the archivolts of the doorway. The cornice rests on a series of lion's heads, separated by horseshoe arches. All the motifs in relief are highly schematic and rough. The church has another door on the north side that juts out from the line of the walls and is brick-built. It has three archivolts supported on stone imposts. Its ornamentation consists of a diamond-point border. Above the doorway there is rose window, its stone surround decorated with the same design. The Modernist tracery was an addition during restorations carried out in the church. Similar to the one described above, but undecorated, is the doorway in the south wall. The rose window above it still has its original tracery. In the interior, the division between the sanctuary and the nave of the church is clearly marked. The aisles are separated by rectangular brick pillars, upon which rest pointed and double arches that rise from stone imposts.

Fundamental elements in the spatial configuration of the church are the chapels open to the side aisles; all of which follows the model of Muslim *qubbas*, the simplest one of which the statue of the Divina Pastora has occupied since 1704. It opens onto the Gospel side aisle, and is square with a recessed arch in the sanctuary. The roof of the central section is formed of a vault of 16 sides on *trompas*. A similar scheme, although of smaller proportions, is used in the Sacramental Chapel, which gives access to the sanctuary.

The entrance roof has mirror vaulting in the Almohad style, and this is repeated in the recessed arch at its head. The square central area has segmented vaulting on *trompas*, which rest on semicircular arches. Both the entrance arch and the recessed arch rest on stone abacuses and late Roman or Visigothic capitals on top of white marble columns. During the restoration carried out in 1964, a triple tomb, covered with vitrified tiling in green, white and manganese, was found underneath the floor of the Sacramental Chapel. The pieces correspond to saltires and stars with eight points, as well as tiles with heraldic motifs in relief, all of which allows us to suppose that this precinct was originally the Memorial Chapel of the Hinestrosa family. These pieces of ceramic, dating from the mid-13th century, now decorate the altar frontal in this same chapel.

The Chapel of la Piedad, which opens onto the Epistle-side aisle is rectangular, with mirror vaulting in the recessed arches on its shorter sides; the central area is covered by a vault divided into 16 sections, on a double system of *trompas*. At the base of these there is plasterwork dating from the restoration carried out in 1885, copying a conserved fragment. The *intrados* of the vault is covered with dense knotwork in brick, which is incrusted with pieces of vitrified ceramic. Plasterwork and *muqarnas* are used at the base of the vaults of the *arcosolios*. The excavation work mentioned above made it possible to locate fragments of a floor and of a bedrock/basement of mosaics forming interlace patterns, as well as small tiles decorated with eagles and castles, corresponding to the arms of the Infante don Felipe, the Archbishop of Seville, between 1249 and 1258. This discovery has allowed the dating of the chapel to the mid-13th century, although it underwent redecoration in around 1415 for the burial of the shipowner Juan Martínez.

XI.1.b Church of Omnium Sanctorum

Peris Mencheta 2. Outside the church of Santa Marina take the street opposite called callejuela del Arrayán. Opening hours: 10.30–12.30 and 19.00–20.00, Sun 10.30–12.00.

Church of Omnium Sanctorum, central aisle, Seville.

This church has so many similarities and elements in common with the churches of San Andrés and San Estéban that they have come to be considered works by the same master. This hypothesis is difficult to prove, since there are also certain elements and circumstances that differentiate them. On the other hand, the relationship with and stylistic dependence upon the Church of Santa María are both so evident that the Parish Church of Omnium Sanctorum can be explained as a direct consequence of it. In relation to the building process, there are records of an important donation by the Infante of Portugal, don Dionís, during his stay in Seville in around 1260. There is also evidence that important renova-

ITINERARY XI   *Temples and Palaces of Seville*
Seville

Church of Omnium Sanctorum, balcony and panel with sebka *work on the bell tower, Seville.*

tion work was undertaken a century later during the reign of Pedro I of Castile.

The church has a rectangular ground plan with three aisles of five bays, separated by eight pillars, which support pointed arches, and a deep polygonal sanctuary. The apse has a roof of ribbed vaulting linked by a keystone rib. On the outside, the apse has brick buttresses and a cornice resting on corbels topped by crenellations. The roof of the sanctuary is accessed via a stairway inside a square turret adjoining the north wall of the apse. Three pointed mullioned windows allow light into this area. The roof of the aisles is formed of wooden structures, put in place during the restoration carried out in 1936.

The square, brick tower is accessed by means of a spiral staircase adjoining the side of the east front of the tower, since the lower floor of the tower is a chapel. On the outside, the window bays on the second floor are semicircular and framed by a multifoil arch inside an *alfiz*. Above these bays, and repeated on all sides of the tower, there is a large panel of *sebka* work enriched with *atauriques* in the Almohad tradition, inspired by the Giralda. A listel moulding marks the transition to the belfry, which has two bays on each side. Stylised corbels support the cornice, over which a pyramid-shaped finial with tiles was erected at the end of the 18th century.

The main door of the church is on the west front; built of stone it juts out beyond the line of the walls. The jambs are slender piers crowned with figurative capitals. The archivolts are pointed with a serrated decoration. Above the entrance there is a window made of thin gauged brickwork enriched with tiling. The other window openings are three stone *oculos*; those in the side aisles still have their original traceries.

In the north and south walls there are two more doorways that, basically, repeat the design of the main door, although the one on the south front has several niches that probably statues would have occupied at one time, which have now disappeared. The brackets for them remain, however, in the shape of pairs of lions with decorative canopies above them. Likewise, the lion's heads and plant motifs worked on the capitals are still visible. From the complex of windows, which originally illuminated the inside of the nave, the one in the south wall near the sanctuary is the most interesting: an *arco tumido* with spandrels decorated with *atauriques*.

ITINERARY XI   Temples and Palaces of Seville
Seville

In the interior, the church chapel that occupies the lower part of the tower is interesting. It follows the scheme of the Muslim *qubba* on a square base and octagonal vaulting on *trompas*. The precinct was given over to Gonzalo Gómez de Cervantes in 1416 as a burial chapel for himself and his descendants.

On account of a fire in the church in 1936 discoveries were made of ancient *arcosolios*, or fragments of plasterwork with *ataurique* and strapwork motifs in the Mudéjar style, dating to around 1400.

XI.1.c Church of San Marcos

Plaza de San Marcos. Take calle Feria as far as calle Castelar, on the left. Opening hours: 17.00–20.00. If closed, visits to the church can be arranged by telephone. Tel: 954 211421.

The unique synthesis between the Muslim Almohad heritage and the Gothic proposals that characterise the Mudéjar art and architecture of Seville from the second half of the 14th century, finds one of its best expressions in this church. Although its general organisation is not substantially different from other Mudéjar churches, San Marcos offers a series of special features that make it a unique example in the city. In fact, the degrees to which Islamic solutions are evident in the building, have allowed classification of it, in error, as a former mosque.

The church has three aisles – with the central nave higher and wider – separated by rectangular pillars that support horseshoe arches, framed in *alfizes* of Almohad proportions. Simple modern structures roof the aisles.

Church of San Marcos central aisle, Seville.

Church of San Marcos, detail of an arch, Seville.

ITINERARY XI   Temples and Palaces of Seville
Seville

Church of San Marcos, detail of the doorway, Seville.

The sanctuary, which is considerably lower than the rest of the church, has two sections: one rectangular, the other polygonal, and both have roofs formed of ribbed vaulting. The chancel arch, which is a pointed Gothic-style arch, rests on reused Roman columns and capitals.

On the outside, the gable wall shows the basilica structure of the aisles. In the centre, there is a notable splayed doorway jutting out from the wall, and above it, a small *oculo* to illuminate the interior. Built of stone, the doorway is decorated with diamond points as well as figurative relief work. A frieze with multifoil arches on small columns and *sebka* work completes the doorway; above it, there is a row of corbels, in the form of lion's heads, to support the cornice. In the three niches, with canopies and lion-head shaped pedestals, there are stone statues from the 18th century, which replace older ones that had deteriorated.

A singular element in this church is its brick tower, with its south and east sides perfectly finished, which has led to the consideration of it as a separate commission. An interior stairway adjoins the perimeter walls, with different types of vaulting covering the various flights. Also unusual is the design of the window arches, which have multifoil and lambrequin borders framed in *alfices* and decorated with *atauriques*. The four sides are finished with a frieze decorated with *sebka* work, which rise above multifoil arches resting on small columns, all of it clearly inspired by the Giralda. The Mudéjar tower finishes in eaves resting on corbels, many of them in the form of lion's heads, above which there is a parapet. An 18th-century belfry tops the shaft of the tower.

XI.1.d Church of Santa Catalina

Calle Almirante Apodaca. Take calle Bustos Tavera. Mass hours: 12.30 and 19.00, Sun 10.30, 12.00, 13.00 and 19.00.

This church must have been built in the second half of the 14th century on the site of an older mosque, since the base of the present tower corresponds to an Islamic building that can be dated between the 9th and 10th centuries. It is a work of cut stone in alternating headers and stretchers, square on the outside and inside, and a spiral staircase around a central cylindrical core. It follows, therefore, the design of the *alminares* of Seville from the Emirate's period.

The new Mudéjar church followed the usual scheme of these buildings: three naves separated by four pillars, which are cruciform in section, and a deep sanctuary of three bays. The

ITINERARY XI   *Temples and Palaces of Seville*
Seville

sanctuary has ribbed vaulting, while the roof of the central nave is formed of wooden structures of *armadura de par y nudillo*, with the side aisles covered by a single pitched structure. The armadura enriches its *almizate* in a decoration of knotwork and pendentives of *muqarnas*.
The church has three doors: the main door is at the foot of the church and is made of brick with interlaced multifoil arches framed in *alfiz*. This design is exceptional in the Mudéjar churches in Seville, since it clearly derives from Almohad designs, which other contemporary churches in the Aljarafe area follow. A similar design was likely to have been used for the doorway in the north front as well, judging by the elements that can still be seen around what today is a doorway with a lintel. The doorway in the south aisle is a simple pointed brick arch.
Nowadays, of these three original doors, only the last mentioned is visible from the outside, since the others have been hidden by other additions through time; the main door was hidden by a new gable wall where, in 1930, a doorway from the disentailed Church of Santa Lucia was inserted. This new façade also concealed some blind openings made of brick with multifoil arches framed in *alfiz*, which today are only visible from the choir loft. The door that was added is of cut stone, with both its design and the sculptural motifs so similar to those on the door of the church of Santa Marina that it can be presumed that it was made by the same craftsmen. A number of small stone statues are placed under canopies on either side, and above the keystone is the figure of the Eternal Father. The

Church of Santa Catalina, interior doorway, Seville.

doorway is finished with corbels of roll-shaped modillions with a central band.
The Mudéjar work of the tower is erected on top of the remains of the original *alminar*. From the outside, it has blind multifoil arches framed in *alfiz*, and sunken panels that must have been decorated with *sebka* motifs, which partially disappeared during the restoration carried out in 1881. The belfry has a horseshoe-shaped opening on each side, framed in *alfiz*, and crowned with a crenellated parapet.
Similar to the multifoil arches of the tower are those which exist on the façade and which, in the form of semicircular apses, correspond to an addition adjoining the north wall. Only the first of these belongs to the original building, the second is from the early part of the 20th century. An important Mudéjar element in this church is the chapel, added in around 1400 to the south wall, which is in

ITINERARY XI   Temples and Palaces of Seville

Seville

Church of Santa Catalina, drawing of the central aisle armadura, Seville.

use at present by the Society of the Hermandad de la Exaltación. This is a structure, which, following the model of the Muslim *qubba* is square with a vault on *trompas*, decorated with strapwork and incrusted with pieces of vitrified ceramic.

XI.1.e House of Pilate

Plaza de Pilatos 1. Take calle Alhóndiga as far as the Plaza de San Leandro and then calle Caballerizas. Entrance fee, except Tues 13.00–17.00. Opening hours: ground floor 09.00–19.00; guided tours of the upper floor 10.00–14.00 and 15.00–19.00.

The *Casa de Pilatos* (House of Pilate) is an architectonic complex started at the end of the 15th century on the initiative of don Pedro Enríquez, the Governor General of Andalucía. Don Pedro Enríquez's widow, doña Catalina de Ribera, continued the project; then their son, the Marquis of Tarifa, took it up; and, finally, the Duke of Alcalá completed it at the beginning of the 17th century.

Although the plan of the *Casa de Pilatos* may give an impression of disorder, on the other hand, it allows the visitor to enjoy an attractive and constantly surprising visit with delicious sensations of light, colour, sounds, smells and views, which are altogether unexpected. Architecture and nature are interwoven to form a whole here, ultimately creating something very similar to other medieval dwellings. However, some forms of ornamentation give the *Casa de Pilatos* a certain "Roman" air, which in many respects is reminiscent of the imperial houses in the nearby city of Itálica more than of the supposed Italian Renaissance models cited as inspiration for it. The fountain in the centre is the vertical axis of the whole space of the patio that earlier in medieval versions, tended towards compositions on longitudinal and horizontal axes. The marble sculptures brought from Italy by the Marquis, the columns ordered from Genoa, the mural paintings on the upper floor and other details, tell a story of the introduction of forms taken from Rome to Seville. Yet, generally, the air of the building gives off a whiff of Oriental perfume, which does not escape anybody, and which we can sum up in a few formal characteristics. The first of these is the indif-

ITINERARY XI *Temples and Palaces of Seville*
Seville

ference of the architect towards the exterior appearance of the complex, which remained "hermetically sealed" until the balconies were opened to give on to the calle Caballerizas in the 17th century. Another Oriental trait is the labyrinth-like design, and the succession of patios of different sizes with fountains and gardens in the interior. A third Islamic charac-teristic is the delicate examples of plasterwork featuring texts in Arabic calligraphy alongside Nasrid themes and some Gothic motifs. Lastly, and above all, there is the decorative ceramic tiling created by Diego and Juan Polido in the 1530s, which completes the image of a palace that was renovated constantly, taking inspiration from Oriental aesthetics.

House of Pilate, detail of the patio, Seville.

ITINERARY XI Temples and Palaces of Seville
Seville

Palace of the Counts of Altamira, cruciform interior garden, Seville.

XI.1.f **Palace of the Counts of Altamira**

Plaza de Santa María la Blanca 1. Go towards the Parish Church of San Esteban, which is also Mudéjar, and take calle Vidrio, which crosses through the former Jewish Quarter and leads to Santa María la Blanca. Next to this is the palace, used at present as the offices of the Consejería de Cultura de la Junta de Andalucía. (Department of Culture of the Government of Andalucía).

This palace, which belonged to the Zúñiga family, Dukes of Béjar and later the Counts of Altamira, is without any doubt the most outstanding example of Mudéjar domestic architecture after the Real Alcázar.
On approach, nothing about the exterior of this building suggests that it has an interior structured like a medieval dwelling. All that is visible on the outside is a monumental façade constructed by an anonymous 17th-century builder. Once inside the door and through the spacious entrance porch, the interior gives off a full medieval flavour, now well restored to its original glory by a comprehensive restoration project intended to convert the buildings for use by the *Consejería de Cultura de la Junta de Andalucía* (Department of Culture of the Autonomous Government of Andalucía).

The interior complex is a palace built for Diego López de Stúñiga on the site of eight or ten land plots, which made up his main property. The complex is on a surprising scale for the time for a construction that was not a royal palace. All the houses formed part of the Jewish Quarter; notable among these were the houses of the Jews Yusuf Pichon and Samuel Abrabaniel. The former was chief accountant and trusted adviser of Enrique III and the latter held the same position at the Court of Juan II and was converted to Christianity before the pogrom of 1391, the year in which the Jewish Quarter, where this palace once stood, was attacked and destroyed. One of the most interesting aspects of these medieval houses, which lie beneath the existing palace, is the extremely rich collection of ceramic floors discovered in the excavations undertaken before the restoration in 1998, which, unfortunately, had to be reburied and are now more than a metre below the present floor level. Floor tiles of alternating red and yellow clay, with extremely varied geometric forms, mixed with small, vitrified *aliceres* in black, white, green or honey colour, make up what now can be considered the best collection of Mudéjar flooring in Spain. Although very few examples have survived, the medieval patterns allow us to imagine the richness of the Mudéjar floors in Seville. The most intense decoration was concentrated on the thresholds between one room and another and in the mat designs at the entrance to the rooms —called *almatrallas* in the Mudéjar language — or "tables of tiles" by the Christians. The most accessible remains otherwise are in a small room where the original fountain has been reinstalled in the centre, raised above the level it was before, and surrounded by a copy of the original floor that was covered up again.

The 15th-century palace was organised around a large colonnaded patio that was subject to alternations in the late 17th century. Despite this, the general Mudéjar structure is still distinguishable, along with some other surviving elements in the same style. The gallery facing east has various Almohad capitals placed on reused Roman columns that show the medieval construction of the gallery. The open space of the patio centres on a long pool or "*alberca perlongada*" as the medieval byelaws of the *alarifes* of Seville call it, reminiscent of that in the *Patio de los Arrayanes* in the Alhambra in Granada, but of a type not known from any other example in Seville. The pool finishes in two fountains or basins at floor level. Occupying the extreme south of the patio is a solemn rectangular chamber with two alcoves, one at each end, separated from the main room by arches of carved plasterwork from the 15th century, and the remains of old *armaduras* from the ceilings exhibited on the walls.

In the west-facing gallery, the great *qubba* or reception room is still intact

Palace of the Counts of Altamira, Patio de los Azulejos, *Seville*.

to see, with its characteristic square shape that, unfortunately, has lost its original ceiling, but it must have been similar to the *qubbas* in other great houses in Seville.

The coverings of the vertical surfaces must also have been notable, although very little remains of them today. The best example is the left jamb of the entrance to the royal *qubba*, with tiling of the Granada-type of very small proportions, which is reminiscent of those in the *Mirador de Daraja* in the Alhambra, although less carefully executed.

The other patio of the medieval palace, built on a square floor plan, smaller in dimension and with arches on pillars, has been identified as that which the documents call the *Patio de los Azulejos*, or Tiled Patio. The name undoubtedly refers to the original ceramic decoration uncovered in recent excavations. The black and white marble tiles seen on the floor today, are the substitute for the alternating white and green tiles from the medieval period. This was probably a small patio for domestic use in contrast to the larger one for public use. This organisation of the palace around a larger patio and another smaller one follows a scheme, also seen in the *Alcázar de don Pedro (Patio de las Doncellas – Patio de las Muñecas)*, and maintained in the palaces of Morocco, where the large and small patios receive the name *wast al-dar* and *dwira*, respectively.

Sited today just inside the first bay of the façade the excavations discovered a beautiful small cruciform garden, one of the most perfect examples to survive of this kind of domestic garden, with four *parterres* divided by two walkways which cross in the centre, where there is a fountain.

XI.1.g Real Alcázar (Royal Palace)

Plaza del Triunfo. Enter by the Puerta de los Leones or Lions' Gate. Take the calle Fabiola and continue down calle Mateos Gago to the Cathedral. Entrance fee. Opening hours: summer 09.30–19.00, Sun and public holidays 09.30–13.00; winter 09.30–17.00, Sun and Public holidays 09.30–13.00.

Here we have what is perhaps the oldest royal palace in Europe still in use today. This building from its earliest beginnings has cast a spell over all those who have visited it, a fascination that drove the constant use of the same model for the royal and noble residences in Seville and Castile.

The Real Alcázar or Royal Palace was the scene of important historical and cultural occasions before and after the Mudéjar period. Here, some of the *Infantes* or royal children were born, and the marriage of the Emperor Carlos V took place here as well.

The complex of the Real Alcázar brings together the best examples of Mudéjar palace architecture, since its buildings are an organic mix of the remains of palaces from the *caliphs*, *taifas* and Almohads and of the Gothic and Mudéjar periods. All of the subsequent and continual interventions have failed to remove completely all vestiges of its former appearance.

The Alcázar Palace is made up of many palaces, among which are four of particular interest within the context of Mudéjar art: the *Cuarto del Caracol* (Snail Chamber), the *Sala de Justicia* (Chamber of Justice), the *Palacio de Pedro I* (Palace of Pedro I) and the *Cenador de la Alcoba* (Garden Pavilion).

To simplify things, it can be said that the *Cuarto del Caracol* – with its cruciform garden – built during the reign of Alfonso X of Sabio in the second half of the 13th century, is an Almohad palace translated into a Gothic one. Its Mudéjar character is evident in this artistic marriage rather than in its style. Unfortunately, reconstruction work in the 18th century destroyed its original appearance. We do not know what it was that created this extraordinary and fascinating complex, whether it was the reuse of structures, which predated the 12th century, or simply the participation of the Muslim *alarifes* in it. Its forms have the Gothic sobriety of the palaces in Burgos, while the spirit and planimetry of the whole is clearly Muslim. No other Gothic palace in the whole

ITINERARY XI   Temples and Palaces of Seville
Seville

of the peninsula matches it, nor is any Almohad palace the same. The U-shaped structure of its solemn vaulted chambers – some in parallel and others at right angles – along with the garden, which all the rooms give onto, makes clear this felicitous mix of two cultures of medieval Spain.

According to the Chronicles of King Pedro, the Palace of the Snail constituted the queen's apartments, while the king resided in the Almohad palace called *Cuarto del Yeso* (Plaster Chamber). The king's palace is where the famous *Cuadra de los Azulejos* (Tiled Chamber) was located, which could have been what now is known as the *Sala de Justicia*, with its restored *azulejos* tiling carried out in the 16th century.

The *Sala de Justicia* is a square pavilion joined to the former *Cuarto del Yeso* and located directly beside the *Corral de las Piedras*, or Stone Courtyard. Known formerly as the *Sala de los Consejos*, or Council Chamber, the supposition is that the monarch met here with his officials and took decisions of state. In fact, it is the area known as *mexuar* in the Muslim palaces, and it seems logical that it should be located close to the chamber where the king resided and yet be relatively far away from the most private areas.

We cannot discard the possibility that the royal *qubba* was erected on top of the Almohad foundations. Carriazo speculated that Alfonso XI built the chamber, but Gómez considers that there is neither historical data nor stylistic traits to indicate that it was not part of the building programme undertaken by don Pedro I, whose style can be seen in the plasterwork covering the walls.

Royal Alcázar, doorway to the palace of Pedro I, Seville.

Royal Alcázar, detail of the doorway to the Palace of Pedro I, Seville.

Temples and Palaces of Seville
Seville

The extraordinary aspect of the Real Alcázar is the above-mentioned Palace of Pedro I, the ancient *al-qsar al-Mubarak* (Palace of the Blessing) from the *taifa* era. Its imposing façade, already visible from the *Patio de la Montería*, is without any doubt the finest in Spanish Mudéjar. It sums up the best in the arts of the time, fusing elements from Seville (the tripartite structure of Almohad origin – the stone base, the blind arcades on both sides of the doorway and the multifoil windows); from Toledo (the lintel of the door); and from Granada (the frieze of smaller blind arcading and the large upper frieze with *kufic* epigraphy with the motto of the Nasrid dynasty). Besides the Muslim inscription, there is another in Gothic lettering praising the king and giving the date of the completion of the building (1364). The later repercussions of this doorway are important, however, not only to the art of Seville, but also in the rest of the Christian and Muslim kingdoms of the peninsula. According to some authors it was the model for the palace in Tordesillas in Valladolid and it might even have influenced Muhammad V to an extent, when, after his visit to Seville, he ordered the construction of the Palace of Comares in Granada. It may also have influenced the interior decoration of the Synagogue el Tránsito in Toledo, a building started by Juan Sánchez de Seville, treasurer to Pedro I.

Inside and through the angled entrance passageway is the *Patio de las Doncellas* or Court of the Maidens. The configuration seen here is the result of multiple alterations, the most important of which were the renovation of the original paving and the substitution of the original marble columns. The original columns, apparently, were very different from each other and so homogeneous Italian ones in the Corinthian style produced in the workshop of the Aprile family in Genoa in the mid-16th century replaced these. Construction of the upper gallery occurred in the 19th century at the same time as modifications were under way, and another modification in the 2000s attempted to restore the original, already partially conserved appearance by using plateresque plasterwork.

The splendid tiled dados always attract the attention of visitors. Although they have been partially restored in various different epochs those in the patio galleries date from the mid-14th century and, after those in the Alhambra, are the most complex in Spain's medieval architectural heritage, acting as the model for the others that were made in later palaces.

Various spaces are grouped around the patio. The oldest, called the *Salon de Embajadores* (Ambassadors' Chamber), would appear to be the remains of the old royal *qubba* of the Palace of al-Mutamid, called then the *Salon de las Pléyades*, and now integrated into the Palace of Pedro I. Pedro I commissioned the wooden doors, in 1363, from carpenters in Toledo, the dados and probably the floors – now lost – from tilers in Granada and the rest of the mural decoration from plasterers who mixed Nasrid and Christian traits. Beautiful poetic inscriptions allude to the palace, the *maecenas* and to Allah alongside medallions with scenes from the *Crónica Troyana* and the *Libro de la Montería*, two books in Pedro I's library, and which must have influenced his education since they deal with two essential facets of the life of a prince: war and hunting.

Among the most spectacular elements in the palace is the great semi-spherical or half-orange cupola constructed by Diego Ruiz in 1427 to replace the original one. Some have considered its knotwork design of stars to be a metaphor of the celestial vault. Beneath this, a frieze depicts portraits of the kings, which refers to the function this chamber must have had in the palace as the *Salon de Linajes*, or Chamber of the Nobility. Triple horseshoe arches give access from the side rooms to the *Salon del Trono*, or Throne Room, the reception rooms for the ambassadors.

The other two galleries of the patio give onto two rectangular rooms with alcoves at each end. These are the *Sala del Techo de Carlos V* (Chamber of Carlos V) and the *Dormitorio de los Reyes Moros* (the Bed Chamber of the Moorish Kings). Both of these are the work of King don Pedro, with the ceilings and some of the dados completed and remodelled at the time of the Catholic Monarchs and the Emperor Carlos V.

Next to the great *Cuarto del Rey don Pedro* (Chamber of King Pedro) in the public area of the palace, is the *Patio de las Muñecas* (Dolls' Court) of more domestic proportions. Here, the galleries on marble columns are outstanding, with caliphate capitals, plasterwork with reminiscences of Granada and tiled dados from the time of the Catholic Monarchs.

Set apart from the nucleus of the palace itself and formerly surrounded by orange groves (which are now mannerist gardens) is today's *Pabellon de Carlos V*, formerly called *Cenador de la Alcoba* (Arbor of the Alcove) or the private dining room, denoting both its function and the name of the garden near which it was situated. Its ground plan is square, while a wooden vault covers its cubic space. The gallery around its perimeter, the high polychrome dado of tiles, the water fountain in the centre of its exquisite tiled floor and the fluid relationship between the interior and exterior, convert it into the latest and most original version of the *qubba* or garden pavilion. Here, inextricably fused, are the Muslim and Renaissance traits that make this one of Spain's last and most refined expressions of Mudéjar art.

NATURE AND ARCHITECTURE

Alfonso Pleguezuelo Hernández

According to Nobert Shultz: "*architecture is the concrete manifestation of man's existential space*". In this sense, one could consider the house one more step on the way to the manifestation of the place occupied by man within the cosmos, and from which he contemplates two other spheres of the natural world: that which refers to his terrestrial position and that which also affects his human condition. In Mudéjar architecture, these traits – a reflection on these three levels of nature – are perceived in a particularly significant way.

The first of these relates architecture to cosmic nature. The architectonic form that most faithfully materialises in the idea of the universe is the cubic chamber, or *qubba*, defined by Islamic art, and adopted by the Mudéjar aesthetic. In it, the cube represents the earth and the semi-sphere that crowns it represents the celestial vault that protects and dominates it. The stars, which are scattered inside these domes, allude to the stars in the firmament. The best example of this architectonic metaphor in the Mudéjar architecture of Seville is in the *Salon de Embajadores* in the Real Alcázar. On the ceiling, the twelve stars that turn around the centre of the vault represent the twelve constellations of the zodiac. Underneath, there is the gallery of royal portraits, an element which adds a component of Christian origin to the space and which converts the Throne Room into the *Salon de Linajes* or Chamber of the Nobility. Here, the effigies of the kings assume both physically and symbolically an intermediate position between the heavenly and the earthly spheres, legitimising the power of whoever occupied the throne. The perfection reached in these *qubbas* meant that every noble palace had one, sometimes called the Room of the Portraits and sometimes the Room of the Half Orange, to distinguish them from the other rooms in the house on account of the shape of the ceiling.

The second level concerns the relationship between architecture and earthly nature. For medieval man, nature in its wild state was the result of the expulsion from Paradise, the reason why the elements became hostile to him. On the contrary, in the Garden of Eden everything was at the service of man, for his use and delight without labour or toil. A prefiguration of this lost Paradise (destined to be regained in the next world) are the gardens within or near the humanised space of the *urbe* and its surroundings. In the vegetable gardens outside the city and in the great gardens that surround the Mudéjar residences, there appears as an essential element the pavilion or *cenador* – a minimal architectonic unit inserted into a tamed area of nature. Here, the garden is understood not in its modern lay sense, but in its accepted medieval and sacred sense of the "enclosed garden" where, in a way even more faithful to the Edenic tradition, the illusion of a space where harmony reigns is created. As well as the pavilion as the minimal architectonic expression inserted into the larger garden, a small fragment of nature is integrated into what is really the house itself: the cruciform garden. The Muslim world received this ancient tradition from the Near East and transmitted the idea of the domestic garden – structured in a rectangle, divided into four parts by two walks, which intersect in the centre – to the West. At the centre, a fountain spurts out water, and from here irrigation channels distribute the water to the four *parterres*. Seville has several examples of these gardens, which testify to their Muslim past and their later Christian iterations.

On the third level, the house itself and the parts that make it up relate architecture to human nature, with the former assuming a final metaphorical value. In the Muslim world and in its Mudéjar derivation, the house is the dominion of the woman, while the street is the dominion of the man. The mystic and unfathomable sense the divinity possesses in the Islamic world is linked predominantly to the sphere of the soul; this, in turn, is embodied in feminine nature, which is simultaneously fluid, diffuse and receptive. From this, it follows that the house, understood as a sacred receptacle, must be, just as the woman is, veiled, hidden and not evident. The soul, the house and the woman are pure interiority without limits and, as a result, the paradigm of a culture that seeks perfection in the intimate. The exterior laconicism of the Mudéjar house compared with its shining and jewelled interior is like the wife who hides herself behind her veil to go out and whose graces are the reserve of the eyes of her spouse only. The obsessive emphasis on honour as the supreme value of the Christian knight and his family may be, in fact, the best testimony of the hybrid nature of the culture of Mudéjar Spain

Royal Alcázar, view of the Cenador de la Alcoba. Seville.

ITINERARY XII

The Aljarafe of Seville

Alfredo J. Morales

This itinerary is part of the programme "**Gateway to the Mediterranean**", co-funded by the European Union within the framework of the Pilot Project Spain-Portugal-Morocco, Art. 10 FEDER.

XII.1 GERENA
    XII.1.a Church of the
        Inmaculada Concepción

XII.2 AZNALCÓLLAR
    XII.2.a Chapel Cemetery

XII.3 SANLÚCAR LA MAYOR
    XII.3.a Church of Santa María
    XII.3.b Church of San Eustaquio
    XII.3.c Church of San Pedro

XII.4 BENECAZÓN
    XII.4.a Church of Santa María
        de las Nieves

XII.5 SHRINE OF CASTILLEJA
    DE TALHARA

XII.6 AZNALCÁZAR
    XII.6.a Church of San Pablo

XII.7 ERMITA DE GELO (optional)

Traditional Muslim Funerary Chapels and Presbyteries

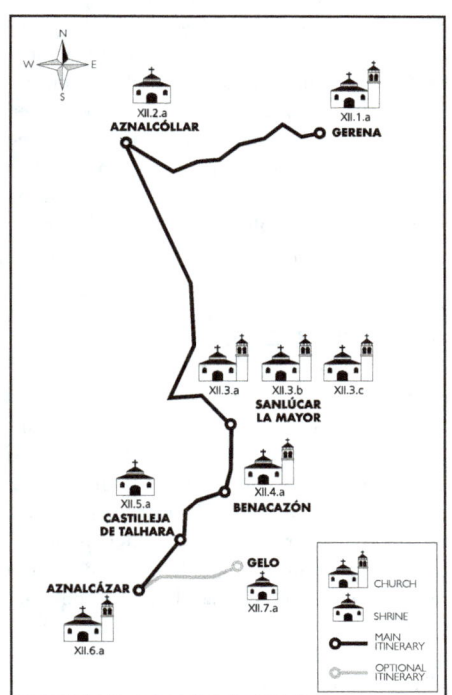

*Church of
San Eustaquio,
side door,
Sanlúcar la Mayor.*

ITINERARY XII *The Aljarafe of Seville*
Gerena

*Church of
La Inmaculada
Concepción,
side door, Gerena.*

One of the most remarkable regions of the province of Seville, and one that has always been the most closely connected with the capital, is the Aljarafe. Its name comes from the Arabic word *as-saraf*, which can be translated as "height" or "a slightly higher place". In fact, this is a sort of *atalaya*, which looks down over the city of Seville and a large part of the valley of the River Guadalquivir. From Muslim times, the chronicles refer to its dense, extensive olive groves, which in turn led to the progressive equating of the term *aljarafe* and "land of olives", a definition that was significantly misleading when it came to establishing the geographical boundaries of the district. Nevertheless, it is generally accepted that Aljarafe coincides with the ridges of land that exist between the valleys of the rivers Guadalquivir and Guadiamar.

In this area, to the west of the city of Seville, there have been many great estates since medieval times belonging to the Military Orders, the Church and the aristocracy. Its population changed significantly because of the Conquest of Seville in 1248, when a large contingent of Christians joined the numerous groups of Muslims who had decided to stay in the district. The situation changed after the uprising of 1264–1266 after the decision was made to expel the Muslims and to confiscate their property. The failure of the resettlement resulted in the serious decline of the population of the area, with groups of people inhabiting a few places and the disappearance of many villages. There was no significant growth in the population until the mid-15th century, and, even then, it accentuated the concentration in the more densely populated areas and the abandonment of the more sparsely populated ones. All of these facts had an important effect on the chronology and character of the Mudéjar work in this district.

XII.I GERENA

Although the River Guadiamar runs through this municipal district of Gerena, it forms part of the district of Sierra Norte. Nevertheless, a visit is recommended as a high point on the route through the Aljarafe because of the exceptional design of the sanctuary of the parish church, which is related to some of the Mudéjar models in the Aljarafe proper.

XII.1.a Church of the Inmaculada Concepción

Opening hours: 06.30–21.00, Sun 09.30–12.30. If the church is closed, a visit can be arranged through the Parish. Tel: 95 5782023.

The Church of the Inmaculada Concepción is a Mudéjar building dating from the 14th century. The rectangular building has three aisles, separated by six cruciform pillars that support pointed arches; it has a flat apsoidal wall at the head of the sanctuary, as well as the two chapels in the side aisles. The sanctuary, in the apse of the main nave, is square, with a roof formed of a large groined vault resting on *trompas* in the corners. In the side apses, the space, which was too narrow and deep, divides into two square sections, the first covered with a false ceiling, while the second repeats the vault of the sanctuary. In this way, the most complicated solution possible was chosen when the configuration of the sanctuary in this church was decided, which was to take the model of the Muslim *qubba*. The roof covering the aisles of this church is a modern structure made intentionally to look like the original Mudéjar wooden one. Another bay was added to extend the church during the second half of the 16th century; this would explain the larger size of the arches nearest the foot of the church, and the fact that their construction is not the same as that used in the rest of the church. This extension was the work of the architect Hernán Ruiz el Joven.

On the outside of the church are three doorways; the two side doors are stone and in the Gothic style, while the door in the south wall has an archivolt decorated with diamond points. Columns and a cornice form an *alfiz*.

The Renaissance-style door in the end wall, at the foot of the church, dates to 1569 and corresponds to the extension of the church by Hernán Ruiz. Its bicoloured brick is a characteristic that should be interpreted as a technical and aesthetic survival of Mudéjar solutions.

The tower rises above the eight-sided vault of the apse on the south side. It has only one section as well as the belfry and the finial spire. Some of the windows, both real and blind, are of considerable interest since they present interlaced multifoil arches similar to those used in the different churches of the Aljarafe district.

XII.2 AZNALCÓLLAR

XII.2.a Chapel Cemetery

12 km on the A477. The cemetery is at the highest point of the town popularly called "Zawira". The cemetery sexton holds the key to the Chapel. Opening hours: summer 08.00–12.00 and 17.00–20.00, winter 10.00–13.00 and 15.00–18.00.

Within what formed at one time the walled precinct of the Muslim city, the Cemetery Chapel, belonging to a Mudéjar building, developed in a reverse way to those in Gelo, Benacazón and Castilleja de Talhara, in that it grew from a sanctuary in the form of a *qubba* and was then completed with the addition of the nave section. The present square-shaped chapel has brick and cob walls and is covered

ITINERARY XII   *The Aljarafe of Seville*
Sanlúcar la Mayor

Cemetery Chapel, general view, Aznalcóllar.

by an eight-sided vault on *trompas*. On the north and the east walls are the remains of windows while on the south wall a complete window has survived in the form of a pointed horseshoe arch resting on piers with a squared *alfiz*. On this same side, a rectangular addition houses the staircase, giving access to the roof terrace. In its interior space, the staircase adopts a polygonal plan, illuminated by a window similar to that described above.

The west front, which is now the façade, originally joined onto the nave. The lines of the double-pitched roof of the nave are still visible, as is the springing of the perimeter walls. Demolishing the aisles meant that the pointed bay framed in *alfiz*, once the chancel arch of the church, had to be partially blocked. This reduced the space, which up until then had allowed access to the sanctuary. With

this operation, the latter recovered its typical *qubba* form as can be seen today.

Stylistically the church can be dated from the end of the 15th century. Its construction may be seen in relation to the sizeable increase in the population that Aznalcóllar experienced in the late years of the same century. It must have been at the end of the 18th century, with the inauguration of the new parish church in the town, when the Mudéjar church was abandoned and the parts that were in ruins, such as the nave and aisles, were demolished. However, the paintings that decorate the vault of the old sanctuary suggest a 19th-century intervention that would have resulted in the definitive abandonment of the sanctuary.

XII.3 SANLÚCAR LA MAYOR

The next town, Sanlúcar la Mayor, is precisely at the point where the steep descent down to the River Guadiamar begins. This is an important strategic position, since it controls the road between Seville and Niebla. There are three important Mudéjar churches here: Santa María, San Eustaquio, and San Pedro. These are three buildings where compositional solutions, plastic resources and a formal repertory – the origins for which must be sought in the Hispano-Muslim art of the Almohad period – can be found. There must have been other important architectonic creations in the same style in Sanlúcar la Mayor, but the only surviving evidence is the imposing remains of the walled precinct.

ITINERARY XII   *The Aljarafe of Seville*
Sanlúcar la Mayor

XII.3.a Church of Santa María

19 km on the A477, in the centre of the town. Visits can be arranged with the layperson in charge of the Parish. Tel: 95 5700107. Opening hours: summer 10.00–12.00 and 19.00–21.00, winter 10.00–12.00 and 19.00–20.30.

While typically seen as the "parish church of Seville-type", the Church of Santa María, in fact, offers some highly interesting peculiarities. As is usual of this type, the sanctuary is polygonal and has two sections with roofs of ribbed vaults. The chancel arch, which links the sanctuary with the nave, is pointed, and rests on superimposed classical shafts with capitals considered Visigothic.
Ten pillars separated the three aisles initially, but during alterations that took place at the beginning of the 17th century, pairs of marble columns replaced these. The arches, clearly of Almohad heritage, were of the pointed horseshoe-type framed in *alfices*, but in an intervention, which probably coincided with the replacement of the pillars, they were lopped off at the springers and transformed into stilted arches.
The three naves' roofs are formed of a wooden structure. The most important is that above the central nave, which follows the model of the Mudéjar *armaduras* of the *par y nudillo* type, although the work is dated 1773 and includes Baroque ornamental motifs.
In the north aisle there is a small square chapel covered by a groined vault on trompas, which follows the model of the Muslim *qubba*.
Of the three doorways in the church, that on the west side lost its original physiognomy during one of the many alterations, perhaps in the 16th century. Nevertheless, on this same façade, there are still two surviving *oculos* and a large window with multifoil arches, which illuminate the interior of the church. The doorway in the south wall is of particular interest, built of brick and with two multifoil arches framed in an *alfiz*, the formula of its composition is of Almohad origin.

Church of Santa María, main door, Sanlúcar la Mayor.

XII.3.b Church of San Eustaquio

If the church is closed, arrange a visit through the Parish. Opening hours: Sun 11.00–13.30.

The Church of San Eustaquio is another typical example of the parish churches of Seville. It has a polygonal sanctuary and three naves. The sanctuary has buttresses on the exterior, a crenellated walkway and windows with multifoil arches.

ITINERARY XII   The Aljarafe of Seville
Sanlúcar la Mayor

Church of
San Eustaquio,
façade and bell tower,
Sanlúcar la Mayor.

Ribbed vaults with a keystone rib and a pointed chancel arch resting on pillars with Gothic capitals grace the interior. Eight pillars, which also act as supports for pointed arches, separate the three aisles with roofs formed of wooden structures: *armadura* of *par y nudillo* in the main nave and single-pitched in the side aisles.

Two of the three doors are in the side walls, both built of brick, and almost identical in their compositional scheme: each has a pointed arch, framed by another double multifoil arch and a large *alfiz*; in other words, they make use of the same solution as in the side door of the Church of Santa María and the church in Castilleja de Talhara. Above both doorways, there is an *oculo*. Four superimposed arches frame the third doorway at the foot of the church: two are pointed and one is both horseshoe and pointed. The shape of the entrance door must have undergone alterations and, originally, must have been a pointed horseshoe arch as well.

XII.3.c Church of San Pedro

Visits can be arranged through the Parish.

The Church of San Pedro is considered the oldest in town and has even been related to an ancient mosque. Although this relationship has no scientific basis, it is clear that its unusual structure, separate tower and its siting within the walls of the original Almohad Alcázar nearby have all encouraged this idea. Nevertheless, it is a Mudéjar church of the "parish church of Seville-type" even though the raised choir for the monks differentiates it; the street passing underneath communicated with the ancient cemetery situated on the left-hand side of the church and enclosed by a wall.

The church has a sanctuary divided into two parts, one rectangular and one polygonal, and both have roofs of ribbed vaulting. There is then a nave with three aisles separated by four slender pillars, which support pointed arches with blind windows in the spandrels, formed by pointed horseshoe arches. Communication between the nave and sanctuary is through a pointed arch that rests on columns with Gothic capitals decorated with plant motifs.

The central nave has an *armadura* of *par y nudillo* roof, while the side aisles have wooden single-pitched structure roofs. Two chapels open from the north side aisle, one in the design of a *qubba*, that is, square, with a vault on *trompas* in the corners.

ITINERARY XI *The Aljarafe of Seville*
Sanlúcar la Mayor

Some remains of the plasterwork survive in the sanctuary and it is probable that originally the whole chancel was decorated in the same way, and that this, along with some pieces of vitrified ceramics, may have embellished the bedrock. In addition to these wall coverings, it is easy to imagine that much of the interior of the church would have had pictorial and figurative decoration, several fragments of which have appeared as successive coats of whitewash have peeled off. This rich and colourful imagery must have been commonplace in Mudéjar churches before the modifications in modern times and some unfortunate restoration works carried out in contemporary times.

Of the church's three doors, those in the south and end walls are of most interest. In these, it is clear how Mudéjar is the result of the assimilation and synthesis of elements derived from Hispano-Muslim, Romanesque and Gothic art.

The south door, which is the most modern, is clearly Christian in origin and juts out from the line of the walls with its splayed arch and archivolts resting on piers. The enormous rose window above it also follows the Gothic model.

The other doorway follows Almohad inspiration. It has a double multifoil arch framed in *alfiz* and a vertex decorated with vitrified ceramic. A later modification altered the door. There are three windows on this wall, the central one of which closely follows the Gothic model, while those at the side are pointed horseshoe arches framed in *alfiz*, in obvious Muslim taste.

The third door follows this same design, since it maintains the pointed door arch. Just above the cornice, an *oculo* provides illumination. The simple lines of this door suggest that this may have been the first door built in the church.

The tower, as mentioned above, is separate. It is on a square ground plan and has various entrances; two of them are next to each other, both offering a throughway. The pointed horseshoe arch openings are repeated in some of the windows higher up the tower. Other openings are simple loopholes.

Church of San Pedro, Sanctuary, Sanlúcar la Mayor.

ITINERARY XII *The Aljarafe of Seville*
Benacazón

Church of Santa María de las Nieves, Sanctuary vault, Benacazón.

XII.4 **BENACAZÓN**

XII.4.a Church of Santa María de las Nieves

5 km on the A477. Opening hours: summer 19.00–21.00, rest of the year 18.30–20.00, Sun 10.00–12.00. Closed Thurs.

The Parish Church of Santa María de las Nieves in Benacazón, was originally a Mudéjar church. The building underwent total restructure during the 17th and 18th centuries and now has a square sanctuary and two aisles. The sanctuary has a vaulted ceiling resting on a double system of *trompas*. On the east and south walls there is a steep staircase, covered with stretches of barrel- and cross vaulting, giving access to the walkway on the roof that has a crenellated parapet. The aisles have wooden ceilings, coffered in the main aisle and single-pitched on the side aisle.

The sanctuary follows the model of the Muslim *qubba*, and, intended as an imposing *atalaya*, it is considerably higher. Originally, there was another aisle adjoining this square structure, which was shorter than the existing ones, but the visual links with the sanctuary would have been unsatisfactory according to this solution, because the reduced-size chancel arch, separating both areas, blocked the view.

The church building can be dated to the end of the 15th century. There does not seem to be any remains of the older church in what is now the main nave, which must have been constructed in the mid-17th century at the same time as the side aisle.

ITINERARY XII The Aljarafe of Seville
Castilleja de Talhara

The wooden structures that comprise the ceilings of both parts of the nave conform to Mudéjar carpentry models. The building of the new nave, which is higher than the original one, and the remodelling of the chancel arch to make the sanctuary more prominent, made it necessary to alter the *trompas* supporting the vault. In its new configuration, these take the form of diamond points that were popular in the plasterwork decorations in the first half of the 17th century.

XII.5 SHRINE OF CASTILLEJA DE TALHARA

4 km along the A477, take a right turn off along an unmade road. It belongs to the Municipal District of Benecazón. The shrine is surrounded by olive and orange groves and the gardens of the chapel itself, which have recently been restored. Visits can be arranged through the Town Hall. Tel: 95 5705173.

This place, established as a Lordship in 1371, became an entailed estate in 1477 when Fernando Ortiz and Leonor Fernández de Fuentes purchased it. The Shrine of Castilleja de Talhara, now incomplete and partially ruined, is built in bricks and adobe with a square sanctuary and nave, divided into three aisles. Originally, the sanctuary roof was formed of a segmented vault on *trompas* and the aisles must have had roofs with wooden structures, although nothing remains of them today. Cruciform pillars supported by pointed arches separate the aisles. The church has two doorways: one in the main façade at the foot, and the other in the left aisle. The former is one of the most attractive of all the Mudéjar doorways in Seville, with its pointed archivolts and a pointed and multifoil arch framed in *alfiz*. In it, elements in fine bare brick are combined with others, which may have been pargeted to imitate a bicoloured bond. This scheme is reminiscent of the doorways of the parish churches in the nearby town of Sanlúcar la Mayor, although, here, a clever combination of materials and the resulting play of textures enriches the style. This

Shrine of Castilleja de Talhara, elevation, Benecazón.

267

ITINERARY XII *The Aljarafe of Seville*
Castilleja de Talhara

Shrine of Castilleja de Talhara, general view, Benecazón.

Shrine of Castilleja de Talhara, ground plan, Benecazón.

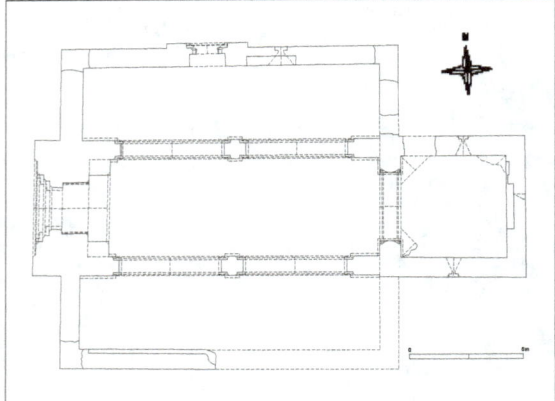

doorway should be considered as one more link in the evolutionary chain of doorways of bare brick with inset or relief strapwork, which appear in many areas of Seville.

The side door is simpler, having an arch with a double surround, straight jambs and *alfiz*. Of the various windows that light the interior of the church, the most interesting is the one on the north wall of the sanctuary, which may have had its design repeated in those on the other walls. This is a pointed horseshoe arch framed in *alfiz*, while inside, which is a pointed bay, it is made of gauged brick and decorated with pieces of vitrified ceramics in green and cobalt blue.

With respect to how the church was constructed, we can establish two different phases: the oldest part is the sanctuary, a structure in the form of a *qubba*, which may have either stood on its own or been joined to a low nave. The connection between the sanctuary and the nave must have been through a small pointed opening, so that the space of the sanctuary had an independent function as is typical of a *qubba*.

The building dates to around 1371, when Alonso Fernández de Fuentes constituted the Lordship of Castilleja de Talhara. The whole building underwent reconstruction a century later; this is likely to have been in response to the increased population, but serves to show the authority of the lords at that time – the only ones in the area – the Ortiz family, who in 1477 had founded an entailed estate. The present nave was constructed at this time, but does not seem to have been connected with the sanctuary, thus it was necessary to alter the chancel arch by raising it and incorporating new supports. In this way, greater visual fluidity and better spatial connection was achieved between the chancel and the nave.

XII.6 AZNALCÁZAR

XII.6.a Church of San Pablo

4 km on the A477. Mass hours: Sat 19.30 (summer 20.30), Sun 10.00 and 12.00. For visits on other days, contact the Parish Priest. Tel: 95 5750635.

The Parish Church of San Pablo is considered one of the finest works of Mudéjar architecture in Seville. The chancel has two sections, one rectangular and the other polygonal, both with ribbed vaulting. The nave has three aisles separated by slender pillars that support pointed arches, over these modern wooden ceilings are inspired by Mudéjar models.

The west door, constructed in brick and framed within a pier moulding, has pointed archivolts finished off with corbelled eaves embellished with corbels and graded crenellations.

The door in the south wall is made of fine gauged brick with alternating ochre and reddish tones. It has pointed archivolts flanked by pier mouldings and splendid strapwork tracery that fills the spandrels. An eave, with corbels and a frieze with lozenges, complete the door.

The separate tower is in the sanctuary of the church. The interior staircase, which climbs around a central square pillar, has a cross- and pointed-barrel vaulting roof. The belfry, which dates from the 18th century, is contemporary with the alterations made throughout the whole building during this period.

This church relates closely to other parish churches in Seville, probably built around 1356, as is the case of Omnium Sanctorum, San Andrés, and San Esteban. Nevertheless, this church is thought to be later; the sanctuary of the church dates from the beginning of the 15th century, while the nave seems to be somewhat later. The last parts built must have been the doorways, in around 1500.

Parish church of San Pablo, side door, Aznalcázar.

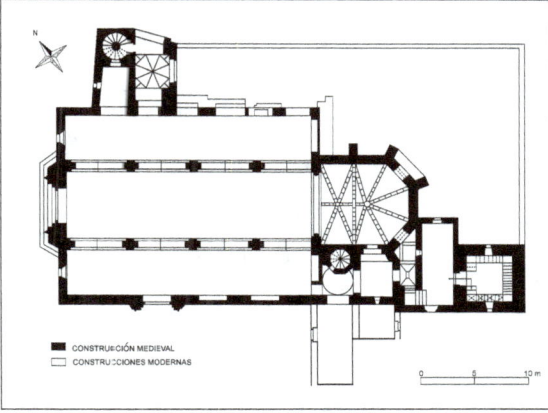

Church of San Pablo, ground plan, Aznalcázar.

Ermita de Gelo

Doñana

There are many reasons for the importance of the Doñana National Park but, essentially, its value lies in its rich fauna and ecology. From the point of view of wildlife, Doñana is a fundamental wintering and migration as well as resting place and breeding area for many species of birds. As far as the landscape is concerned, there are three differentiated ecological areas – the sand dunes, game reserve and marshes – giving Doñana a unique diversity and wealth of avifauna.
The Visitor Centre "José Antonio Valverde" *is recommended and can be reached from Aznalcázar along the signed track. There are other interesting ways to visit the Park such as in a Land Rover from El Rocío (Tel: 959 430432) or by boat aboard the Buque Real San Fernando up the River Guadalquivir from Sanlúcar de Barrameda (Tel: 956 363813).*

Centro de Interpretación del Corredor Verde
(Green Belt Visitor Centre)
At the end of the 1990s, there was a spill of toxic residues from a mine near the marshes of Doñana when the deposit that held them burst. The great landslide of highly toxic slime made its way all along the valley of the River Guadiamar and reached several parts of the National Park. The effects of the spillage are still evident today in spite of the incessant cleaning-up operation, which is still underway.
At present the Comunidad Autónoma de Andalucía *(Autonomous Community of Andalucía), with funding from the EU, is developing one of the most ambitious and complex programmes of landscape restoration ever carried out in Europe. Specialists from all fields of environmental studies are carrying out numerous analyses and suggesting proposals that the hope is will allow the River Guadiamar to flow with clean water again and recuperate the original vegetation and avifauna. The documentation of the whole operation will remain on display in a Visitor Centre in Aznalcázar.*

XII.7 ERMITA DE GELO (optional)

4 km on the A474. It belongs to the Municipal district of Benecazón. Visits can be arranged through the Town Hall in Benecazón.

This building, an outstanding example of Mudéjar religious architecture, is practically all that is left of what was once a village property of the Canons of the Cathedral of Seville until its sale in the mid-15th century to the Knight of Seville, don Gonzalo of Saavedra and his wife, doña Inés de Ribera.

This recently restored little church has a rectangular ground plan with three aisles separated by rectangular pillars. It has a square sanctuary adjoined at one side by the sacristy and a house. Modern wooden structures that reproduce the ancient Mudéjar roof forms cover the three aisles, and over the sanctuary is an eight-sided vault on *trompas*. Among the outstanding elements of this building is the doorway in the west wall, built of brick with pointed archivolts, finishing in a crenellated cornice. Also noteworthy is the blind window in the front wall; this has a pointed multifoil arch resting on piers, which is framed in an *alfiz* decorated with strapwork motifs.

The present building is the result of a long historical process that divides into four basic stages. The first phase resulted in a single nave church covered by a wooden structure, and a square sanctuary, which followed the model of the Muslim *qubba*. The vault of this part must have appeared in the *extrados* and emerged onto a flat roof. The entrance must have been through the west door. This door, along with the window in the front wall, allows this first phase to be dated to the late 15th century.

During the second stage, the church was extended to three aisles and the chancel arch was enlarged to improve the flow between the sanctuary and the nave. The height of the nave meant that the walls of the sanctuary had to be raised, and the original flat roof was replaced by a hip roof. In addition, a bell gable was erected over the west doorway of the church. This phase of the work must have been carried out in the first third of the 17th century.

Another phase in the history of the building corresponds to the 19th century when the whole structure was repaired and the bell gable and side door were rebuilt. The work done in the 20th century was even more decisive and corresponds to the fourth phase in the history of the building. There was an intervention in the 1940s that from a historical point of view fundamentally affected the wooden ceilings and the floors. The decision to carry out the most recent restoration work, which took place in 1998, sought to rectify the abandoned and almost completely ruined state of the building. This complete restoration recuperated the old structures and other elements maintaining the contributions of the different phases.

The recommended route back to Seville is along the Seville-Huelva motorway.

*From Seville a link can be made to the Moroccan MWNF exhibition: "**Andalusian Morocco: Discovery in Living Art**", or this itinerary can be continued to Granada.*

Shrine at Gelo, elevation, Benecazón.

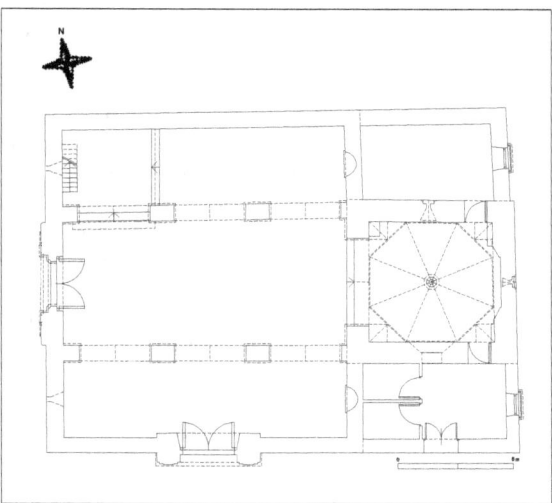

Shrine at Gelo, ground plan, Benecazón.

TRADITIONAL MUSLIM FUNERARY CHAPELS AND PRESBYTERIES

Alfredo J. Morales

A number of Seville's noble families had memorial chapels built in parish churches that copied the formula of the Muslim *qubba*: a space with a dome and versatile in character, which often serves as burial space, adopting a square ground plan configuration and increased in height by a vaulted ceiling on *trompas*. This type of structure, which became widespread at the beginning of the 15th century, extended throughout the Archdiocese of Seville and into Castile. Opening from the side aisles of these churches the memorial chapels were autonomous units, which contributed to the widening of the internal space and enriched the volume of the exterior profile of the churches.

In their simplest form, the chapels are normally square with ceilings arranged as ribbed vaults, which rest on corner *trompas*. This schema was then progressively enriched by fragmenting or doubling the system of *trompas*, and multiplying the number of intercrossing ribs in the *intrados*, until they developed into complex compositions dominated by strapwork. On the exterior, normally there is a covering over the vault, while the walls are finished by a walkway with crenellated merlons. The few window openings provided light; these were normally simply loopholes, but are interesting because of the different types of arches, normally contained within an *alfiz*, which frame them.

At present that the oldest surviving memorial chapel of this type is considered to be in the Parish Church of San Pedro in Seville, where an inscription dates it to 1379. However, the Chapel of la Quinta Angustia in the former Convent of San Pablo, now the Parish Church of the Magdalena, could possibly be even earlier, since we know that it was rebuilt after a fire that destroyed the convent church in 1353. The most outstanding chapel of this type, leaving aside the question of age, is that called de la Piedad, in the Church of Santa Marina, dated to around 1415.

Although not all the chapels here reach the decorative richness of this latter one, there are many others in the Archdiocese of Seville of equal splendour, for example, in San Pedro in Sanlúcar la Mayor, San Pablo in Aznalcázar, San Jorge in Palos de la Frontera, and San Marcos in Jerez de la Frontera.

The use of these memorial chapels spread to Córdoba; here, examples have survived in the Churches of San Miguel, San Pablo, and Santa Marina. By the time the stylistic properties of these churches had reached Castile, the model had recovered the complexity and rich ornamentation of the finest ones in Seville. Examples of these are the Chapel of San Jerónimo in the Franciscan Convent of La Concepción in Toledo, La Mejorada in Olmedo, and the "Capilla Dorada", or Gilded Chapel, in the Convent of Santa Clara in Tordesillas.

At a later date, and now with their memorial character forgotten, these structures in the form of a *qubba* were used as the model for the design of the sanctuaries in some of the Mudéjar

churches in Seville, especially in the district of the Aljarafe. The most complex and original solutions are those of the Parish Churches of Hinojos and Gerena.

Church of la Magdalena, Chapel de la Quinta Angustia vault.

ITINERARY XIII

First day

Rodrigo de Mendoza, Marquis of Zenete – from La Calahorra Castle to El Albaicín

Rafael López Guzmán, Miguel Ángel Sorroche Cuerva

This itinerary is part of the programme "**Gateway to the Mediterranean**", co-funded by the European Union within the framework of the Pilot Project Spain-Portugal-Morocco, Art. 10 FEDER.

XIII.1 LA CALAHORRA
    XIII.1.a Castle-Palace
    XIII.1.b Church of La Calahorra

XIII.2 LANTEIRA
    XIII.2.a Church of Lanteira

XIII.3 JEREZ DEL MARQUESADO
    XIII.3.a Church of Jerez del Marquesado

XIII.4 GUADIX
    XIII.4.a Church of Santa Ana
    XIII.4.b Church of Santiago
    XIII.4.c Church of San Miguel
    XIII.4.d Church of San Francisco
    (optional)

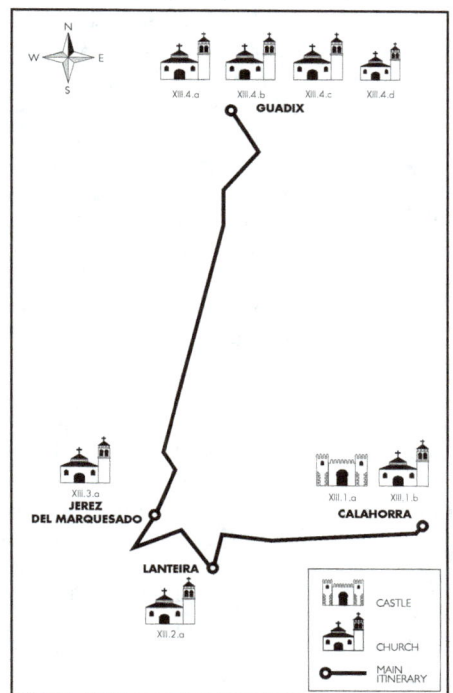

Palace of the Madraza, Chamber of the Twenty-Four Gentlemen, detail of the coffered ceiling, Granada.

ITINERARY XIII   *Rodrigo de Mendoza, Marquis of Zenete — from La Calahorra Castle to El Albaicín*

San Miguel Bajo, entrance to the aljibe *or water cistern, Granada.*

Royal Hospital, detail of the staircase ceiling in the Patio de los Mármoles, Granada.

This two-day itinerary recreates to some extent the historical route between the district of the Marquesado, or estates of the Marquis of Zenete, and the city of Granada. This route linked Rodrigo de Mendoza in retirement in his Castle Palace, La Calahorra, with the two properties he began to build in Granada: a villa on the outskirts of the city on the site of a Moorish *almunia*, or garden, and a palace with Mudéjar characteristics in the very centre of the Albaicín.

We are going to visit a conjunction of buildings, both civil and religious, which show how the Mudéjar was integrated into the process of subjection and control of a particular area; and how this system of working offered quick, cheap and safe architectural solutions for the reuse of medieval spaces. This system, based on an artisan structure and the use of a very precise terminology, with roots in the system of guilds, and based on the established practice of apprenticeships, was the perfect response to the complexity and specific nature of the rich Mudéjar heritage that we are about to visit.

The north side of the Sierra Nevada became a magnet for the Spanish Muslims from the end of the 15th century until the expulsion of the *Moriscos* in the 17th century. The result of the safe-conduct policy issued by Cardinal Mendoza in 1490, which invited any Muslims fleeing the frontier with Castile to settle in this area of the Granada province, meant not only the survival and perpetuation of Mudéjar art, but also motivated Mendoza's confrontation with the crown over its announced tolerance policy.

Countryside around Lanteira.

Characterised by the unique way of using wood for ceiling panels and frameworks for roofs, the Mudéjar building system is reflected in the urban physiognomy and in the buildings of a whole series of places in the province of Granada, providing evidence of a past characterised by cultural symbiosis. The son of the Cardinal and Primate, don Rodrigo de Mendoza was particularly fond of this district and was named heir and Marquis of it in 1491. Don Rodrigo was one of the most important personalities in the kingdom of Granada during the transition from the Middle Ages to modern times and the protagonist in a series of interesting events, which were apparently contradictory. While on the one hand he fought to maintain the medieval feudal structures, confronting the power of the king, on the other, he attempted to become one of history's most innovative patrons of the art of the Renaissance with the work he carried out in his castle – the Palace of La Calahorra.

There, in the centre of the Marquis of Zenete's land, he built one of the most extraordinary constructions of the modern age. Built on top of an ancient Muslim fortress, the Castle-Palace of La Calahorra must have allowed him to control the through-traffic across the region from the neighbouring Alpujarras and the city of Almeria. A cartel on the gate of the castle displayed the challenge: *"In the defence of knights whose kings would do them wrong"*. These words infuriated King Fernando el Católico, who sent an army under the command of the Count of Tendilla, the Marquis's kinsman. The encounter between the cousins ended with the removal of the offending text and a family feast.

ITINERARY XIII   *Rodrigo de Mendoza, Marquis of Zenete — from La Calahorra Castle to El Albaicín*

La Calahorra

Castle-Palace
of La Calahorra,
general view.

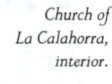

Church of
La Calahorra,
interior.

XIII.1 LA CALAHORRA

XIII.1.a Castle-Palace

From the Castle there is an extraordinary panoramic view over the surrounding countryside, thick with almond trees, and of the Sierra Nevada in the distance. Opening hours: Wed 10.00–13.00 and 14.00–18.00.

Commissioned by Rodrigo de Mendoza in 1509 and finished in 1512, the Castle became one of the most outstanding examples of Renaissance architecture in 16th-century Spain. Its construction went against the tendency of the time, imposed by the power of the king, who felt that he needed to destroy the existing fortresses to be able to consolidate his power over all of his subjects, including the ancient feudal nobility. In this sense, the attempt of don Rodrigo was an anachronism, explicable only by the political and strategic interests of the

crown, which believed the old feudal and military caste was still needed.

The exterior of the castle is forbidding and military and in complete contrast to the interior, which is refined and courtly, a reflection of the Italian humanist ideals. This spirit of the Renaissance is evident in the patio with galleries on two levels, where five arches rest on Corinthian columns at each level. The upper columns rest on pedestals and the galleries are closed with a marble balustrade. The monumental staircase that occupies the centre of the west side determines the proportions of the rest of the space; a model copied by most of the Renaissance buildings throughout Spain.

In terms of decoration, the doors, windows and friezes are outstanding and develop a rich sculptural scheme. The Latin inscriptions, referring to the patron and his wife, alternate with sculptures inspired by classical mythology, obliging the viewer to interpret the building in humanist terms. The wooden ceilings, seen in various rooms, introduce us to a style of woodwork that will be much evident from here on in, in the itinerary.

Many Spanish and Italian artists worked on this building. Among these, Michele Carlone stands out. He directed the work, first from Genoa and then from inside the palace itself. In Genoa, Carlone supervised the cutting and working of the Carrara marble that arrived by boat at the Port of Almeria. Once he had arrived in La Calahorra the Italian architect made sure that the design of the materials used, whether local or not, was related to the world of Classical Antiquity which the Renaissance was trying to recapture.

XIII.1.b Church of La Calahorra

Opening hours: Mon Tues and Sat 19.30–21.00, Fri 17.00–21.00, Sun 11.00–13.00. If the church is closed, contact the Parish. Tel: 958 677126.

The Church of La Calahorra stands out above the houses of the village. Built in 1550, to the plans and conditions of Francisco de Antero who presented them in 1546, the tower, built in brick, is one of the best examples to be found in the area. Once inside, the church has a single nave, with a choir loft at the foot. The ceiling is one of the most successful of the Mudéjar type: double *limas* with single cross braces and five paired anchor ties, decorated with strapwork, on corbels. There are two brick portals, one at the foot of the church and another at the side, giving onto a square. The sanctuary, separated from the rest of the building by one of its main arches, was modified in the 18th century.

Church of Lanteira, interior.

Lanteira

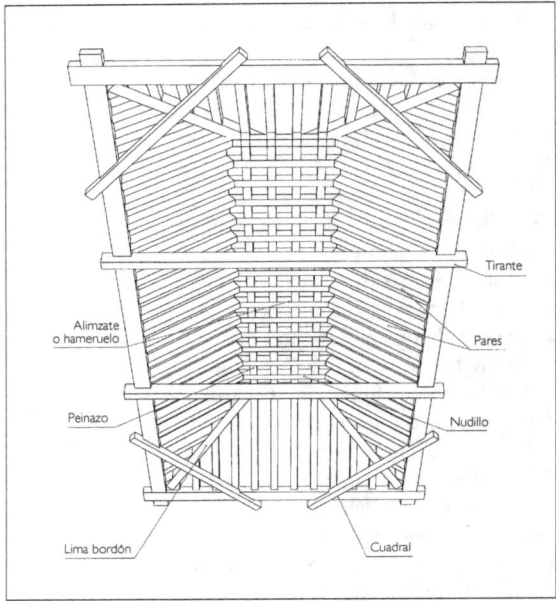

Schemes of armaduras de lima bordón.

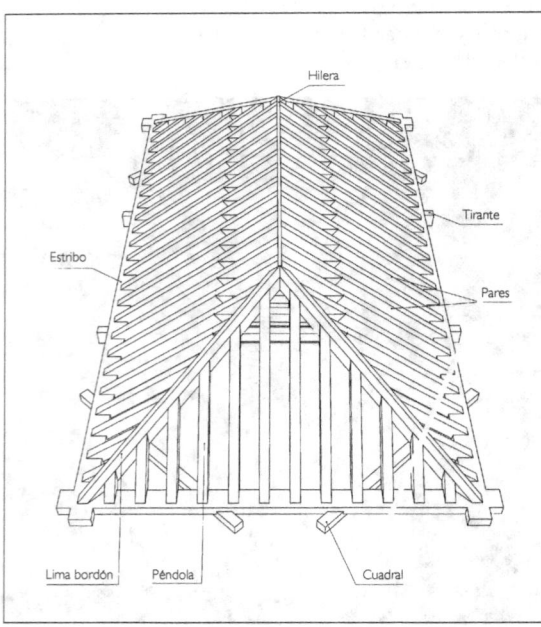

XIII.2 LANTEIRA

XIII.2.a Church of Lanteira

7 km on SE19. Opening hours: Tues, Wed, Thurs and Sat 17.30–18.30, Sun 11.00–12.30. If the Church is closed, ask for Sra. Angelina. Tel: 958 673699.

This church, rebuilt after 1626 from the ruins, has one of the finest Mudéjar ceilings of the area. Its existence proves that the techniques of the Mudéjars in the construction of ceilings were used before the expulsion of the *Moriscos* in 1610, making it clearly part of the Islamic cultural heritage. The structure of the ceiling is single *limas* with cross braces and four paired anchor ties with strapwork of knots-of-eight on corbels. The *arrocabe* still shows remains of the original polychromy; the complexity of the geometric forms and arabesques provide an eloquent demonstration of the richness of the artistic techniques of Arabic origin. The sanctuary, separated by a segmental main arch, is covered with a ceiling of *armadura de limas bordones*, with cross braces on inverted Mannerist corbels; in the centre, the *almizate* is decorated with a pinecone-shaped *muqarnas*. It has a choir loft and a balcony next to the sanctuary, which was the reserve of the most important families of the area. On the outside, the two portals are worthy of note: one at the foot of the church and the other on the side of the square. Adorned with simple mouldings, they fit naturally into the sober surroundings of the village.

Rodrigo de Mendoza, Marquis of Zenete – from La Calahorra Castle to El Albaicín

XIII.3 JEREZ DEL MARQUESADO

XIII.3.a Church of Jerez del Marquesado

6 km on the SE19. Visits can be arranged through the Parish. Tel: 958 672110.

This church, one of the most important examples of Mudéjar architecture in the province has, along with that in Lanteira, two portals. The doorway at the foot of the church is brick, while the side door is in the Renaissance style and has a semicircular arch with Corinthian columns, an entablature and a niche. The spandrels, decorated with the Episcopal coats of arms, identify this church as the real institutional and religious centre of the district. Its central geographical situation, and the number of *Moriscos* who were part of the population, were undoubtedly the relevant factors here. The interior has three aisles separated by brick pillars with attached half columns. This multiplicity of space allows a divided view of the whole church, which is only complete at the end of the visit to the interior. The adornment of the different chapels and retables are suggestive rather than excessive, reflecting the varied popular devotion in the area. The monumental wooden ceilings are emphasised with a pictorial programme that is somewhat obscured today from the smoke off candles and the passing of time. Renaissance *grutescos* appear on Mudéjar strapwork, and geometric designs link the Italian traditions introduced by the Marquis of Zenete with the Muslim heritage of carpentry techniques.

Church of Jerez del Marquesado, side door, Lanteira.

Sierra Nevada National Park
The imposing peaks of the Sierra Nevada reach their highest point in the 3,481 m. of the Mulhacén; there are more than 20 other peaks over 3,000 m. The Park has an extension of more than 170,000 hectares and includes more than 60 villages.
The height of the mountain range favoured the development of glaciers in the Pleistocene so that the most southerly glaciation of the Iberian Peninsula is evident here. The moulding action of the ice has resulted in interesting relief, gouging out arêtes, U-shaped valleys, cirques, moraines and various groupings of residual lakes, typical of an alpine landscape.

ITINERARY XIII   Rodrigo de Mendoza, Marquis of Zenete – from La Calahorra Castle to El Albaicín

Guadix

Church of Jerez del Marquesado, elevation.

Church of Jerez del Marquesado, ground plan.

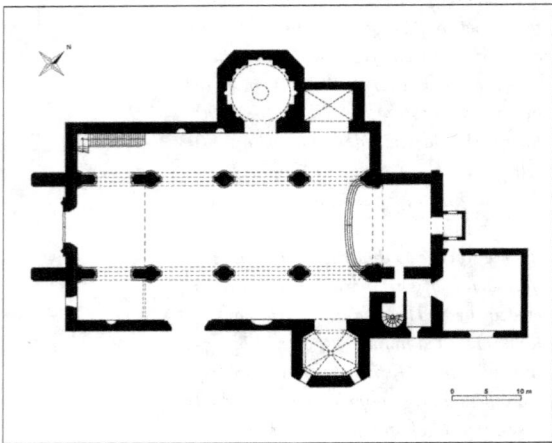

XIII.4 GUADIX

During the Islamic period, Guadix was an important urban centre. It was even the capital on various occasions when civil war divided the kingdom into factions, such as when it was the seat of power of the Zagal against Boabdil in the 15th century. The conquest took place in 1489 and afterwards the Catholic Monarchs founded a completely new Islamic city. A stout wall surrounded the whole city, comprising an *alcazaba* or citadel, a medina with the great mosque and various outlying districts.

XIII.4.a Church of Santa Ana

11 km on the SE19, in the calle Santa Ana. Opening hours: Mon 18.00–20.00, Tues 18.00–21.00, Wed 16.30–20.00, Thurs 17.00–20.00, Fri 16.00–20.00, Sat 16.30–20.00 and Sun 08.30–13.30.

One of the gates in the Muslim wall, now called *Arco de la Imagen*, is the entrance to the area occupied by the Church of Santa Ana. Constructed on the site of an old mosque, once it had been consecrated it was used as the Parish Church until 1500.
On a basilica ground plan, it is divided into three aisles, with a choir loft at the end and an octagonal sanctuary. The supporting arches and those at the entrance to the chapels are Gothic, as are the supports. In the interior, the Mudéjar ceilings are notable with their *armaduras de limas* retained in natural wood, providing a sharp contrast with the brightness of the whitewash, which covers the walls, supports and chapels. The sobriety of its elements and the chromatic con-

ITINERARY XIII Rodrigo de Mendoza, Marquis of Zenete – from La Calahorra Castle to El Albaicín

Guadix

trasts make this church a good place to rest before venturing to the centre of the city where the Muslim *zocos* or marketplaces were, and which are as busy and noisy as is to be expected in a provincial capital.

XIII.4.b **Church of Santiago**

In the Plaza de Santiago. Opening hours: 17.30–20.00. If the church is closed, contact the Parish. Tel: 958 661097.

The Church of Santiago, next to where the *Bab Rambla* or the Gate of the Rambla once was, was constructed over a former mosque, of which part of the baths that still survive are incorporated into the present building. The general plan of the church is a well-known one in the buildings of Guadix, with three naves and side chapels, separated by Gothic arches and brackets of whitewashed brick. The ceilings of the side aisles are single-pitch structures with beams decorated in black and white, and curved – like the nave – towards the sanctuary to increase the potential of the visual space. The roofing of the chapels are the same as the side aisles, with the exception that the two nearest the main altar have *armaduras* of *limas moamares* with only three pitched sides, which are *apeinazados* with eight-strand knotwork.

The roof of the sanctuary – a half-barrel vault in wood with coffers in the shape of stars – is reminiscent of that in Santa Isabel la Real in Granada. It is finished with a venerable carpentry structure of coffers decorated with rosettes. The decorative scheme continues in the main doorway on the Gospel side. Attributed to Diego de Siloé who probably designed it, and

Church of Santa Ana, interior, Guadix.

Church of Santiago, doorway and tower, Guadix.

Guadix

executed by Rodrigo de Gibaja, it has two parts. The higher one rises above a semicircular arch over double pairs of Corinthian columns on pedestals. In the centre, under the arms of Carlos V, a niche presides over the decorative whole, which is decidedly Renaissance.

Bishop don Gaspar de Avalos financed the building with the intention of using it as a pantheon for himself and his family. This clergyman, one of the great builders of the diocese, was responsible for the Renaissance design of the Cathedral. His artistic interests are reflected in the Church of Santiago, where Italian tendencies are adapted to the Mudéjar possibilities.

XIII.4.c Church of San Miguel

In the calle San Miguel. Opening hours: Tues and Wed 17.00–20.30, Thurs, Fri and Sat 16.00–20.30, Sun 09.00–12.00. If the church is closed, contact the Parish. Tel: 958 660151.

In the calle Real de Santo Domingo, the Church of San Miguel occupies the former building of the Convent and Church of Santo Domingo, which moved to the outskirts of the town to an area with an Islamic population that needed to be indoctrinated. The establishment of the Parish of San Miguel at its present site took place in 1958, after the reconstruction carried out by the Dirección General de Regiones Devastadas in 1955. Founded by the Catholic Monarchs at the end of the 15th century, the original church is earlier than other churches in the town, such as Santiago, or Santa Ana. In 1560, a new church was built, which was still unfinished in 1589 when the master Juan Huete was working on it.

Entry to the church is through a semicircular arch with Doric pilasters and an entablature with the symbols of the Predicant Order of the Dominicans, dogs and angels, set within a simple façade. It has three aisles with pointed arches on pillars, a choir at the foot and a sanctuary with a pointed chancel arch. The separate side aisles are in three individual spaces, which each has a roof of semicircular vaulting perpendicular to the axis of the church itself.

Outstanding among the whole are the eight-part Mudéjar ceilings in the nave, the sanctuary and the old chapel of the Virgin del Rosario, on the Gospel side near the main altar, as is usual in the other Mudéjar churches in Guadix. The first of these is a magnificent example of an eight-part rectangular *armadura de limas moamares* decorated in polychrome, and with the *almizate* decorated with strapwork. Displayed at both ends are the arms of the Order of Santo Domingo and four pairs of interlocking anchor ties on corbels.

The natural-wood *armadura* in the sanctuary is also eight-sided and of *limas moamares* on a square base, completely *apeinazada* and with a pinecone of *muqarnas* in the *almizate*.

The *armadura* of the Old Chapel of the Virgin del Rosario, again eight-sided but cupula-shaped, is *apeinazada* with ten-strand knots, and a pinecone-shaped *muqarnas* in the centre.

The Baroque Chapel of the Virgin del Rosario completes the interior of the church, added and funded by the Bishop Fray Clemente in 1690. The polygonal plan, inspired by the Chapel of San Torcuato in the Cathedral of Guadix, appears to be two-levels high, simulated by means of Ionic entablatures.

This very simply decorated church has undergone various restorations in more recent times. These, above all, have affected the interior walls and highlighted the magnificent examples of the ceilings preserved in the interior.

XIII.4.d Church of San Francisco
(optional)

In the Plaza de San Francisco and currently under restoration. Opening hours: Sun 10.00–12.00.

The Church of San Francisco, one of the best examples of Mudéjar in Guadix, follows a well-established conventual plan with a central rectangular nave and an eight-sided sanctuary at the head. At the other end is the choir loft, accessed directly from the convent. The design is completed with various chapels opening off the side aisles, which have roofs of various different systems of vaulting.

This building occupies the centre of the most aristocratic district of Guadix. The chapels in its interior responded to the nobility's desire at the time to perpetuate their memories with architectonic decoration where family heraldry would never be lacking. With burials in the interior of the churches banned at the end of the 18th century, the construction of municipal cemeteries went ahead in accordance with the royal decrees related to public hygiene. The aristocrats in Guadix responded by burying their loved ones in the cemetery outside the city walls in the morning and then bringing them back by the light of torches to the centuries-old Chapel of San Francisco in the dead of night. This constant protection of the church on the part of the most powerful families of the city explains why the *armaduras* – some of the most decorated and complex constructions in the whole province of Granada – are preserved. The *lazos*, or knots, interlaced with eight-pointed stars, and the cone shapes of *muqarnas* occupy all of the space; a representation of the great starry sky that would still be visible if the magnificent ceiling of the church were not there, with its prodigious colouring in blue, white, red and gold.

Church of San Miguel, ceiling, Guadix.

Rodrigo de Mendoza, Marquis of Zenete – from La Calahorra Castle to El Albaicín

Guadix

Leaving Guadix in the direction of Granada, through the district with the caves of San Miguel and la Magdalena, and then passing through a desert-like territory, get ready to witness villages with magnificent Mudéjar churches. These churches are a reflection of the policy of occupation of the territory, which the Crown of Castile carried out. This is the case in Purullena, Cortes de Guadix, Graena, and La Peza, where the splendid wooden ceilings of their parish churches still survive.

The Caves of Guadix
This unique habitat is interesting from both the social and the geographical point of view. A cave town, it occupies an extension of approximately 200 hectares of land, the soil of which is predominantly soft clay, which is impermeable, but hardens with the action of the air. This material is perfect for excavating cave dwellings, as the damp does not penetrate. The temperature inside the caves remains at a constant 18° C at all times throughout the day and all year round. The whitewashing of the interiors provides additional light and acts as a disinfectant. Exactly when people first started inhabiting the caves is unknown, but the present population is still about 2,000, which makes it the largest troglodyte settlement in existence.

ITINERARY XIII

Second day

Rodrigo de Mendoza, Marquis of Zenete – from La Calahorra Castle to El Albaicín

Rafael López Guzmán, Miguel Ángel Sorroche Cuerva

XIII.5 GRANADA
- XIII.5.a Hospital Real (Royal Hospital)
- XIII.5.b Madrasa Palace
- XIII.5.c House of los Tiros
- XIII.5.d Church of Santa Ana and San Gil
- XIII.5.e Church of San Pedro and San Pablo
- XIII.5.f House of Castril – Provincial Archaeological and Ethnological Museum
- XIII.5.g House of Lavadero de Santa Inés
- XIII.5.h Church of San José
- XIII.5.i Church of San Miguel Bajo
- XIII.5.j Church of the Monastery of Santa Isabel la Real
- XIII.5.k Palace of the Marquis of Zenete

Education and Scientific Knowledge

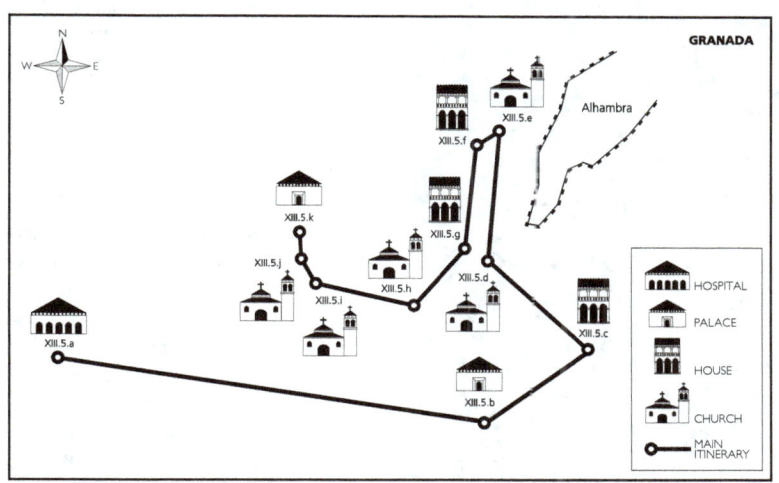

ITINERARY XIII   Rodrigo de Mendoza, Marquis of Zenete — from La Calahorra Castle to El Albaicín
Granada

XIII.5 **GRANADA**

Reaching the city of the Alhambra, this urban itinerary continues to the edge of the city, outside the walls of Islamic Granada, to the *medina*. Climb up through the winding streets of the Albaicín to the Palace built by the Marquis of Zenete, at the very heart of the Moorish city.

XIII.5.a **Hospital Real (Royal Hospital)**

54 km on the A92. The Hospital is situated in the Cuesta del Hospicio. Enter Granada by the Camino de San Antonio as far as the calle Real de la Cartuja. This building is now the Rectorate of the University of Granada. Opening hours: 09.00–21.00, Sat 09.00–12.00. Closed Sun.

The Catholic Monarchs founded the Hospital Real (Royal Hospital), intending to make the state responsible for problems of hygiene and public health. The Hospital was built outside the Islamic city on top what had been a Muslim cemetery. To find the architectonic model followed here we have to look beyond the Iberian Peninsula, namely to the Renaissance hospitals of Milan and Florence. The ground plan is a large square divided by a central cross that forms four interior patios. The cross was probably reserved for the wards and the exterior square for medical consultations, the pharmacy, storerooms, kitchens, and so on.

In the interior elements from the Gothic tradition are found, such as the *cimborrio*, or rib vaulting of the lower floor of the cross, as well as Renaissance forms in the windows of the main façade, in the *Patio de los Marmoles* (Marble patio) and in the Chapel. Mudéjar craftsmanship can be seen in the wooden ceilings that cover wide spaces, whether as flat *alfarjes* on the ground floor or double pitch *armaduras* on the upper floor. The decoration of the staircases situated in the *Patio de los Marmoles* and the *Patio del Archivo* (Archive patio) is outstanding: it is known that artists of the category of Juan de Plasencia or Melchor de Arroyo took part in the decoration of them. While the formerly used designs were clearly Islamic in origin, the later decorative models were imports from Italy. We find this ambivalent language again in the cross on the upper floor, which is now the Central Library of the University of Granada. Here, carpenter Melchor de Arroyo explored the possibility of using geometric coffers in

Royal Hospital, general view, Granada.

perspective to design a "half-orange" dome as a solution to the problem of the inside of the great *cimborrio*, making the Hospital Real stand out above the whole of the rest of the city. In 1552, Melchor de Arroyo's solution for the roof was approved by Diego de Siloé, the architect of the Cathedral in Granada and renowned as an artist in Spain and Italy at the time.

XIII.5.b Madrasa Palace

Calle Oficios. Go up the calle Gran Vía de Colón, opposite the Cathedral. This is now the University of Granada. Opening hours: Mon-Fri 09.00–22.00, Sat 10.00–14.30 and 17.00–20.30. Closed Sun.

The itinerary now heads to the Madrasa or Arabic University. Founded by the Sultan Yusuf I (1333–1354), it was the first institution of its type in al-Andalús and is the only one where excavations have unearthed interesting architectonic remains. The subjects taught in this *madrasa* were medicine, calculus, astronomy, geometry, mechanics, literature, philosophy and subjects in the area of religious laws and practice.

The building gave onto the square of the Great Mosque, part of which is still visible now between la Lonja and the Capilla Real. In the interior, the space occupied by the prayer hall with its *mihrab* and the splendid plasterwork decoration have survived. A fire in the 19th century destroyed the wooden ceiling and the architect Mariano Contreras rebuilt it in 1893. Among alterations to the interior to adapt the building to function as the Town Hall, the *Sala de Caballeros Veinticuatro* on the upper floor, is outstanding. Its name – Chamber of the Twenty-Four Gentlemen – comes from the 24 councillors who made up the Town Council of the time and who used the room for meetings.

The room has one of the city's most important Mudéjar *armaduras*, but in addition to the expert technique of the carpenter, there is also the exquisite work of the painter, Francisco Fernández, who finished the decoration in 1513. This is a rectangular ceiling of double *limas moamares*, covered entirely with strapwork in geometric designs, which the Renaissance decoration, painted with *grutescos* and *candelieri*, compliments. In addition, there is an inscription praising the Catholic Monarchs, whose portraits preside over the chamber: *"The most high, magnificent and most powerful seigneurs don Fernando and Doña Isabel, King and Queen, our lords, won this great and most noble city of Granada and their kingdom by force of arms in two days in the month of January, in the year of our Lord Jesus Christ one thousand four hundred and ninety two."*

Palace of la Madraza, ceiling in the Chamber of the Twenty-Four Gentlemen, Granada.

ITINERARY XIII   Rodrigo de Mendoza, Marquis of Zenete – from La Calahorra Castle to El Albaicín
Granada

XIII.5.c House of los Tiros

Plaza del padre Suárez. From the Plaza de Isabel la Católica take the calle Pavaneras. Converted into a museum, it also has a temporary exhibition space. Opening hours: Mon–Fri 14.30–20.00.

The Casa de los Tiros is situated in what was once the Jewish Quarter of Granada. After the expulsion of the Jews in 1492, the nobility of Castile divided the city up between them. This social redefinition of the urban space gave rise to numerous palaces like this one in the area we are considering. The fabric of the building itself corresponds to the union of two lineages, one Castilian and the other Muslim, which is evidence of the cultural symbiosis that took place in Granada. The daughter of Comendador Gil, Vázquez Rengifo, who married the grandson of Sidi Yahya, personified this process of unification. A tower was added to the Muslim dwelling, and the exterior was renovated gradually until it developed into the present structure. Although some remains of the Nasrid building can still be seen in the interior, on the façade there is an interesting design of mythological figures (Jason, Hercules, Theseus, Hector and Mercury) which, mixed with the motto of the house, "*El corazon manda*" (the heart rules), indicates that there was a return to medieval chivalric ideals.

The *zaguán*, or entrance porch, has an *alfarje* with huge beams resting on keel-shaped corbels. In this simple ceiling, there is an outstanding pictorial group of wild beasts and fantastic monsters in fighting attitudes. Another series of lesser ceilings are seen in the rooms on the ground floor, and a splendid patio leads to the upper floor and the principal room of the palace, known as the *Cuadra Dorada* or Golden Chamber.

Here, one of the most complete iconographic projects of Renaissance Granada is realised on a Mudéjar *alfarje*. The beams rest on corbels in anthropomorphic shapes and, on the underside are carved swords and the same family motto as seen at the entrance, "*El corazon manda*".

In the quirks of the *alfarje*, quadrangular spaces hold busts in bas-relief and explanatory inscriptions about the personalities represented. Inventing a whole family tree for themselves, the owners recounted the deeds of their forebears. From the Roman world and Trajan, the medieval world and Recaredo, Alaric, Hermenegildo and Fernando III, to the present, where – alongside the most illustrious person-

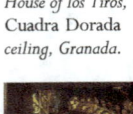

House of los Tiros, Cuadra Dorada ceiling, Granada.

alities of the time, Gonzálo Fernández de Córdoba, don Iñigo López de Mendoza, the Catholic Monarchs or Carlos V – their own immediate ancestors join the pantheon: Juan Vázquez Rengifo and Alonso de Granada.

The development of this historical and mythological tale on a Mudéjar *alfarje* clearly communicates the ideological interests behind this mixed and unequal marriage; that is, to link the Christian present with the Christian past, leaving out the Muslim era of the city. The new lords of Granada were themselves depicted beside the kings and emperors without mentioning the Islamic princes who had governed the city for eight centuries. This aristocratic and military ideal was given a cultural and dilettante twist in the 16th century when an Academy in the Italian style was set up in the palace, in which the Venegas Family of Granada brought together the most cultured people of the city to celebrate poetry readings and contests.

XIII.5.d Church of Santa Ana and San Gil

Take the Avenida de los Reyes Católicos towards the barrio del Albaicín. The church is in the Plaza Nueva, at the beginning of the Carrera del Darro. Mass hours: from 18.00.

This is a typical example of the capacity of Mudéjar techniques to define grandiose spaces in simple structures with a single nave. Constructed on top of a former mosque, work on the Church of Santa Ana finished in around 1548. Integration with its surroundings was a later project car-

Church of Santa Ana and San Gil, façade and tower, Granada

ried out by means of a Renaissance doorway, the work of Sebastían de Alcántara. A magnificent tower was another later addition of between 1561 and 1563, with the fundamental intervention of the master bricklayer Juan de Castellar. The whole is a splendid lesson in the possibilities of the use of brick mixed with a polychromatic range of tiles and glazed roof tiles.

On the inside, built with the approval of Diego de Siloé, a main arch differentiates the sanctuary from the rest of the church. The great nave, with an *armadura* ceiling signed by the carpenters Benito de Córdoba and Alonso Hernández Barea, is of a rectangular shape; the roof has double *limas moamares* and a great *almizate* of interlocking eight-strand knots and four pinecone-shaped *muqarnas*. The double anchor ties, also with knots, lead the way to the sanctuary, with its eight-sided ceiling embellished by prominent squinches elongated into

ITINERARY XIII Rodrigo de Mendoza, Marquis of Zenete – from La Calahorra Castle to El Albaicín

Granada

Church of San Pedro and San Pablo, general view with the Alhambra in the background, Granada.

triangular forms and ten-strand knots. The whole complex, completed with five- and ten-point strapwork, presents a global image of the great starry sky.

XIII.5.e Church of San Pedro and San Pablo

Head along the Carrera del Darro. Opening hours: Mon-Fri 17.30–18.30, Sat 18.00–19.30, Sun 10.00–13.00.

Overlooking the River Darro is the Church of San Pedro and San Pablo. Building work began here in the second half of the 16th century and, designed by Juan de Maeda, shows clearly how the organisation of spaces in Mudéjar churches provides a concrete alternative to the classical solutions. Here, we find a nave with transept and side chapels opening off the main area. The result is a rectangular ground plan and an elevation

ITINERARY XIII   Rodrigo de Mendoza, Marquis of Zenete – from La Calahorra Castle to El Albaicín

Granada

that has different levels, with windows that ensure the illumination of the interior. The various wooden ceilings, created by the carpenter Juan de Vilchez, are outstanding. Among them is the *armadura* of the nave, a great rectangle of *limas moamares* with *almizate* decorated with four bunches of *muqarnas*, while the *armadura* over the transept has 16 sections and rests on four coffered squinches. The Sanctuary ceiling, as the one described previously, develops into a cupola decorated with knots of ten strands. In the side chapels of this church, the various tombs of the principal families of Granada in the 16th century enrich the artistic heritage of the whole. Similarly, the palaces of these same families, such as the Casa de Castril, enrich this lower area of the Albaicín.

XIII.5.f House of Castril – Provincial Archaeological and Ethnological Museum

Opposite the church, in the Carrera del Darro 43. Opening hours: Tues 15.00–20.00, Wed–Sat 09.00–20.00, Sun 09.00–14.00. Closed Mon.

The house belonged to the family of don Hernando de Zafra, who was secretary to the Catholic Monarchs. Possibly built by Hernando de Zafra's grandson after 1539, the façade, worked in stone, is an ample discourse on the possibilities of the Renaissance language imported from Italy. This is a mixture, or a kind of anthology, with motifs of *grutescos*, *candelieri*, heraldry and symbolic forms, which tell us much about the skill of the sculptors in Granada and of the culture of their patrons. Several of the interior spaces lead off the central Renaissance patio, most of them covered with *alfarjes* decorated with geometric forms, which in some places echo Renaissance coffered work. The most outstanding ceiling is the one over the staircase; here we find a magnificent rectangular *armadura* of five sections, with *limas moamares*. The whole ceiling is covered with interlocking strapwork of ten-strand knots with the *almizate* decorated with three pinecone-shaped *muqarnas*. The outlines are marked in white, red and black and the centre of the stars are gilded. A highly stylised plant motif completes the decoration.

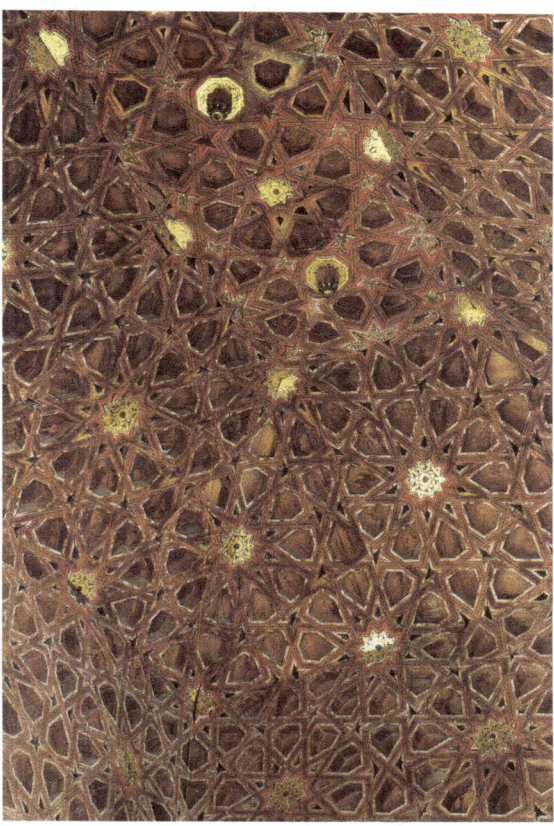

House of Castril, main staircase ceiling, Granada.

293

House of Lavadero de San Inés, main room ceiling, Granada.

*Church of San José, tower-*alminar*, Granada.*

XIII.5.g House of Lavadero de San Inés

Go up calle Zafra and, on the left, take calle Portería Concepción to the Cuesta de Santa Inés. Then take a right into calle Lavadero. The house at Nº 9 is now the Hotel Palacio de Santa Inés. Open (for visits): 12.00–19.00.

The owner of this 16th-century building must have been a highly cultured person, perhaps a doctor, to judge from the remains of the pictorial representations on the walls of the patio galleries, where there are – although now difficult to distinguish – allegories of Prudence and Wisdom, as well as Samson and Delilah.

Besides the simple *alfarjes* of the galleries and of some of the smaller rooms in the house, in the main first-floor chamber there is an outstanding rectangular *armadura* of *limas moamares* with three paired anchor ties. The *almizate* is decorated on the extremities and in the centre with eight-strand knot strapwork and cupolas of *muqarnas*. Details in polychrome differentiate elements of the geometric decoration, including gold in the most significant parts.

The conversion of the building into a hotel and some painstaking restoration has ensured that this house remains to be appreciated as part of Granada's heritage, allowing us to contemplate an artistic whole that had for many years been forgotten.

XIII.5.h Church of San José

In calle San José Alta. Return to the Cuesta de Santa Inés and continue along San Juan de los Reyes. Opening hours: Mon–Sat 19.00–21.00, Sun and public holidays from 10.30.

It was here in the lower part of the Albaicín where the first administrators of the recently conquered city established themselves, giving the streets names such as *los Oidores*, the Judges, where the officials of the Chancellery lived. Continuing from here, heading up the calle San Juan de los Reyes and then turning along the Cuesta de San Gregorio, we find the Church of San José, built in around 1525 by the architect Rodrigo Hernández on top of the former Mosque *al-murabitin*, or Mosque of the Almoravids.

Of the Islamic building, still surviving are the *aljibe* or water tank, which must have supplied water to the fountain for ablutions, and the *alminar*, which was repurposed as the bell tower. Inside, the church is organised with four pointed arches that support the pitched roof decorated with geometric motifs. The sanctuary roof comprises magnificent strapwork *armadura* made by the carpenter Domingo de Frechilla, and financed by doña Leonor Manrique, the widow of don Pedro Carrillo de Sotomayor, as a burial place for the family. The Memorial Chapel of the Nuñez de Salazar family also has a notable *armadura*, richly decorated with strapwork.

XIII.5.i Church of San Miguel Bajo

Go up calle San José as far as the Plaza de San Miguel Bajo. Opening hours: Sun and public holidays from 12.30.

The construction of this church progressed in two distinct stages corresponding to two different architectural projects, but without compromising the special unity, which results in a compendium of Mudéjar ceilings.

The first stage, from 1528 to 1539, includes the sanctuary at the top of a flight of steps and two sections demarcated by diaphragm arches similar to those in San José, while the foot of the nave, realised between 1551 and 1557, is finished with an *armadura de limas* with strapwork. The increased space needed for religious services most probably relates to the increase in the population of the district, while the Mudéjar construction techniques made it possible to undertake the successive additions without affecting the unity of the whole.

The exterior is completed with two doorways in stone, made by the stonemasons Juan de Alcántara and Pedro de Asteasu, following models by Diego de Siloé. The door at the foot in the Corinthian style is interesting, made up of a semicircular arch over which there is a niche holding a

Church of San Miguel Bajo, detail of the Sanctuary ceiling, Granada.

ITINERARY XIII Rodrigo de Mendoza, Marquis of Zenete – from La Calahorra Castle to El Albaicín

Granada

Church of the Monastery of Santa Isabel la Real, façade and tower, Granada.

XIII.5.j Church of the Monastery of Santa Isabel la Real

In calle Santa Isabel la Real.

The convent complex is a good example of what the monastic foundations were like in Granada in the 16th century. The construction was a result of the crown's intention to accomplish completely its religious control of the town in addition to the cathedral and the parishes. Founded by the Catholic Monarchs, it arose from the regrouping of already existing buildings.

On the outside, the church has a Gothic portal attributed to Enrique Egas and a Mudéjar tower, similar to that of Santa Ana. In the interior, the single nave has an *armadura de limas dobles*, completely covered with strapwork, with three pairs of anchor ties, and cross braces in the corners. In addition, the sanctuary has one of the most interesting examples of Gothic *armaduras*, comparable with models in Castile and even with those of Central Europe.

XIII.5.k Palace of the Marquis of Zenete

Opposite, in the calle Santa Isabel la Real, on the corner of calle de la Tiña. At present, the Palace houses the Foundation of Nuestra Señora del Pilar. A Visit can be arranged by telephone: 958 278307.

The itinerary finishes with the property that belonged to Rodrigo Díaz de Vivar, Marquis of Zenete, which remained in the family until 1662, when it was converted into a hospital for patients with ringworm. Its palace structure complies with the character-

sculpture of St Miguel. The arms in the spandrels, *grutescos* and an acanthus leaf on the keystone, complete the decoration of the door. The church's water tank is on the side that gives onto the square; dating from the 13th century, the opening has a pointed horseshoe arch framed in *alfiz*, resting on shafts of Roman columns, which is a reminder that this space was a mosque during the Islamic era.

Rodrigo de Mendoza, Marquis of Zenete – from La Calahorra Castle to El Albaicín

Granada

General view of the Albaicín from San Miguel, Granada.

istics of the original Islamic building, which was transformed in the 16th century. A forecourt covered by a simple *alfarje* leads us onto a courtyard of spacious dimensions in which the rhythm of the lower level is arranged by columns from the ancient Nasrid building, providing the basis for the Mannerist lintels. The upper floor has balustrades, piers turned in the style of Ionic columns, and lintels, which repeat the design of the lower ones, although now smaller.

Recent excavations have uncovered the various historical sequences of the building, thus allowing appropriate understanding and appreciation of its artistic and historical value.

In the Nasrid palace belonging to the reigning dynasty, Boabdil was acclaimed monarch for the second time in 1482, after he had taken refuge in the Alcazaba. In the hands of the Marquis of Zenete, the building became another example of the symbiosis between the Muslims and the Christians. Its new owner, being a man of his time, lived astride the two cultures, and this, definitively, is what we recognise as Mudéjar.

EDUCATION AND SCIENTIFIC KNOWLEDGE

Rafael López Guzmán, Miguel Ángel Sorroche Cuerva

The *Madrasa* in Granada was possibly the only building of this typology in al-Andalús. In all likelihood it was built in the mid-14th century by the Sultan Yusuf I, which may explain why the Arabic texts call it Madrasa Yusufiyya or Madrasa Nasriyya (in reference to the Nasrid dynasty). In fact, even if the sultan was the founder, the real driving force behind the project was his Prime Minister, Ridwan, whose role, as well as the prestige of the institution, is reflected in the text of Ibn al-Jatib:

"He founded the Madrasa of Granada, where there was none before, and gave it funds; he established in it permanent dwellings [for the students] and nobody favoured it more than he did; it became the only and best one in its splendour and charm and he brought the water to it of the habiz [pious bequest] in an unending supply."

The *madrasas* originated in the Islamic East; the founding of the first *madrasa* in the institutional sense was in 1067 by Nizam al-Mulk, the *vizier* of the Seljuk Sultans, Alp Arslan and Malik Chah. This *madrasa* directly adopted the building model of the Turkish Seljuks, which style then gradually extended throughout Arabia, Syria, Palestine, Anatolia, North Africa and finally the kingdom of Granada.

In the *madrasa*, the students were provided lodgings if they came from other cities, food, and sometimes, small amounts of money. Its facilities included accommodation for the students, as well as study rooms, a library and a small mosque.

Most of the information we have about the teaching in the *Madrasa* in Granada comes from Ibn al-Jatib. We know that the majority of the teachers there came from Granada itself or from other towns in its kingdom, although there were also scholars from other Islamic areas, especially from the Maghreb.

As regards the *madrasa*'s curriculum, we do not have any documents that specify exactly what it contained. As a result, we have to look at the biographies of the teachers who taught there to find out which subjects they offered. The most common subjects taught were in the areas of law and religion, or philosophy and literature. Among the former there were, above all, the principles of Islamic law, jurisprudence, laws of inheritance, readings of the Qur'an, Muslim theology, commentary on the Qur'an and *Sufism*. In the second subject area, the principle teaching was in language, philology, metrics and Arabic literature. The scientific subjects taught included medicine, calculus, astronomy, geometry logic and even mechanics.

Among the teachers who gave classes in Granada we can mention by name: Abu Zakariyya, from Archidona in Malaga, one of the most eminent scholars of the period, whose knowledge included medicine, geometry, astronomy, calculus, Islamic law and literature.

Another scholar was Abu Alí Mansur al-Zawawí, from Tremecén in Algeria. Al-Zawawí was contracted by the *madrasa* in Granada in 1332 at a high salary. He had many disciples to whom he taught the different branches of law and *Tafsir*, or commentary of the Qur'an.

La Madraza, Oratory, Granada.

Glossary

Ajimez	Overhanging balcony made of wood and enclosed in latticework.
Alarife	Architect or master craftsman.
Albanega	Triangular space or spandrel between the arch and the *alfiz* in Muslim architecture.
Albarrana	Tower situated outside the walled precinct, joined to it by bridges, arches or walls, which can be eliminated if the tower falls into enemy hands.
Alfarje	Flat ceiling made of carved or artistically interlaced wood, which may also be a floor.
Alfiz	Rectangular surround to the Arabic arch, which frames the *albanegas* and starts either from the imposts or from the base.
Alicer	Band or ceramic frieze with different work in the lower part of the walls.
Almizate	Panel of the *par y nudillo* ceiling parallel to the floor.
Angrelado arch	Arch that has the intrados ornamented with small lobes, cut to form points.
Cairelado arch	Arch decorated with small arches in the intrados.
Mixtilíneo arch	Arch formed by straight and curved lines.
Túmido arch	Pointed horseshoe arch.
Armadura	Composition of pieces of wood that make up the roof structure of a building. It may take the following basic variant forms: *de parhilera y mojinetes; de par y nudillo, de limas* or *de artesa*.
Armadura apeinazada	Wooden ceiling in which the ornamental strapwork is assembled without using nails.
Armadura de limas o de artesa	Wooden ceiling of trapezoidal cross section, in the shape of inverted troughs, in which the pitched sides are joined by one or two beams placed at the corner or border of the sections of the ceiling.
Armadura de par y nudillo	Wooden ceiling in which, for increased strength and to avoid the rafters warping, a horizontal collar beam or *nudillo* is placed between the corresponding rafters. The succession of these horizontal beams with the boards in between gives a flat surface: the *almizate* or *harneruelo*.
Armadura de parhilera o mojinetes	Wooden ceiling, double-pitched with a triangular cross section, made of a series or pairs of principal rafters, called *pares* or *alfardas*, above which is the ridge or *hilera* and below which rest the tie-bar or *estribado* that is supported by the walls.
Arrocabe	Decorative band of wood or plaster, which covers the upper part of the wall where it meets the ceiling.
Artesonado	Ceiling or roofing system made of coffers or caissons.
Atalaya	Watch tower or vantage point, normally built in a high place to keep watch over and control the countryside or the sea.
Ataurique	Stylised plant motif ornamentation inspired by the Classical acanthus; much used in Hispano-Muslim art.

Glossary

Caravansarai	Inn situated on the main communication routes for the caravans or convoys of travellers to rest in safety.
Cimborrio	Lantern over the transept, normally in the shape of a square or octagonal tower, ending in a spire.
Cuenca o arista	Ceramic with sunken-relief designs obtained by the pressure of a mould and then coloured completely with the enamels deposited in the hollows or *cuencas* delimited by a lip or *arista*.
cuerda seca	Ceramic technique that consists of the separation of different coloured enamels by means of a line of oil-based paint.
Don	The equivalent of "Sir" in English.
Engobe	Mixture of non-vitrifiable earth and water applied over the whole or part of a clay object to mask its colour and trace designs onto it.
Estribo	Tie-bar or strap sometimes placed horizontally over the tie beams that the rafters fit into and rest on.
Funduq	In North Africa, an inn for merchants and their pack animals; warehouse for merchandise and a commercial centre equivalent to the *caravanserai* or *khan* of the Islamic east.
Grutesco	Decorative motif based on fantastic beings, plants and animals. So called because it imitated the style of those found in the grotto of the Palace of Augustus.
Guadameci	Leather adorned with painting or designs in relief.
Habus	Donation of buildings under certain conditions to the mosques or other Muslim religious institutions.
Hammam	Turkish bathhouse.
Hégira/Hijra	Islamic era from the emigration (*hijra* in Arabic) of the Prophet Muhammad from Mecca to Medina in 622 of the Christian era. The Muslim year comprises lunar months and has 354 days normally and 355 days in a leap year.
Iwan	Vaulted hall, walled on three sides.
Khan	Stopping place on the great communication routes. Inn and warehouse (see *funduq* and *caravasarai*) in towns of certain importance.
Khanqa	Monastery or hostel for *sufis* or dervishes.
Kufic	Angular form, stylised, often highly decorated, Arabic script used in early Qur'ans and foundation inscriptions supposedly attributed to Kufa in Iraq.

Glossary

Lima	Rafter, placed in the dihedral angle, formed by the sloping or pitched sides of the ceiling upon which rest the short or jack rafters.
Madrasa	(Madraza in Granada). School of Islamic sciences (theology, law, the Qur'an) and a residence for students.
Medina	City. In North Africa, the old part of town in contrast to the European extension of the cities.
Mexuar/Meshwar?	Council hall of the *viziers*.
Mihrab	Niche in the *qibla* wall of the mosque to indicate the direction of Mecca.
Mimbar	Pulpit in a mosque from which the *imam* preaches the sermon to the faithful.
Mocárabes	Decoration of prisms in the form of stalactites with a concave lower surface.
Morisco	In the Christian kingdoms of the Iberian Peninsula was the name given to Muslims converted to Christianity after the reconquest.
Mozarab	*Mozárabes* is the name given to the Hispanic minorities who were allowed by Islamic law to remain as tributaries and lived in Muslim Spain until the end of the 11th century, retaining their Christian religion and even their ecclesiastical and judicial organisation.
Mudéjar	Name given to the Muslims allowed to remain among their Christian conquerors without changing their religion, in exchange for a tribute. The adjective, Mudéjar, is also used for the art and architecture; to describe traditional craftsmanship begun under Islamic domination that continued for Christian clients after the Christian conquest of a particular area.
Muezzin	He who calls the Muslims to prayer from the minaret of a mosque.
Muladí	Spanish Christians who converted to Islam and lived as Muslims during the domination of the Arabs in Spain.
Naskhi	(Literally "copied") one of the most widespread styles of calligraphy used in Arabic script.
Olambrilla	Decorative tiles, with sides of approximately seven centimetres, which are combined with rectangular floor tiles, generally red, to form flooring.
Par y nudillo	See *armadura de par y nudillo*.
Parhilera o mojinetes	See *armadura de parhilera o mojinetes*.
Peinazo	Board inserted between the beams and within the lanes of the wooden *armadura* to complete the knotwork decoration.

Glossary

Qubba	Cupola. By extension, a monument raised over the tomb of a marabout.
Qibla	Direction of the *Ka'ba*, (literally "cube"), the temple in Mecca that is the centre of the Muslim religion, and towards which the faithful must face to pray.
Real	Spanish coin in the Middle Ages.
Ribat	Fortress constructed in the frontier zones from which the Muslim warriors who lived in it set out on the holy war.
Taracea	*Intaglio* decoration based on notches in the wood that are later filled with small pieces of different materials, which fit exactly into the spaces, creating a polychromic effect. The colours are always the natural ones of the pieces inserted.
Taujel/Taukhel	Flat wooden ceiling completely covered with strapwork decoration, which conceals the beams; cf. *alfarkhe*, where the beams are exposed.
Trompa	Squinch or semi-conical arch with the vertex in the interior angle of two walls and the broad part overhanging. It is used in order to move from a square structure to an octagonal one, adding four chamfered sides in the interior.
Turbe	Private burial place. Architectonic practice introduced by the Turks into Tunisia.
Zaquizamí	Wooden ceiling.
Zawiya	Religious establishment dedicated to teaching, under the control of a guild or society.
Zellij	(Tiling) Small pieces of glazed ceramic combined to make geometric and knotwork forms, used as decoration on the exterior or interior of monuments. Some have their own names: *sino* or star, *azafate*, *almendrilla* or almond, *candil* or oil lamp.

Historical Personalities

Alfonso VIII (1155–1214)
Led the Battle of the Navas de Tolosa (1212), which caused the collapse of the Almohad Empire and opened the route across the Guadalquivir River for the Christians. He founded the monastery of Las Huelgas Reales in Burgos.

Alfonso X (1221–1284)
His reign was of great historical significance in various ways, such as foreign and economic policy, relations with the different estates, conquering and resettlement policies, and areas related to legislation and culture. Notable in the cultural arena, are the increased activity of the School of Translators in Toledo and the literary production of Alfonso X himself, his *Cantigas de Santa María*.

Benedict XIII (1328–1424)
Don Pedro Martínez de Luna was crowned Pope under the name of Benedict XIII and was known as Pope Luna. A great patron of the arts, he raised the apses and rebuilt the *cimborrio* of the Parroquieta Chapel in the Seo. His work served as a model for other ecclesiastical patronage. He built his principal residence in Daroca (1411), probably under the direction of Mahoma Rami.

Enrique II (1333–1379)
Led the Rebellion against his brother Pedro I of Castile in 1366, with the support of France and Aragón.

Fernando II de Aragón (1452–1516) – **Ferdinand of Aragón**
Married Isabella of Castile (1474) and they reigned together as the Reyes Católicos, or Catholic Monarchs, from 1479–1504. From the 14th century until the possession of the Kingdom of Aragón in 1479, the Meseta of Castile and the Valley of the River Ebro lived in a situation of instability. As well as establishing the unity of Castile and Aragón, they transformed and enlarged the Aljafería and the Royal Alcázar in Seville.

Francisco Jiménez de Cisneros (1436–1517)
A Cardinal whose cultural activity had its maximum manifestation in the creation of the University of Alcala in 1507, with a new orientation compared to the traditional scholastic and juridical outlook of the University of Salamanca.

Isabella I of Castile (1451–1504)
(See Fernando II de Aragón).

María de Padilla (d.1361)
Lived as the concubine of Pedro I of Castile in the palace in Astudillo. As a result of the threat of excommunication, brandished by the Pope against Pedro I, she began the conversion of the palace into the Convent of the Poor Clares.

Mahoma Rami (15th century)
Master craftsman in the service of Benedict XIII. On account of the transcendence of his work, he is considered to be one of the most important Mudéjar masters ever.

Muhammad V (1354–1391)
Nasrid king of Granada. His reign and that of his father, Yusuf I, represent the apogee of the Nasrid dynasty, whose splendour is reflected in the Alhambra and in the Patio of the Lions and the adjoining rooms. A great friend of Pedro I, who restored him to his throne, he sent him craftsmen who worked in Astudillo (1356), Tordesillas (1363), Seville (1364–1366) and Toledo. His visit to the Royal Alcázar in Seville may have influenced his decision to order the building of the Palace of Comares in Granada.

Pedro Gumiel (1460–1519)
Architect to Cardinal Cisneros. He controlled and supervised all that the Cardinal built in the first decades of the 16th century.

Pedro I de Castilla (1334–1369)
Nicknamed "The Cruel" he carried on a border war for 13 years with Pedro IV of Aragón. His most important cultural work was the building of the Mudéjar palace of the Royal Alcázar (1364–1366).

Pedro IV de Aragón (1319–1387)
Nicknamed "The Ceremonious" he was a great patron of the arts He ordered the building of the Mudéjar palace of the Aljafería, as well as the Chapels of San Martín and San Jorge.

Pedro Tenorio (d.1399)
Archbishop of Toledo and partisan of the Trastamara in the wars between Pedro I and Enrique II. He reconstructed the walls of the city and especially the Puerta del Sol or Sun Gate, the bridge of San Martín and the Castle of San Servando.

Bibliographic References

ABAD CASTRO, M. C., *Arquitectura mudéjar religiosa en el arzobispado de Toledo*, Toledo, Obra Social Caja Toledo, 1991, 2 vols.

Actas de los Simposios Internacionales de Mudéjarismo (organised since 1975 in the city of Teruel and then taking place every three years since 1981): I (1975); II (1981); III (1984); IV (1987); V (1990); VI (1993); VII (1996); VIII (1999), Instituto de Estudios Turolenses.

AGUILAR GARCÍA, M. D., *Málaga mudéjar. Arquitectura religiosa y civil*, Universidad de Málaga, 1979.

ANGULO ÍÑIGUEZ, D., *Arquitectura mudéjar sevillana de los siglos XIII, XIV y XV*, Seville, 1932; 2nd rev. ed., Municipality of Seville, 1983.

BORRÁS GUALÍS, G. M., *Arte mudéjar aragonés*, 3 vols, Saragossa, Cazar-coaata, 1985.

BORRÁS GUALÍS, G. M. (ed.), *El arte mudéjar*, Saragossa, Unesco-Ibercaja, 1996.

DELGADO VALERO, C. and PÉREZ HIGUERA, M. T., "El periodo islámico y mudéjar", in VV. AA., *Arquitecturas de Toledo*, Toledo, Servicio de Publicaciones de la Junta de Comunidades de Castilla-La Mancha, 1991, vol. I, pp. 59–405.

"Estudios Mudéjares y Moriscos", *Sharq al-Andalus*, no. 12, 1995 (monograph).

FRAGA GONZÁLEZ, C., *Arquitectura mudéjar en la Baja Andalucía*, Santa Cruz de Tenerife, 1977.

HENARES CUELLAR, I. and LÓPEZ GUZMÁN, R., *Arquitectura mudéjar granadina*, Granada, Caja General de Ahorros y Monte de Piedad de Granada, 1989.

LAVADO PARADINAS, P., "Tipología y análisis de la arquitectura mudéjar en Tierra de Campos", *Al-Andalus*, XLIII, 1978, pp. 427–454.

LLEÓ CAÑAL, V., *La Casa de Pilatos*, Seville, Caja San Fernando de Sevilla y Jerez, 1996.

MARTÍNEZ CAVIRO, B., *Mudéjar toledano. Palacios y conventos*, Madrid, 1980.

MOGOLLÓN CANO-CORTÉS, P., *El mudéjar en Extremadura*, Universidad de Extremadura – Institución Cultural "El Brocense", 1987.

PALACIOS LOZANO, A. R., *Bibliografía de arquitectura y techumbres mudéjares, 1857–1991*, Serie Estudios Mudéjares, Teruel, Instituto de Estudios Turolenses, 1993.

PAVÓN MALDONADO, B., *Arte mudéjar en Castilla la Vieja y León*, Madrid, Asociación Española de Orientalistas, 1975.

PAVÓN MALDONADO, B., *Arte toledano islámico y mudéjar*, Madrid, Instituto Hispanoárabe de Cultura, 1973; 2nd ed., 1988.

PÉREZ HIGUERA, M. T., *Arquitectura mudéjar en Castilla y León*, Junta de Castilla y León, Consejería de Cultura y Turismo, 1993.

TORRES BALBAS, L., *Arte almohade. Arte nazarí. Arte mudéjar*, vol. IV of the "Ars Hispaniae" collection, Madrid, Plus Ultra, 1949.

VALDÉS FERNÁNDEZ, M., PÉREZ HIGUERA, M. T. and LAVADO PARADINAS, P., *Historia del Arte de Castilla y León*, "Arte mudéjar", vol. IV, Valladolid, Ámbito Ediciones, S. A., 1994.

VALDÉS FERNÁNDEZ, M., *Arquitectura mudéjar en León y Castilla*, León, Colegio Universitario-Institución "Fray Bernardino de Sahagún", 1981; 2nd ed., 1984.

Authors

Gonzalo M. Borrás Gualís
Professor in the Department of the History of Art in the Faculty of Philosophy and Letters in the University of Saragossa, where he teaches Mudéjar Art in the History of Art degree programme. His area of research is Mudéjar Art. Member of the Scientific Committee for the Centre for Mudéjar Studies (Comité Cientifico del Centro de Estudios Mudéjares) and of the International Symposiums of Mudéjarism of Teruel (Simposios Internacionales de Mudéjarismo de Teruel), he is also the Co-ordinator of the programmes of Mudéjar Art for UNESCO and MWNF.
Among his publications the following can be highlighted: *El Arte Mudéjar*, Teruel, Instituto de Estudios Turolenses (1990); *El Islam. De Córdoba al Mudéjar*, Madrid, Silex (1990); *El Arte Mudéjar*, Saragossa, Ibercaja-Unesco (1996) and *Arte Mudéjar Aragonés*, 3 vols, Saragossa, Cazar-coaata (1985).

Pedro Lavado Paradinas
Doctor in History of Art from the Faculty of Geography and History of the Complutense University in Madrid (1978). The subject of his Doctoral thesis was *Mudéjar Art in Castilla-León* for which he was awarded the Special Prize. His experience includes the following posts: teacher of the History of Spanish and Hispano-American Art at the University of Heidelberg 1979–80; teacher of History of Art in the School of Applied Arts and Crafts in Santiago de Compostela; and civil servant in the Ministry of Education and Science since 1982; Departmental Head and Head of the Education Section of the National Archaeological Museum in Madrid 1986–1992. Since 1980, he has taught History of Art in the Associate Centre of the UNED in Madrid, and since 1992, he has been the Head of Works of the Art Department at the Institute for the Conservation and Restoration of the Cultural Heritage of Madrid.
He has published more than 100 works on various subjects, including Mudéjar art, Hispano-Muslim art, medieval archaeology, iconography, ethnography, education in museums, Didactics and so on.

Rafael López Guzmán
Teacher of History of Art in the Faculty of Philosophy and Letters at the University of Granada, where he teaches undergraduate and doctoral courses on subjects related to Muslim and Hispano-American art. He has been the Director of the Cultural Extension Programme of the University of Granada, and was the General Co-ordinator of the Project "El legado Andalusí" (The Andalucían Heritage).
Among his numerous publications are: *Tradición y clasicísmo en la Granada del Siglo XVI: arquitectura civil y urbanismo*, Granada (1987); *Arquitectura Mudéjar Granadina*, Granada (1990); and *Arquitectura y carpintería Mudéjar en Nueva España*, México (1992).
In addition, he has participated in joint projects among which are: "La Medina musulmana" in *Nuevos Paseos por Granada y sus contornos*, Granada (1992); "Las primeras construcciones y la definición del Mudéjar en Nueva España" in *El Mudéjar Iberoamericano. Del Islam al Nuevo Mundo*, Madrid (1995).

María Pilar Mogollón Cano-Cortés

Graduated in History of Art in 1979 from the University of Extremadura. She was awarded the Premio Fin de Carrera *"Publio Hurtado"* and became a teacher of History of Art in the Faculty of Philosophy and Letters. She was awarded her Doctorate from the same University five years later and since 1988 has been a teacher in the Department of History of Art in the Faculty of Philosophy and Letters at the University of Extremadura.

Among her publications are: *El Mudéjar en Extremadura* (1987), the subject of her doctoral thesis; *Cáceres: la busqueda de una ciudad eternal* (1987); *La sillería de coro de la catedral de Plasencia* (1992); *Por tierras de Cáceres y castillos de Cáceres* (1992); *El Gótico en Extremadura* (1995) and *Monumentos artísticos de Extremadura* (1986).

Alfredo Morales Martínez

A teacher in the Department of History of Art, Faculty of Geography and History of the University of Seville. First prize "Archivo Hispalense" of the Provincial Government of Seville (1975). Technical Adviser to the Department of Historical and Artistic Heritage of the Archdiocese of Seville. Member of the Andalucía Committee for movable assets. Member of the Scientific and Executive Committee of the exhibition "El Mudéjar Iberamericano. Del Islam al Nuevo Mundo", Malaga (1995). Between 1989 and 1991, he was Sub-Director General of movable assets at the Ministry of Culture.

María Teresa Pérez Higuera

Professor of the History of Medieval Art, Faculty of Geography and History of Art I (Medieval) at the Complutense University in Madrid, where she teaches Hispano-Muslim and Mudéjar Art.

Among her many published works those on Islamic themes are the most important: *Objetos e imágenes de al-Andalus* (1994); "Arte en época almorávide y almohade" in *Historia de España* by Menéndez Pidal (1997); *Arte Mudéjar en Castilla y León* (1993), "Arte Toledano" in *Arquitecturas de Toledo* (first ed. 1991, second ed. 1993) as well as her collaboration on the same subject in *Casas y palacios en al-Andalus* (1995); *El Mudéjar Iberoamericano* (1995); *Arte Mudéjar* (1996) and the chapter on "Mudéjar en la Corte" in *Historia del arte en Castilla y León* (1996).

Alfonso Pleguezuelo Hernández

Studied History of Art at the University of Seville between 1973 and 1978 and was awarded his Doctorate there for his work "Arquitectura Sevillana de principios del siglo XVII". At present, he teaches History of Art in the Faculty of Fine Arts in Seville. As well as his interest in proto-Baroque architecture he has also specialised over the last 20 years in the history of Spanish ceramics, a field he has approached from several different methodological perspectives related to historical archaeology, architectonic expression or a more strictly historical-artistic perspective. In relation to this thematic area, he has published various books, articles, exhibition catalogues and has presented papers at both national and international congresses.

Miguel Ángel Sorroche Cuerva

Graduated in History of Art from the University of Granada and was awarded his Doctorate in 1997 for his thesis: *Urbanismo y arquitectura popular en las altiplanicies de Granada*. At present, he teaches in the Department of History of Art at the same University and his main work centres on the study and evaluation of the traditional heritage, in its urban and architectonic expression. A result of this are his publications on the theme and his study visits to international centres such as the Centro de Documentación de Arquitectura Latinoamericana in Argentina, the C'a Foscari University in Venice or his work with Town Councils and official Organisations in Andalucía, Aragón and the Basque Country.

Museum With No Frontiers Exhibition Trails and related Travel Books
ISLAMIC ART IN THE MEDITERRANEAN

The following titles have been published in the series:

Egypt
MAMLUK ART
The Splendour and Magic of the Sultans *236 pages*

Under Mamluk domination (1249–1517), Egypt became a prosperous commercial-route crossing centre. Great riches came to the country. Cairo was one of the most powerful, secure and stable cities of the Mediterranean basin. Scholars from all over the world came to settle there, attracting their followers and students. Mamluk architecture and decorative art displays the vitality of commerce, the intellectual energy, and the military and religious force of this period. Characterised by elegant and vigorous simplicity, the purity of line is similar to modern models. The works selected between Cairo, Rosetta, Alexandria and Fuwa represent the height of Mamluk art.

Italy – Sicily
SICULO-NORMAN ART
Islamic Culture in Medieval Sicily *328 pages*

An Island in the middle of the Mediterranean, Sicily is a land of encounter, where various cultures have coincided and adjusted mutually, reaching a new harmony. Unique in the European panorama, Arab-Norman architecture, relatively speaking, is different from that found in the Islamic world. The exhibition presents it from the standpoint of its uniqueness and provides some codes for interpretation permitting better identification. An attentive visitor will better appreciate the admirable fusion of elements, originating from Byzantine, Arab and Norman cultural spheres, employed in this art, which is as original as it is refined.

Jordan
THE UMAYYADS
The Rise of Islamic Art *224 pages*

Following the Arab-Muslim conquest of the Middle East, the seat of the Umayyad Dynasty (661–750) was moved to Damascus, where the new capital inherited a cultural and artistic tradition dating back to the Aramaean and Hellenistic Periods. Umayyad culture benefited by this move from the frontier between Persia and Mesopotamia and between the countries of the Mediterranean world. The position was favourable for the emergence of an innovative artistic language, in which a subtle mixture of Hellenistic, Roman, Byzantine and Persian influences, produced architectural order and decorative originality. Through the diversity of the works presented, the exhibition also offers the opportunity to reflect on the Iconoclast phenomena.

Morocco
ANDALUSIAN MOROCCO
Discovery in Living Art *264 pages*

From the beginning of the 8th century, Islamic Moroccans looked beyond the Pillars of Hercules (Gibraltar) and settled in the Iberian Peninsula. From then on, both shores shared the same destiny. From continual cultural, social and commercial exchange animating this extreme of the Maghreb for more than seven centuries, sprang one of the most brilliant facets of Muslim civilisation. Authentic Hispano-Maghreb art left its stamp not only on resplendent, monumental architecture, but also in the characteristics of the cities and traditions of extreme refinement. The exhibition reflects the historic and social wealth of the Andalusi (Andalucían) civilisation in Morocco.

Palestinian Authority
PILGRIMAGE, SCIENCE AND SUFISM
Islamic Art in the West Bank and Gaza *254 pages*

During the reigns of the Ayyubid, Mamluk and Ottoman Dynasties, numerous pilgrims, from all over the Muslim world came to Palestine. This dynamic tide of religious fervour gave a decisive impulse to the development of *Sufi* thought, through the *zawiya*s and *ribat*s, which multiplied all over the country. Various study centres welcomed the most distinguished scholars. In this way, they obtained considerable prestige and conditions became favourable for the expansion of refined art, which conserves its power to fascinate, even today. The monuments and Islamic architecture proposed for the exhibition clearly reflect these great dimensions of pilgrimages, science and Sufism.

Portugal
IN THE LANDS OF THE ENCHANTED MOORISH MAIDEN
Islamic Art in Portugal *200 pages*

Eight centuries after the Christians reconquered their lands from the Muslims, towns of the ancient "Gharb al-Andalus" (western Andalusia) have preserved the Legend of the beautiful enchanted Moorish maiden whose spell was broken by a Christian prince; the artistic route of Muslim presence in Portugal also expresses, through a subtle interdependence between constructive techniques and decorative programmes, popular regional architecture. The exhibition gives the visitor a clear view of five centuries of Islamic civilisation (the Caliphate, Mozarabic, Almohad and Mudéjar periods). From Coimbra in the confines of the Algarve, palaces, Christianised mosques, fortifications and cities, all affirm the splendour of past glories.

Spain | Andalucía, Aragon, Castilla La Mancha, Castille and Leon, outskirts of Madrid
MUDÉJAR ART
Islamic Aaesthetics in Christian Art   *316 pages*

The art of the Mudéjars (the Muslim population remaining in Andalucía after the reconquest) has an unquestionably unique place among all expressions of Islamic art. It deals with the visible manifestation of a splendidly cultured cohabitation with a unique understanding between two civilisations that, in spite of their political and religious antagonism, lived a fructiferous artistic romance. Applying schemes, although rigorously Islamic, the Masters of Works and Mudéjar artisans, famous for their outstanding knowledge in the art of construction, erected for the newly arrived Christians innumerable palaces, convents and churches. The selected works, chosen for their variety and abundance, testify to the exuberant vitality of Mudéjar art.

Syria
THE AYYUBID ERA
Art and Architecture in Medieval Syria   *288 pages*

Bilad al-Sham testifies to a thorough and strategic programme of urban reconstruction and reunification during the 12th and 13th centuries. Amidst a period of fragmentation, visionary leadership came with the Atabeg Nur al-Din Zangi. He revived Syria's cities as safe havens to restore order. His most agile Kurdish general, Salah al-Din (Saladin), assumed power after he died and unified Egypt and Sham into one force capable of reconquering Jerusalem from the Crusaders. The Ayyubid Empire flourished and continued the policy of patronage. Although short-lived, this era held long-lasting resonance for the region. Its recognisable architectural aesthetic – austere, yet robust and perfected – survived until modern times.

The book was conceived not long before the war started. All texts refer to the pre-war situation and are our expression of hope that Syria, a land that witnessed the evolution of civilisation since the beginnings of human history, may soon become a place of peace and the driving force behind a new and peaceful beginning for the entire region.

Tunisia
IFRIQIYA
Thirteen Centuries of Art and Architecture in Tunisia   *312 pages*

Since the 9th century, without breaking with traditions inherited from the Berbers, Carthaginians, Romans and Byzantines, Ifriqiya was able to assimilate and reinterpret influences from Mesopotamia, through Syria and Egypt, and from al-Andalus (Andalucía). This is a unique form of syncretism, of which numerous vestiges prevail even today in Tunisia, from the majestic residences of the Muslim sovereigns in the capital, to the architectonic rigor of the "Ibadism of Jerba". The visitor is invited to look at existing *ribat*s, mosques, *medina*s, *zawiya*s and *gurfa*s (large rooms containing bedroom suites) to witness their imprint on a land abounding with history.

Islamic Art in the Mediterranean

Turkey
EARLY OTTOMAN ART
Legacy of the Emirates   *252 pages*
Highlighting this exhibition are the works and monuments most representative of the finest period of western Anatolia, the cultural and artistic bridge between European and Asian civilisations. In the 14th and 15th centuries, the transition to a Turkish-Islamic society led artists of the Turkish Emirate to elaborate on a brilliant artistic union culminating in Ottoman art.

In preparation

Algeria
AN ARCHITECTURE OF THE LIGHT
The Arts of Islam in Algeria
A provisional publication of the French version is available for free download at this link: http://www.museumwnf.org/images//books/40/fr/31/book/sample.pdf (21 MB)

www.ingramcontent.com/pod-product-compliance
Lightning Source LLC
Chambersburg PA
CBHW071812230426
43670CB00013B/2438